PLAYING FOR UNCLE SAM

★ THE BRITS' STORY OF THE NORTH AMERICAN SOCCER LEAGUE ★

DAVID TOSSELL

MAINSTREAM
PUBLISHING
EDINBURGH AND LONDON

First published in Great Britain in 2003 by
MAINSTREAM PUBLISHING (EDINBURGH) LTD
7 Albany Street
Edinburgh EH1 3UG

ISBN 1 84018 748 4

A catalogue record for this book is available from the British Library

Typeset in Gill Sans and Giovanni

Printed in Great Britain by
Creative Print and Design Wales

Contents

Acknowledgements

One of the most enjoyable aspects of the preparation of this book was discovering how many people shared my enthusiasm for telling the story of the British involvement in the North American Soccer League (NASL). My huge gratitude is due to all of those listed as interviewees at the end of the book, many of whom were also kind enough to put me in contact with former colleagues. In addition, a lot of people opened doors through the sharing of telephone numbers and e-mail addresses or the delivery of messages, notably Mal Butler, Roy Collins, Christopher Davies, Roger Davies, Paul Donovan, Paul Futcher, Richard Green, Frank Juliano, Paul Mace, Alan Merrick, Mike Preston, Neil Rioch, Michael Signora, Paul Tinnion, Roger Wash, Dave Wasser, Phil Woosnam and Gary Wright.

Special thanks are due to Bob McNab and Richard Whitehead, for their input and detective work, and to Vince Casey and Alan Merrick, who generously made their photographic collections available for my use. Jack Huckel and Colin Jose at the American Soccer Hall of Fame deserve mention for their assistance, while all of this would have been for nothing without the backing of everyone at Mainstream Publishing.

Some people contribute in ways beyond the practical, like Sally, whose long-term support and organisation of family life have helped to make projects like this possible.

To Pete Abitante, thanks for professional guidance and personal friendship. Lucy, this book could not have been undertaken without your encouragement, nor completed without your patient proofreading. Finally, thanks to my mum, for unwavering support in all areas of my life.

Introduction

The BBC's Kenneth Wolstenholme may have declared famously that it was 'all over' as Geoff Hurst slammed the ball into the West Germans' net for the third time, but for the North American Soccer League the emphatic underlining of England's World Cup triumph was just the start.

When Bobby Moore led the red-shirted English heroes into the Wembley sunshine on that memorable July afternoon in 1966, eight million viewers were tuning in on their televisions in the United States. Considering that they had either forgone their weekend lie-in if they were on the west coast or were fitting the game around their brunch arrangements on the eastern side of the country, NBC's audience for the events being played out several thousand miles away was considered an outstanding success. And it offered final, indisputable confirmation of what several influential and wealthy American folks had been suspecting for a while: that their country was ready to embrace the world game of football. The nation's long wait for a top-tier professional 'soccer' league was about to come to an end.

The appearance of Alf Ramsey's men on American screens could not have been better timed. The '60s were a boom time for sport in the US, the pervading mood one of expansion and experiment. Improved communication and travel had opened up geographical areas until recently unexplored by the professional leagues, while increased and enhanced television coverage was giving sport more exposure than ever before. The American public had more disposable income and were keen to find ways of spending it. Sport offered a popular option and a welcome diversion from years of civil unrest, a debilitating war in Vietnam and a series of shocking assassinations of major political figures.

In American football, the gridiron version, the established National Football League (NFL) had faced a challenge from the newly formed American Football League, forcing a merger that brought about the advent of the Super Bowl and pushed the league to heights of popularity no other US sport could match. Not that the others were struggling. The decade saw every major sports league increase by at least six teams as burgeoning cities lobbied for franchises. Into such a climate of pioneering came professional soccer, beginning a saga that, over the course of almost two decades, would mix high drama with comedy, sporting excellence with moments of pure farce.

This book does not set out to be the definitive history of the NASL (a thorough examination of the reasons behind the league's collapse could fill a volume on its own). Rather, it is the tale – much of it anecdotal – of the British players, coaches and administrators who were part of the league. And, whatever the headline during the NASL's roller-coaster existence, the Brits were never far from the heart of the story.

From the moment America opened its sporting borders to soccer, those from the British Isles were at the front of the check-in line. Some, like George Best and Rodney Marsh, would make the journey because they felt English football had nothing left to offer them. Others went to prove a point, like World Cup goalkeeper Gordon Banks, who demonstrated that it was possible to keep the best forwards in the world at bay with only one eye. But it was not just the big-name internationals that crossed the Atlantic to join up with their peers, Pelé, Beckenbauer and Cruyff. A whole legion of First Division players and lower-league journeymen extended their careers or forged new ones in the NASL. Men like Peter Beardsley, Peter Withe and Alan Brazil used it as a finishing school for great things back home, while some, like Alan Willey and Paul Child, virtually unknown in their homeland, stayed on to perform feats that rank alongside those of any of the NASL's most recognisable names.

Across the water they went, the celebrity and the unknown, the young and the old, the richly talented and the poorly appreciated. An 18-year procession of players lured by the opportunity to play in the land of Uncle Sam. This is their story.

1. ☆ An Uncivil War

As the bright, crisp sunshine of spring gave way to the hazy days of the summer of 1966, it was a good time to be a sporting underdog in America. Many of the nation's headlines were being created by those who had previously been written off, counted out or simply ignored. The battle to crown the champions of the ice hockey world saw the Montreal Canadiens come from two games down to overturn the Detroit Red Wings in the final series of the Stanley Cup. Golfer Billy Casper was turning around an even greater deficit, making up seven shots on the final nine holes of the US Open in San Francisco before beating the great Arnold Palmer in a play-off. In tennis, 22-year-old Billie Jean King overcame former champion Maria Bueno at Wimbledon to win an overdue first Grand Slam singles title, three years after qualifying for her first final. Meanwhile, baseball underdogs everywhere toasted the descent of the mighty New York Yankees towards last place in the American League. Even the United States Soccer Football Association (USSFA), perhaps the biggest sporting no-hoper of all, was about to have its day.

Dramatic events on the greens of California and the courts of south-west London had done little to quicken the sedate pace of activity in the New York offices of the USSFA. As Americans cheered Casper and King, the organisation's part-time employees went quietly about their business, which consisted mainly of administering the national team's hapless attempts to qualify for the World Cup finals and overseeing semi-professional competitions like the American Soccer League, whose clubs paid the USSFA a meagre yearly fee of $25. The prospect of a World Cup in which the United States was once again merely a distant spectator was not much more than an interesting distraction. That was, however, until letters began dropping into the USSFA's mailbox from men with money to spend and the inclination to lavish it on an idea they felt could not miss: a new professional soccer league.

Without having done a great deal to invite such attention, the USSFA suddenly had at its fingertips a scheme apparently so certain of success that three consortiums were fighting to win approval to put it into practice. Potential investors included major corporations like Madison Square Garden and the RKO General Corporation, while interested individuals included Lamar Hunt, the owner of American football's Kansas City Chiefs, Jack Kent Cooke of the Washington Redskins and several others with controlling interests in major sports franchises. Professional soccer, so the theory went, would help to feed the public's insatiable sporting appetite and enable the stadium and team owners to turn days when their buildings had previously stood empty into profitable trading opportunities.

Rubbing their hands with considerable glee at this sudden surge of interest in what was still regarded largely as the 'foreign sport', the USSFA sprang into action. In conjunction with the Canadian Soccer Football Association (CSFA), its first response to the requests for permission to set up an officially sanctioned league was to demand from each consortium a franchise fee of $25,000 for every proposed team, plus a cut of gate receipts and television revenue. When disapproval was voiced at the level of the fee, USSFA committee member Jack Flamhaft commented, 'It makes me laugh. Here come millionaires who own some billionaire businesses in other fields. Did *they* want a franchise for $25?'

While the world watched the events in England in July 1966, representatives of the three competing groups travelled to San Francisco to plead their case to the USSFA's annual convention. In the end, the choice was simple. The group led by Jack Kent Cooke, the only one to accept the USSFA terms, was given official recognition and prepared to begin play in 1968 as the North American Soccer League. But the two rivals, their conviction about the sport hardened by America's interest in Geoff Hurst and his pals, decided not to go quietly. Joining forces to call themselves the National Professional Soccer League (NPSL), they announced that ten teams, with or without permission from the authorities, would begin play in the spring of 1967, thereby beating their rivals onto the field by a full year. The NPSL added that it was now prepared to accept the USSFA's terms and produced a cheque for $250,000. By now, though, it was too late to find a place under the wing of the USSFA, which had given Cooke's NASL group the exclusive rights to operate a professional league in North America.

The NPSL, dubbed the 'outlaws' to the NASL's 'in-laws', pushed on with its plans, buoyed by a television contract with CBS, yet facing a potential recruiting problem. The lack of local talent meant that the bulk of the players would have to come from outside the United States. However, any player signing with the renegade outfit faced the threat of being placed on a FIFA blacklist. One bizarre rumour even began to circulate that any player going to play in America was liable to be drafted into the army and sent to fight in Vietnam.

One of the first players signed by the NPSL was a 31-year-old English forward, Ron Newman, whose 12 seasons in the Football League had taken him finally to Gillingham, where he was waiting for news of a possible coaching post in South Africa. 'I knew my career was coming towards the end and I had itchy feet,' he recalls. 'Before my legs gave out I wanted to go to an exotic place. While I was playing for Gillingham and waiting for things to develop in South Africa I started reading about an old friend of mine, Phil Woosnam, who was going to coach a team in Atlanta. I knew Phil from when I moved from Portsmouth to Leyton Orient. I moved into his old house after he had gone to West Ham and I kept getting his bloody post! Phil contacted me and asked me to go with him instead of going to South Africa.

'The way I heard it was that there was another league that had been given authenticity and we were classified as an outlaw league, so I called the players' union in England and asked if there was a problem. Their reply was, "If you have permission from Gillingham and are not breaking your contract there is no problem."'

Newman was to find out that he had been given false information when the NPSL's lawyers asked him to volunteer to be a test case at the end of the season. 'There were law suits going on like crazy and I was asked if I would write to the Football Association to be reinstated. That letter became a major tool in the legislation. The FA wrote back and said I was quite welcome to come back – as soon as I had sat out a one-year suspension! I thought that was bullshit. It was diabolical. The idea had been to see if I was going to be punished for playing in the NPSL, so the answer from the FA was the one the league's lawyers wanted.'

While the NPSL had set about stocking its teams with men like Newman, the NASL, stung by its rival's determination to launch first, decided to act. The league's name was changed to the United Soccer Association, allowing it to revel in a patriotic acronym and avoid confusion with its similarly titled rival. Then plans were announced to kick off in 1967 after all. Unable to sign players of sufficient calibre at the eleventh hour, the USA opted for the novel solution of simply contracting 12 teams from around the world to spend the summer playing in the United States in a different guise.

As the winter of 1966 approached, Kenneth Wolstenholme, England forward Jimmy Greaves, ex-Nottingham Forest striker Roy Dwight and London businessman Jim Graham were called in to help with the recruitment of teams from the British Isles. With plenty of money to spend on the USA's behalf, their Christmas shopping list consisted of three teams from England, three from Scotland and one from each side of the Irish border. So it was that Wolverhampton Wanderers traded the Black Country for California to become the Los Angeles Wolves, while Stoke City left the Potteries to become the Cleveland Stokers and Sunderland were re-invented as the Vancouver Royal Canadians. From Scotland, Aberdeen journeyed to America's capital city to become the Washington Whips, Dundee United were to play as the Dallas Tornado and Hibernian prepared for life as Toronto City. After Linfield turned down their invitation because of the possibility of having to play games on a Sunday, Glentoran accepted the chance to represent Northern Ireland and play the role of the Detroit Cougars. The Republic's Shamrock Rovers inevitably went to the Irish-dominated city of Boston to play as the Boston Rovers.

The process of allocating the teams to cities was based largely on ethnic demographics, although most of the pairings stretched that point rather thinly and some franchises were undoubtedly left feeling that they had been short-changed for the $250,000 each was paying to its imported club. Some of the better sides targeted by the USA had been unavailable, such as Pelé's Santos in Brazil, leaving the field to be filled by Uruguay's Cerro (New York Skyliners), Brazil's Bangu (Houston Stars), Den Haag of Holland (San Francisco Golden Gate Gales) and Italian side Cagliari (Chicago Mustangs).

Instead of a couple of weeks on the beach with their families, what lay ahead for the players was a 12-game schedule that would last almost two months and take in most corners of North America. In modern times, such a proposal would cause uproar among leg-weary and well-travelled players, not to mention their agents and medical advisers. But Aberdeen goalkeeper Bobby Clark, in the early stages of a career that would bring him 13 Scotland caps, recalls the tour as the opportunity of a lifetime.

'Players weren't spoiled back in those days,' he says. 'We were a lot happier about things like that. We were a young side, looking to get better, and this was an opportunity to play against good teams like Wolves, Sunderland and Cagliari, who were champions of Italy a couple of years later. We were about to play in Europe so it was a chance for us to experience playing against different types of teams.

'And America was an exciting, far-away place, somewhere we had never had the chance to play before. To go there and live in the Washington Hilton for a couple of months, to play in an indoor stadium like the Houston Astrodome, to be flying to every game, to go to Disneyland and see Andy Williams in concert – it was all so different to anything we had known before. Personally, it was fantastic as well. I was looking to establish myself in the team and I had just finished a physical education course. I was allowed to get off school three weeks early as long as I came back and did a month's unpaid teaching.'

The welcome extended to the teams when they arrived in the US lived up to the travellers' hopes. Glentoran's players were led to the airport terminal across a red carpet by the St Andrews Pipe Band of Detroit. While such receptions were designed to make their guests feel at home, it was going to take more than modified kits, with gridiron-style numbers on shirt-fronts, to make the players think of themselves as Cougars or Stokers. 'We knew we were representing Washington and in public we talked about the Whips,' says Clark. 'But we still thought of ourselves as Aberdeen playing against Dundee or Hibernian.'

And the Americans' lack of knowledge about the sport was still very evident. Clark adds, 'People would see our Washington Whips bags with the WW logo and the words "soccer team" and not even know what that was. They'd ask us, "What's a *saucer* team?" I think it went over their heads when we told them we were playing in the Cup!'

Newman experienced similar bewilderment among the people of Georgia. 'As soon as we got to Atlanta they wanted us to go into a parade through town. We rushed to get into our uniforms, got on the parade float and a horse and cart started pulling us down the road. People were looking at us as though we were circus freaks. Nobody there had even seen a soccer ball. I thought, "This is ridiculous." I jumped off the float, got a ball and started to interact with the people along the route, flicking and heading the ball backwards and forwards to the kids. A couple of the other lads saw what I was doing and followed suit. We became the hit of the parade.'

One of Newman's teammates was former Northern Ireland winger Peter McParland, who recalls, 'The first thing the locals taught us was how to eat a hamburger properly. The follow-up was that we got invited to all these barbecue evenings and all these ladies would come up and say they played soccer at school. It seemed to be only ladies playing over there.'

The NPSL's persuasive arguments to potential recruits about future FIFA recognition put it in a position to launch a month before the rival league's imported teams arrived in the US. Woosnam, who in his joint role of coach and general manager was responsible for signing up players for the Chiefs, says, 'Maybe we were all put on a blacklist. But I believed we were doing it right, whereas the other league was just bringing in teams and therefore not doing anything of any value to the community. I thought our league would be in the stronger position with FIFA. Not one player we tried to sign turned us down.'

McParland adds, 'They told us that it was always on the cards that FIFA would recognise the league in the long run and that we would not be on a blacklist. I was coming towards the end of my career anyway, so I didn't feel I was taking a gamble. And it was not a bunch of cowboys who were backing the league.'

Doubts remained, however, about the quality of the players whose services had been secured. The ten NPSL teams were stocked mostly by signings from Latin America, the Caribbean and Europe, the dominant nations being West Germany and Yugoslavia. Only eight genuine American players would get on the field during the season.

The British contingent was small and included few recognisable names. Several of them had already been in North America, playing semi-professionally in Canada, and most of the better-known Football League exports found themselves at Atlanta under Woosnam, the former Wales forward. Capped 17 times by his country, Woosnam had played more than 100 League games for each of West Ham, Leyton Orient and Aston Villa and his influence was obvious in the composition of the Chiefs squad. Goalkeeper Vic Rouse was a fellow Wales international, earning one cap while playing 238 league games for Crystal Palace. Brian Hughes had racked up more than 200 games for West Ham and ex-Aston Villa wing-half Vic Crowe had played 16 times for the Welsh side. Winger Ray Bloomfield boasted a handful of games for Villa, while the biggest name on the roster was McParland, another Villa veteran. Scorer of 98 goals in 293 League games, he was one of Northern Ireland's most celebrated players, having earned 34 caps after being spotted in the League of Ireland at Dundalk. His finest hour had been the 1958 World Cup, when he scored five goals as his country reached the quarter-finals. A year earlier he had scored both Villa goals in the FA Cup final victory against Manchester United, although he was more widely remembered for the challenge on Ray Wood that left the United goalkeeper hobbling on the wing.

A fast, direct goal-scoring winger, McParland also won the Second Division title and League Cup with Villa before moving on to Wolverhampton and Plymouth. Woosnam recalls, 'He had been playing for Worcester when I played with him in a kick-around game in some kind of summer celebration and I thought, "Peter can still play." He was only 32 when he came out to America and he did exceptionally well. He had a wobbly knee and we had to leave him out for certain games, but he had two great years.'

Elsewhere, the New York Generals' line-up included George Kirby, who had scored 188 goals in a seven-club Football League career, and Roy Hartle, who played 446 League games for Bolton. In goal was former Wolves and Aston Villa man Geoff Sidebottom, whose renowned bravery would eventually force his retirement in 1971 after suffering a third concussion in two seasons with Brighton. Coaching the team was Freddie Goodwin, the former Manchester United and Leeds wing-half, who would soon become manager of a Birmingham City team that won promotion to Division One and reached the semi-finals of the FA Cup.

The Oakland Clippers fielded former Brentford and Chelsea centre-half Melvyn Scott and ex-Brentford and Millwall winger Barry Rowan, while the Philadelphia Spartans included Liverpool-born wing-half John Best, whose six games for Tranmere were the extent of his Football League experience. Alongside him in defence was Peter Short, another Liverpudlian, who would score both the Spartans' goals in their opening-game victory over Toronto. Best and Short were destined to join the group of players who would carve out long and successful careers in the US. While Best would go on to serve as a coach and general manager, Short would end his playing career ten years and seven teams later and then undertake three stints as an NASL head coach. (In February 1984, Short was shot dead in Los Angeles at the age of 39 after discovering two teenagers breaking into his car.)

Playing the majority of the games in goal for the Toronto Falcons was former Scotland international Bill Brown, the last line of defence in the Spurs team that completed the Football League and FA Cup Double in 1961. After losing his place in the side following Pat Jennings's arrival from Watford, he had spent one season at Northampton before trying his luck in America.

The most recognisable figure among the British ex-pats was former Manchester United forward and 'Busby Babe' Dennis Viollet, now 33 years old. A survivor of the Munich air crash, which had taken the lives of eight of his youthful and talented teammates, Viollet totalled 159 goals in 259 League games for Manchester United, including a club record 32 in a single season. It was a mystery that he was rewarded with only two England caps, and it was his love of socialising that was thought to be behind United's surprise decision to sell him to Stoke City in 1961.

The new era of professional football in the United States kicked off on 16 April 1967, the day after Scotland's 3–2 victory over England at Wembley had them proclaiming themselves champions of the world. In the NPSL's season opener, Woosnam's Chiefs met Viollet's Bays in front of a modest crowd of 8,434 in Baltimore. It was hardly the kind of game to have the fans battering at the doors of the ticket office for future presentations. A dour defensive battle was won 1–0 by the home side – exactly the kind of game the NPSL had hoped to guard against by adopting a scoring system that had the purists cringing. Teams would receive six points for a win, three for a draw and a bonus point for every goal scored, up to a maximum of three per game.

CBS approached its weekly live broadcasts of NPSL action with the slogan 'Just For Kicks!' But, sitting alongside respected American commentator Jack Whitaker, Tottenham and Northern Ireland legend Danny Blanchflower was in no mood to patronise the viewers. As a man who had captained Spurs to the Double and won 56 international caps, he had his credibility to protect and told it like it was – which meant week after week of often-brutal criticism of the games. It did not help matters when referee Peter Rhodes admitted that 11 of the 21 free-kicks he awarded in the televised Toronto–Pittsburgh match were to allow CBS to work in commercial breaks. At one point he even appeared to push down a player who was trying to get up because the ad break had not finished. Television ratings and crowds slumped as the season progressed, producing a final average attendance of 4,879 per game.

But, for all its faults and in-fighting, at least soccer was back on the US scene. While Hurst's hat-trick had sewn the final seeds of what would eventually become the NASL, it was, strictly speaking, only a rebirth of the sport on the professional level in America. The first guys to be paid for kicking a round ball in the United States had picked up their pay cheques more than three-quarters of a century earlier.

Largely a game played by upper-class college types as the second half of the nineteenth century came around, soccer had established itself at elite colleges like Yale, Columbia and Cornell, only for those establishments to follow Harvard's lead in switching to rugby, which developed into America's own helmeted version of football. But the working-class communities, their populations increased by the influx of large numbers of immigrant workers, ensured that soccer continued and regional leagues developed across the country.

The involvement of corporate sponsors meant that some players were being paid to play on a semi-professional basis and, buoyed by America's participation in the 1904 Olympics, the NASL operated from 1906 to 1921, the first professional league to achieve any longevity in North America.

The American Soccer League arrived on the scene in 1921, built around the richer clubs from the existing semi-professional circuit, and regularly achieved crowds of 10,000. The ASL even provided a taste of things to come in the NASL by signing several British players. Scotland international Tommy Muirhead arrived from Rangers as player-manager of the Boston Wonder Workers and then secured the services of national teammate Alex McNab from Morton, who was paid $25 a week and given a job at the Wonder Works factory.

By the end of the 1920s, however, the ASL had fallen out with the USSFA over the scheduling of fixtures and was suspended by the governing body, thereby becoming an unauthorised competition. As clubs jumped from one league to another and the stock market crash took away financial backing, the first coming of professional soccer in the US was on borrowed time. Before long, the sport was back to a structure of regional amateur competitions. Even the famous 1950 victory of the USA team over England in the World Cup finals in Brazil failed to bring any significant change. Although the International Soccer League, a competition between visiting foreign teams, began in 1960 and continued for six seasons, it did so in a low-key manner that gained little attention inside or beyond the North American borders.

The 1966 World Cup, however, had apparently changed all that, yet soccer's summer of '67 failed to make the anticipated impact. Anyone heading to San Francisco, for example, did so with flowers in their hair, a Gales soccer game coming a poor second to hanging out in the Haight-Ashbury district listening to The Beatles. The trend was repeated around the country.

For those who cared enough to notice, the NPSL's Western

Division was dominated by the Oakland Clippers, who won 19 of 32 games and finished 29 points ahead of the St Louis Stars. The Eastern Division featured a much closer race, with Baltimore and Philadelphia finishing with identical records of 14 wins and 9 draws and the Bays qualifying for the two-legged final by virtue of their bonus points. George Kirby proved to be the most prolific scorer among the British contingent, netting 14 goals for New York and adding two assists, the name given to key contributions in setting up a goal.

Baltimore, with former Derby County and Torquay United goalkeeper Terry Adlington between the sticks, had kept ten clean sheets during the season and did so again in the first leg of the final as Viollet's individual effort produced the only goal in front of 16,619 fans in Baltimore. Coached by former Ipswich Town inside-forward Doug Millward, the Bays were overpowered in the second leg as Oakland's Yugoslav midfielder Dragan Djukic scored a hat-trick in a 4–1 win.

The USA, with its traditional points-scoring and 'teams-in-disguise' format, was a little more successful than its rival at the gate. On 1 May, the day after Muhammad Ali had been stripped of his world heavyweight title for resisting the US military's call to go and fight in Vietnam, almost 35,000 saw Wolves draw against the Brazilian Houston Stars in the opening game. The season would produce an overall average attendance of 7,890, with Houston the biggest draw at 19,802 per game and the Boston Rovers trailing in last with an average of 4,171, proving that it needed more than an Irish team to bring out the crowds. Boston's home game against San Francisco attracted only 853 paying customers to the Manning Bowl in Lynn, Massachusetts, but even that beat the 648 who turned out in a Detroit thunderstorm for the all-Irish battle between the Cougars, from Glentoran, and the visiting Rovers.

Northern Irish champions Glentoran, despite enjoying only moderate success with three wins and six draws, were one of the more colourful teams on the circuit. In their first game, at Boston, player-manager John Colrain was accused of having punched a linesman after he ruled out a goal for offside late in the 1–1 draw. It was the second Detroit goal the linesman had disallowed. Colrain, a former Celtic and Ipswich forward, claimed he had merely shaken his fist and inadvertently made contact with the flag, but he was suspended indefinitely by the USA. Glentoran argued there had been no official investigation and took their case to FIFA, yet Colrain was still banned for the next two games.

There was a controversial finish in the rematch, with Boston bitterly protesting the penalty award that gave Detroit victory, but that was nothing compared with the chaos when Brazilian side Bangu (Houston) visited the University Stadium of Detroit. The Brazilians held a 2–0 lead with 17 minutes left in a bad-tempered game and eventually the contest degenerated into a free-for-all, with some of the Bangu players even grabbing corner flags to use as weapons. The referee abandoned the game and the USA, apportioning blame equally between the two teams, allowed the result to stand. The same evening saw the match between Cagliari (Chicago) and Uruguayan team Cerro (New York) called off with three minutes remaining at Yankee Stadium after a disputed foul led to both sets of players exchanging punches. Even members of the 10,000 crowd invaded the pitch to participate as the referee and his linesmen fled the scene. There was more fighting in Glentoran's meeting with Stoke, which saw the Irish forward Danny Trainor and Stoke defender Tony Allen dismissed six minutes from time.

Meanwhile, four wins in their first six games meant the Los Angeles Wolves were always on course to take the USA's Western Division title. Their angular Northern Ireland centre-forward Derek Dougan scored in three successive victories and Ernie Hunt finished as the team's top scorer with four goals. The defence never conceded more than one goal until the division title was just about wrapped up. Near the foot of the division, Sunderland won only three games as the Vancouver Royal Canadians, while Dundee United had only three victories in the colours of the Dallas Tornado. 'We took it seriously enough,' says Sunderland striker John O'Hare. 'We just weren't a very good side at that time. It was not through lack of commitment.'

In the Eastern Division, the Cleveland Stokers remained unbeaten in their first seven games before winning only one of their final five matches to finish second in the table. Peter Dobing's seven goals made him the leading scorer among the British teams, while Hibernian's Peter Cormack was on target five times for third-placed Toronto City. Winners of the division were Aberdeen, the Washington Whips, for whom Jim Storrie top-scored with five goals.

'We had a group of very good young players at that time,' recalls goalkeeper Bobby Clark. 'Martin Buchan was on his way to becoming a world-class defender and was later transferred to Manchester United. Jimmy Smith, who went on to Newcastle, was a terrier in midfield, and at the back Francis Munro had a great summer. One of the reasons Wolves signed him was because they saw how well he played against them in America.'

Fans back in Scotland followed their team's exploits closely. 'I did a daily report for the *Daily Record* and somebody else did one for the *Press and Journal*,' Clark explains. 'People were very excited about hearing where we were playing. It was pretty big news at the time for a team like Aberdeen to be over there playing at places like the Astrodome.'

In other British cities, interest in their team's overseas exploits was less evident. 'Hardly anyone from Sunderland knew we were even out there,' says O'Hare. 'We didn't have any press travelling with us and I don't remember any coverage.'

Having won their divisions with identical records, the Wolves and the Whips tossed a coin to see who would host the one-off final, with the Los Angeles Coliseum emerging as the venue. The final brought together teams who had been involved in some of the tournament's many controversial incidents. During their meeting in Washington, Wolves player David Burnside had aimed a throw-in at Aberdeen's Munro, hitting the Scottish defender on the head. Munro retaliated by throwing punches and it was Wolves chairman John Ireland, fearful of a public relations disaster, who risked copping a few blows himself by stepping in, pipe still in his mouth, to halt the duel. The teams' first meeting had ended in a 1–1 draw, but when the Washington management complained that Wolves manager Ronnie Allen had used three outfield substitutes, instead of two plus a goalkeeper, a replay was ordered. The additional game, won 3–0 by the Whips, was slotted into the schedule four days before the sides met again in the final.

Six months after more than 61,000 sat in the Coliseum to watch the Green Bay Packers beat the Kansas City Chiefs in gridiron's first Super Bowl, a crowd of 17,824 gathered to witness the USA's inaugural championship game. It turned out to be a remarkable match. After 63 minutes the teams were locked at 1–1, goals by midfielders Peter Knowles, for Wolves, and Jimmy Smith cancelling each other out. But suddenly the game exploded with four goals in the space of less than four minutes. Clark recalls, 'There were penalties saved and scored, good goals and bad goals. It was a bizarre situation in a way. It was like a basketball game with all that scoring. But it was one of those games you desperately wanted to win.'

Twice Wolves hit back to level through Burnside after Munro and Jim Storrie edged their team ahead. According to Munro, 'Neither side had seemed desperate to make it much more than an exhibition match for the benefit of the locals. Then the burst of goals wiped away the "take it easy" atmosphere. The stadium was in turmoil.' There was no doubt about how seriously the teams were taking it when Smith was sent off after 80 minutes following a clash with Wolves winger David Wagstaffe, after which Burnside edged Wolves into a 4–3 lead. But with only seconds remaining, Munro equalised for ten-man Washington to take the game into extra-time.

Wolves scored first in extra-time through Dougan and could have wrapped up victory had Terry Wharton not been denied from the penalty spot by Clark. Once again, it was left to Munro to save the day for Washington, converting a last-gasp penalty to complete his hat-trick and set up a period of sudden-death play in which the first team to score would win. After a total of 126 minutes, Wolves defender Bobby Thomson crossed from the left and Aberdeen defender Ally Shewan deflected the ball off his shins past Clark.

The Los Angeles Wolves had taken the USA's first final 6–5. But by the time the champions were boarding their plane back to England, soccer's accountants were confirming that there had been no real winners in the first year of the sport's American revival.

2. ☆ Staying Alive

The return of professional soccer to the United States had clearly not gone according to plan. Some of the teams in the NPSL and USA had returned losses of $500,000. The problem was the age-old one when it came to soccer in the United States. Quite simply, most Americans understood little and cared even less about the sport being served up by the two organisations. Watching the 1966 World Cup on television had been one thing; the audience had bought into the global significance of the event. But that did not mean they would rush out and buy season tickets for their 'local' team. Furthermore, the clubs had no real connection to the community. John O'Hare, part of the Sunderland team that represented Vancouver in 1967, says, 'We didn't do much to market the team to the Canadians. We should have done more. It was really just the British ex-pats who came to see us.'

 The teams had no history, few American heroes and, as was clear to those who did understand their football, a poor-quality version of the game was being offered. The ethnic groups who had been expected to turn out to watch the sport of their homeland knew a sub-standard product when they saw one.

The US soccer community could see that on the field there was a clear choice to be made between the fast-track route of bringing in greater quality and quantity of foreign players or taking the more conservative path of growing slowly by developing American players and encouraging greater participation in the sport. The first concern for the team owners, however, was how many of them would still be competing in 1968. The consensus was that the problems of the previous season had been caused by the competition between the two organisations spreading the sport's fan base too thinly. In December 1967, the leagues took the sensible step of merger and adopted the name originally favoured by the USA.

The North American Soccer League was born, although it had not been a painless labour. Talks about the proposed merger threatened to become long and drawn out, until an $18-million law suit filed by the NPSL against those established football authorities who had tried to isolate them hastened matters to their conclusion. Initially, the new NASL had two commissioners, Dick Walsh and Ken Macker, who had held the posts with the USA and NPSL respectively. Neither came from a soccer background, with Walsh, a renowned baseball administrator, admitting, 'I hardly even know what a soccer ball looks like.'

Only 17 of the two leagues' combined 22 franchises remained, with some teams being moved to prevent having more than one in any market. On the field, a compromise approach was adopted in an attempt to boost the number of home players involved, while at the same time increasing the quality of play. In short, it meant fewer, but better, foreigners, with the number of Americans in the league rising to 30.

The British contingent at Atlanta was largely unchanged, with Newman moving to Dallas during the season after losing his place in the team. Cleveland retained the name of the Stokers and continued to wear red and white stripes, even though most of their players were no longer from the Potteries. The exception was Stoke's reserve goalkeeper Paul Shardlow, who played in all 32 games and would die a couple of years later after suffering a heart attack during training in England. With former Liverpool, Newport and Norwich centre-half Norman Low in charge of team affairs, Cleveland were one of eight clubs that had British coaches for at least part of the season.

Former England international and future national team manager Bobby Robson seemed destined to swell that number after reaching an agreement with the Vancouver Royals before the merger of the two leagues. Meanwhile, however, the San Francisco Gales had made a similar deal with the Hungarian legend Ferenc Puskas. When San Francisco folded and the team's owners bought a controlling interest in the Vancouver club, it was their man who won the coach's job. Robson turned down the role of assistant, Vancouver's loss being Fulham's and, eventually, Ipswich Town's gain.

The situation caused inevitable discomfort among the English players Robson had talked into signing for the club. Among them was Huddersfield defender Peter Dinsdale, who reveals, 'I left England thinking that I was going to play for Bobby Robson and got to Canada to find I was playing for Puskas. I had met Bobby on a course at Lilleshall. We got talking and I decided it was a good time to go over. I was going over on a ship with my family when I heard that Bobby was made manager of Fulham. It disappointed me when I heard that Puskas was the manager because I wanted to play for Bobby.'

Among Puskas's other English charges were full-back Bobby Cram, formerly with West Brom and later to be part of the Colchester United team that upset Leeds in the 1970–71 FA Cup, and former Fulham and Crystal Palace winger Brian 'Pat' O'Connell. After winning their first three games, the team finished bottom of the Pacific Conference's Western Division.

Dinsdale continues, 'Bobby had got half the team together and Puskas had got the other half. We got on well, but our playing styles were different. All those years ago, there were two different styles of games. The continental players that Puskas signed were ball players and we were runners and because of that we didn't gel. Puskas had signed older players who didn't have the legs any more. The language was a problem as well. We were just not a team. We were two halves put together.'

Gordon Jago, a former Charlton centre-half from London's East End who had been coaching at Fulham, jumped at the chance to exchange Craven Cottage for Memorial Stadium in Baltimore to coach the Bays. He explains, 'I came over the previous year with Fulham to play in the San Francisco area. Well, that's not a bad city for your first experience of America and I fell in love with what I saw. I got a call from Clive Toye, the former *Daily Express* writer, who was general manager at Baltimore. He asked if I would like to coach the team and I thought it was a hell of an opportunity. It turned out to be the most difficult two years of my soccer life. We couldn't spend any money on players. But it hardened me up as a person.'

The Boston Beacons were coached by former Brighton and Portsmouth full-back Jack Mansell and, one year before he signed for Chelsea, right-back Paddy Mulligan was back in Boston after playing there with Shamrock Rovers the previous summer. The Detroit Cougars line-up featured Jim Standen, whose six seasons at West Ham had brought him a pair of Wembley victories, in the 1964 FA Cup final and the next year's European Cup-Winners' cup final. Roy Cheetham had played 127 League games in ten years as a wing-half at Manchester City, while teammates included former Motherwell and Arsenal winger Tommy Coakley and Portsmouth and Millwall centre-half Brian Snowdon. Beginning the season as player-coach was centre-forward Len Julians, whose last English team had been Millwall, where he scored 58 League goals in three seasons.

In Los Angeles, an all-English defensive unit was being built by coach Ray Wood, the former Huddersfield and Manchester United goalkeeper. Centre-half Tony Knapp, a veteran of more than 200 games for Southampton, was the most experienced of the group. The New York Generals retained Freddie Goodwin as coach and, significantly, included Gordon Bradley, an English wing-half who had not played in the Football League since finishing a stint of 129 League games for Carlisle seven years earlier. The Generals finished out of the play-off picture, but Bradley was to become one of the key figures in New York soccer over the following decade.

The season's tale of the bizarre was the Dallas Tornado, who, having been represented by the players of Dundee United the previous year, needed to build a team from scratch. Owners Lamar Hunt and Bill McNutt hired Yugoslav coach Bob Kap and charged him with recruiting a squad. Kap's approach was to hire a group of inexperienced youngsters, mostly amateurs, from England, Holland and Scandinavia. By the time the Dallas Tornado took the field for their first game of the 1968 NASL season they had already played 45 games on an exhausting winter-long world tour that was designed to turn them into a coherent unit. Travelling through Spain, Morocco, Turkey, Cyprus, Iran, Pakistan, India, Ceylon, Burma, Malaysia, Indonesia, Vietnam, Taiwan, Japan, the Philippines, Australia, New Zealand, Fiji and Tahiti, the Tornado won only ten games. As they trekked around the world they waved the US flag and acted as representatives of a country most of their players had not yet seen.

Ron Newman heard the tales of Kap's unorthodox methods when he arrived following his mid-season trade from Atlanta. 'He was weird. The way I heard it, he would put an ad in the local paper wherever he was going, asking for people who had played football. A load of guys would turn up and when he asked who they played for they would say, "Liverpool" and add in a whisper, "Gasworks". One guy's mate even turned up with him one day and Kap asked him if he wanted to go on a world tour. It turned out he didn't even play football! I guess it seemed like a great idea to send the team off all over the world to get experience but later on the money seemed to have disappeared.'

Whether through inexperience, incompetence or travel sickness, results proved the folly of Kap's approach. It was not until the 22nd game of the NASL schedule that Dallas gained the first of only two victories. Inevitably, Kap did not last the season, being replaced by Englishman Keith Spurgeon, who had coached Ajax Amsterdam after suffering a serious injury playing for Tottenham. A total of 36 players represented the Tornado in 1968, while Newman, injured early in the season at Atlanta, acted as assistant coach after his arrival.

The season started with a significant change in the CBS commentary booth, where the network bosses decided they'd had enough of Danny Blanchflower's straight talking. Had he been retained, however, he would have been passing comment on a vastly superior product. 'It was a very good standard,' recalls Phil Woosnam. 'It was the highest standard we had in the league until the mid-'70s.'

The league was split into two conferences and four divisions, with Atlanta winning the Eastern Conference's Atlantic Division on the back of the league's best defence. The Cleveland Stokers captured the Lakes Division ahead of the Chicago Mustangs, while the Kansas City Spurs prevailed in the Western Conference's Gulf Division, thanks in part to the 17 goals scored by Irish forward Eric Barber, who had played just three games for Birmingham after signing from Shelbourne. The Pacific Division saw a triumph for the San Diego Toros, whose co-coach was George Curtis, the former Southampton wing-half. The Toros had an identical record to the Oakland Clippers, but San Diego gained one more bonus point to head into a two-legged Conference Championship meeting with Kansas City. In the same division, Los Angeles retained the gold strip of the Wolverhampton team that had won the USA title, but there were few other similarities as they won only 11 of 32 games.

Having disposed of the Spurs, San Diego's opponents in the final were Atlanta, who drew 1–1 at fellow division winners Cleveland before winning 2–1 at home three days later with goals by Peter McParland and the South African Kaizer Motaung, later to return to his homeland to form the famous Kaizer Chiefs club. Motaung had been the Chiefs' top scorer in the regular season with ten goals, one more than former Bournemouth forward Graham Newton. Woosnam had discovered Motaung at Johannesburg's Orlando Pirates. 'I had been invited to coach the Zambian team in the summers of 1963 and 1964 and one of the guys I worked with said I ought to go down to Johannesburg to look at a couple of players,' he explains. 'One of them was Kaizer. We could hardly hide the fact that we were there watching him because we were the only two white faces in a crowd of 30,000. He made the difference to our team that year. He had immense ability around the box.'

San Diego went into the final with the ageing Brazilian Vava, a World Cup-winner in 1958 and 1962, accompanied in midfield by Englishman Ray Freeman. After a goalless draw in California, the second leg was played on a rainy night in Georgia, with just under

15,000 in attendance. 'There was a great atmosphere,' says McParland. 'The crowd was very enthusiastic because the city of Atlanta had never won a national title in any sport.'

It was McParland who scored the first goal in a 3–0 victory, enabling Woosnam to add the NASL title to the Coach of the Year prize he had been awarded. 'In those days I had a great belief in overlapping defenders,' he says. 'One goal came from the full-back going wide on one side and the second came down the other side. For the third goal, Kaizer picked the ball up in the centre circle and went all the way before putting it in the back of the net.'

Barely had celebrations died down in Atlanta before the realities of the season began to hit home. The league's budget had been set with a break-even average crowd of 20,000 in mind, yet only 3,400 per game had attended. Vancouver were among the teams in dire financial straits, which meant a shock was in store for Dinsdale and his teammates. 'We were playing in the Empire Stadium, which held about 40,000, and because we were only getting a few thousand at our games there was talk about the future of the team. But I had a contract for three years and I thought that if I had a contract it would be paid up. But they tore up our contracts and left us with no money and no one to go after to get what we were owed. It turned out that the team was owned by a shell company that had no money in it so our contracts were never paid.'

Several other owners were poised to desert the NASL's sinking ship. John Best, who had moved to the Cleveland Stokers after seeing the Philadelphia Spartans close down following the 1967 season, could see the writing on the wall as his new team rattled around with 4,000 fans in a stadium that held 80,000. But he argues, 'I felt the owners should have been more patient. You have to earn the attendance of fans. There is no God-given right to demand that they come and watch. You have to put all those little building blocks in place, and the pace of growth was a very important thing when you were looking at what was trying to be accomplished.'

Few, however, were prepared to show such patience in the face of losses that were estimated at $20 million over two years. Besides, at the end of a year that had seen the escalation of the conflict in Vietnam, the assassinations of Martin Luther King and Robert Kennedy, ongoing civil and racial unrest and the presidential election victory of Richard Nixon, there were more important priorities than propping up a 'foreign' sport. America's new soccer league was on the brink of collapse and it was up to a Welshman to save it.

3. ☆ Man for All Seasons

Phil Woosnam had always been a little different to most of his peers in professional football. While others spent their late teens and early twenties establishing themselves at their clubs, or falling by the wayside, Woosnam had his nose buried in books as he gained a B.Sc. in physics and maths from the University of Wales in Bangor. And by the time the NASL's 1968 season ended with the league facing the prospect of collapse, the articulate and intelligent Welshman had shown enough vision, foresight and passion about soccer in America to land himself the role of the sport's reluctant saviour.

Woosnam remembers, 'They kept the league's problems under wraps until a couple of weeks before the end of the season. I used to attend the league meetings because I was general manager at Atlanta as well as coach, and late in the season was the first time I found out we could be going down from seventeen teams to five. The ringleaders of the remaining clubs at that time were Lamar Hunt, who owned Dallas, and Dick Cecil, who was president of the Atlanta Braves baseball club and the guy I reported to. They asked me to go round the country to all 17 owners and try to persuade them to keep going.'

It was a far cry from the career Woosnam had imagined for himself when he was turning out as an amateur for Manchester City's second and third teams – and playing one League game – during his college days. Born in the small Welsh village of Caersws in 1932, Woosnam did not start playing League football regularly until his early twenties when he appeared for Leyton Orient while stationed in London as part of the national service duties that followed his graduation. 'Orient weren't Manchester City but they were still a good Third Division team and were up at the top with

30

Alec Stock as manager,' Woosnam recalls. 'When I came out of the army I taught at Leyton County High School as well as playing, but I realised that if I didn't teach any more I might be able to play for a First Division club. So I retired from teaching and when West Ham came in for me I moved five miles across town.'

When Woosnam arrived at Upton Park in 1958 he found a club crackling with innovation, debate and sharp footballing minds – many of whom used to spend hours in a local café discussing tactics with the help of salt cellars and ketchup bottles. Woosnam's teammates included future managers and coaches like Malcolm Allison, John Bond, Ken Brown, Malcolm Musgrove and Noel Cantwell. 'It was a marvellous time and a great environment to be a part of. My first game was Malcolm's [Allison] benefit game after he had lost a lung. He was still around the club a fair bit so I got to know him pretty well. There were others in the club who were outstanding football people, strong personalities who didn't crack when the pressure was on.'

The culture of Upton Park clearly made its mark on Woosnam, as evidenced by the measures he would introduce to instil a West Ham-type positive attitude in the NASL in future years. 'We played an attractive brand of soccer at West Ham and it was my best experience in the professional game. The whole attitude of the players towards the game was different to anywhere else. It was the perfect club and a most enjoyable time. You always felt you were learning something. We didn't win anything but the team was good enough to have won . . . we were leading the First Division for a long time but didn't sustain it throughout the season.'

Woosnam already had his eye on a career in management and had qualified as a coach when, in 1960, he was given the chance to take charge at Upton Park. 'They asked me if I was interested in being player-manager. I said no, but I recommended two people: Ron Greenwood, who I knew from Lilleshall, and Joe Mallett, who had been a coach during my Orient days. Ron got the job.'

In 1962, Woosnam was on the move, signing for Aston Villa for his final four-year stint in the Football League. He worked as an FA staff coach throughout his spell at Villa Park, but still considered himself a player when the call came to head to America. It was only his desire to keep his word that saw him board the plane for Atlanta after being offered a transfer to Chelsea.

He explains, 'The last couple of years at Villa had been hard and I was at that age when I didn't feel I was in the league to battle relegation every year. It was the summer of 1966 and I thought I had another two or three years and I hoped I could get back into London with a club there. When I couldn't get a team, I saw a piece in the paper by the sportswriter Clive Toye saying people were coming over to America to start a professional league.'

Woosnam travelled to London to meet representatives of the new organisation and arranged to visit them in the US. 'I told Villa I would be going over to America on the Sunday after the opening game of the new season. They didn't select me for the game because they thought I might not come back.'

Having attended a league meeting in New York, Woosnam flew south to visit the Atlanta Chiefs. 'I stayed a week and was impressed. I thought I could learn a lot from the promotion of sports and so on and thought if I stayed a couple of years I could go back into management in England. I felt confident about the success of the Chiefs. The baseball club owned them and that brought other benefits. I felt that we could achieve something with their backing, using their relationship with the public and media.'

But when Woosnam returned home to tell Villa he was heading to Atlanta as player-coach of the Chiefs he discovered that wheels had been turning in his absence. 'Tommy Docherty wanted me to sign for Chelsea. He said to Villa that he would like Tony Hateley and me to join him because he had a young team that was developing and needed some experience. Now, I had not signed anything with Atlanta, but I had committed myself verbally and, as much as Chelsea would have been my first choice, I felt I had to go back to Atlanta. They were nice people and I felt obligated to them. By that time I had already asked Vic Crowe and Peter McParland to come over.'

Woosnam believed that the impending collapse of the sport after the 1968 season would see him heading back to Britain. 'I thought it was the end as far as most of us were concerned. I didn't know what to tell the players. Would we be able to play another season? If we did, would they be invited to stay on? I was prepared to go back home.'

Then came the plea to Woosnam to make a last-ditch effort to keep as many of the 17 NASL teams in the fold as possible. 'I went to see all the owners and told them, "Don't give up yet. You can't expect it to happen in two years." Because the salaries weren't enormous in those days they couldn't have been losing that much money. Some believed and some didn't.'

As he embarked on his rescue mission, Woosnam admitted to reporters that his club had lost $250,00 in two years, less than some. He added, 'We have developed the Atlanta area as we expected, but this has not happened elsewhere.' Woosnam's comments were directed at those teams who had expected instant returns and were not prepared to invest in the future by getting more youngsters involved in the sport. 'In about 50 per cent of the cities they had set up grassroots programmes but in the others they just wanted to win a game and that was it.'

The approach taken by Woosnam had received endorsement during the summer of 1968 by his old friend Malcolm Allison. Having observed the American scene at close quarters, the Manchester City coach commented, 'Phil Woosnam in Atlanta is probably the only one with the right idea. He has gone and got kids interested. It's what you must do and what the Americans will have to do if they want the game to survive.'

Ironically, Allison's City had experienced the improved on-field quality of the NASL during 1968, losing twice to Atlanta and also to Oakland. After the initial 3–2 loss against the Chiefs, Allison claimed their opponents had been of Fourth Division standard and that such a freak result could not happen again. It did, the Chiefs winning 2–1. Peter McParland remembers, 'We wanted to beat them badly because Malcolm was shooting his mouth off and we thought we had better shut him up. We had something to prove.'

The Chiefs' efforts to introduce soccer to children in Atlanta had been driven, not by the club as a long-term tactic, but by the players themselves. Woosnam recalls, 'We taught the club exactly what they needed to do off the field. The club leadership was among ourselves, the players. The guys had great personalities and were outstanding in the community. Ron Newman led the charge to establish youth soccer in the city – maybe because of need, as there were a number of players with sons who wanted to play. We recruited players who were interested in that side of things.'

Unsure whether his Dallas team would last the winter, Newman decided to use his time fruitfully instead of sitting around waiting for the results of Woosnam's tour. Having been the instigator of the Atlanta youth programme, he set about developing a similar movement in his new home town. 'You couldn't get uniforms, balls or anything in the stores at that time,' Newman recounts. 'My young son, Guy, who had just started playing in England before I moved over, came to me one day with a list of names. He had recruited these kids to play, but there was no one to play against. An American friend said, "Let's start a league." He put an ad in the paper and we told people to report at seven o'clock and pretty soon we were overflowing. I had to rush off and get some teammates to help out. We counted out 12 boys and gave them to this player and 12 to the next.'

Having also recruited fathers to help out with coaching and refereeing, Newman's next task was to find somewhere to play.

'There were no soccer fields. I went with Ronnie Foster, who played for Leyton Orient when I was there, to make one at my son's school. The principal said we could use a field at the back of the school. I remember marking out the pitch in the freezing cold on a Monday. Then it pissed down on Wednesday so I had to do it again ready for Saturday. But by Saturday, the school district had put a baseball diamond in the middle of the field! I remember the head man of the recreation areas of Dallas saying to me, "If you could see all the teams looking for baseball fields you would know why I did it." I said, "In a few years' time all those fields will be obsolete because soccer here is going to be bigger than baseball." Three years later I bumped into him and he said, "You were right. I can't get enough soccer fields. I thought you were something from outer space saying that." I used to be a carpenter in the dockyards at Portsmouth so I ended up making the goals for our first game. I thought I did a pretty good job, but then vandals broke them all up. Not out of spite but because they were good to swing on.'

Newman's reward would come in the number of soccer balls being kicked around in years to come. By the end of the decade, Atlanta and Dallas had joined the traditional hotbed of St Louis as the focal points for soccer participation in the States. 'We had more than 60,000 playing in Dallas five years later,' he explains. 'It was like giving away five-dollar bills for a dollar. As soon as kids began to play they could not get enough of it. I went to England in our off-season and went to Birmingham to see Umbro. I brought back all these uniforms. I worked out a cost of about five dollars a set and was selling them to the kids for the same price we got them. But I had no idea about the import duty or anything. The socks were nylon and there was a high import duty on that so it turned out costing us more than we were selling the uniforms for. Then I found out we had American mothers coming in and saying the sleeves were short or the shirt was too long. Back home if I had to play centre-forward for Pompey I had to wear a shirt that was twice the size as me and if I was on the wing the shirt was too small. The mums wanted them to fit like Saville Row. I thought, "Just pull them up, tuck them in or cut a bit off!"'

While Newman was building goalposts and ordering uniforms, Woosnam was having a frustrating time in meeting rooms. In early January 1969, he addressed the ten owners who had not yet abandoned the NASL. Joe Namath and the upstart New York Jets were preparing that week to upset America's sporting equilibrium by beating the heavily favoured Baltimore Colts in Super Bowl III, which meant that it passed virtually unnoticed when only five of ten teams allowed themselves to be counted in for the 1969 NASL season.

Ten of the previous season's seventeen franchises folded completely during the winter of 1968–69, while Oakland, renamed as the California Clippers, embarked on an exhibition schedule and the Chicago Mustangs dropped down to the semi-professional National Soccer League. Not surprisingly, CBS cancelled its NASL television contract.

The five remaining NASL owners took the inevitable step of asking Woosnam to run the league in the position of commissioner. It appeared a thankless task, but the Welshman accepted eagerly. 'I looked on it as a great challenge and I wouldn't have done it unless I believed we were going to succeed. Vic Crowe took over at the Chiefs, so I knew the club was in great hands.'

The one offer from home that could have changed Woosnam's decision never materialised. 'There was a group of people threatening to buy Villa, who had got into serious financial trouble. They were talking about me as manager but in the end they didn't make a decision and didn't buy the club. At that time I probably would have taken that job.'

Woosnam enlisted Clive Toye, the former *Daily Express* writer and Baltimore general manager, as his second-in-command. Toye had abandoned Fleet Street in search of a new challenge after the excitement of reporting on England's World Cup triumph and had remained close to Woosnam during his battles to keep the NASL afloat. 'We ended up opening the new league office in the visitors' locker room of Atlanta stadium,' he explains. 'We spent hours on the phone talking and it seemed natural we would end up working together. Phil, being a mystical Welshman, felt a sense of mission and in my case it was plain bloody-mindedness, a determination to make people like soccer.'

Toye had been offered his position in Baltimore through his close relationship with those setting up the original NPSL, but admits to surprise at how undeveloped the soccer scene had been when he arrived in America. 'I'd had no idea of just how unknown and unwanted soccer was. There was an absolute lack of knowledge. They couldn't even spell "soccer". East of Mississippi there was only one store where you could buy soccer equipment. I felt that in the first two years a number of owners were in it only to have more dates in the stadium and as a self-protection measure just in case it took off. Once it was apparent it was not going to spread like wildfire they said, "Sod it. Let's get out."'

With owners having done exactly that, Woosnam and Toye demanded that the five surviving clubs drastically reduce player salaries and other operating costs so that annual budgets could be held at a manageable $200,000 per team. The next task was to construct a season, but the uncertainty over the future of the league meant that clubs did not have complete rosters. Woosnam played for time by splitting the season into two halves, the first of which was a throwback to the USA season of 1967 with each club to be represented by an imported team from Britain. The hope was that the high quality of play would help create momentum going into the second half of the season.

Woosnam spent the early part of 1969 visiting Britain to line up teams to play in the US. Gordon Jago, with whom he was now coaching America's World Cup team, accompanied him. The first half of the season was to be staged as the International Cup, with the Atlanta Chiefs represented by Second Division Aston Villa. West Ham turned out on behalf of the Baltimore Bays, flying out their World Cup heroes Geoff Hurst, Bobby Moore and Martin Peters after England's 4–1 thumping of Scotland in the Home International Championship. Two years after winning the USA crown for Los Angeles, Wolves were back as the Kansas City Spurs. Kilmarnock became the St Louis Stars, while Dundee United reprised their role of two years earlier as the Dallas Tornado. 'The teams got good money to play out there and we used our personal contacts to get the ones we wanted,' says Jago. 'With his background, Phil obviously wanted Aston Villa, while I had always supported West Ham and their manager, Ron Greenwood, was a personal friend.'

FIFA gave approval for the tournament to be used as a testing ground for a change to the offside law, with no player ruled offside from a direct free-kick. The results would be inconclusive and the response mixed. West Ham manager Ron Greenwood said during the event, 'We see no real advantage in ruling out offside as the kick is taken. The Americans are confident they can sell this idea but I have my doubts.'

A typical view of the NASL's tinkering was expressed by Wolves coach Sammy Chung, who said, 'It seems crazy that the Americans are looking for ways to change a sport that is fast enough for millions everywhere else while they leave the sport of baseball untouched. For some reason, no one has ever thought of speeding that up.'

Woosnam's belief that the International Cup would deliver success at the gate was mistaken. West Ham, who had finished eighth in Division One, opened up against Wolves in front of just over 5,000 fans in Baltimore. The low point came in Dallas, where Dundee United and Kilmarnock, fifth and fourth respectively in the previous Scottish League season, fought out an exciting 3–3 draw in front of fewer than 200 people. Jago recalls, 'We thought that West Ham, with Bobby Moore and their World Cup players, would be a massive draw but they weren't to the Americans. Sports fans in America relate so much to money, which is why in later years people went to see Pelé. They heard how much money he was earning so they thought he must be an attraction.'

On the field, Wolves repeated their success of two years earlier, winning six of their eight games in the colours of Kansas City and scoring twenty-five goals in the process. Five of those goals were scored by England Under-23 international Peter Knowles in what was virtually the swansong of his career. The talented midfielder, whose good looks had made him something of a heart-throb with female fans, would play his last game for Wolves in September of that year, claiming that he had lost faith in football and found it outside the game. He retired to devote himself to life as a Jehovah's Witness. Those religious beliefs also caused an etiquette problem in the States as he refused to stand for the American national anthem before kick-off.

With Knowles in full flow, Wolves enabled Kansas City to finish five points ahead of Baltimore's Hammers. Greenwood's side won five games, including a 6–1 win against Dundee United (Dallas) that featured a Trevor Brooking hat-trick. The Wolves players were made honorary citizens of Kansas City for their efforts, while Chung put their success down to the serious way in which they had approached the games. 'I consider there is no such thing as a friendly,' he stated. 'One has to drill the killer instinct into the side.'

The failure of the international teams to attract sufficient fans claimed a victim even before the second half of the season kicked off when, at a league meeting in Dallas, Baltimore owner Jerold Hoffberger broke the news that the team would finish the season and then close.

'Hoffberger said quietly to me that we would be closing and told me not to tell anyone,' says Jago. 'He felt that if we couldn't draw with West Ham we wouldn't draw with our own players. It was purely a business decision. Like other teams, the owners in Baltimore had seen the 1966 World Cup on television and thought, "This looks good. Let's get on with it. If it doesn't work we can just go back to baseball." The plan was to cut back everywhere and quietly close down at the end of the season. It was a deliberate move to take the sport under.'

Hoffberger was the owner of the Colt 45 beer company and the Baltimore Orioles baseball team and Jago, whose lame-duck side won only two of their sixteen games, believes he was forced to play the fall guy to protect the owner's credibility and the image of his other business concerns. 'The Baltimore owners felt they did not want criticism. They moved us from Memorial Stadium to a high school and then tore up the car park there for repairs. It was a rough inner-city area and people would not go to the games there and leave their cars on the street. I respected the owner, respected his decision, and I took a lot of stick. I remember at one game hearing a foreign voice shout, "Go home to your Queen Elizabeth!" I was getting stick in the papers as well, but I couldn't just say, "Sorry, we don't have any money because we are closing down."'

By the end of the season, the Bays were attracting fewer than 500 for their home games. 'It was easy to close down then,' says Jago. 'We had lost games, not drawn fans and moved into a small stadium. They probably did it the right way. The beer sales and the baseball team didn't suffer.'

The 16-game NASL season saw Newman assuming charge of the Dallas Tornado, coaching them to a modest third-place finish. The final table demonstrated the effects of the NASL's unique scoring system. Atlanta had the best record, with eleven wins and three draws, while Kansas City won ten and drew four. But the Spurs' 53 goals eclipsed Atlanta's 46 and the resulting bonus points gave them a 110–109 edge over Vic Crowe's team to earn their second title of the summer. The St Louis Stars, reflecting the summer's wave of patriotism that surrounded the success of the Apollo 11 moon mission, chose to include 14 home-grown players in their 18-man squad but won only three games and trailed in attendance with only 2,274 per game. At this stage of the sport's development, some things were still a giant leap too far.

4. ☆ Bright Lights, Big Cities

Football fans around the world have little trouble in remembering 1970 as the year of the breathtaking Brazilians. In America, however, the World Cup made little impact. As the tournament neared, an appalled nation was reeling from the killing of four Kent State University students in anti-war demonstrations and watching in grim fascination as Charles Manson and members of his 'family' were sentenced to death for the grisly murders of actress Sharon Tate and others. But, unknown even to the country's soccer faithful, events down Mexico way were about to ensure that the NASL's tide would turn, eventually carrying some of the world's biggest stars to America's shores.

The demise of the Baltimore Bays had left Phil Woosnam with the task of preventing the NASL being reduced to four teams. He succeeded by persuading the Rochester Lancers and Washington Darts to part with $10,000 each for the privilege of stepping up from the American Soccer League. Ironically, they were to be the two leading teams in the expanded 24-game campaign.

Coventry City were invited to be a part of the new season, one of four international teams who played against each of the six NASL clubs. The home teams' results in the four games were to count in the standings. Hertha Berlin, Portugul's Varzim and Israeli team Petah Tikya were the others who participated, although Dallas Tornado asked to be excused a game against Israeli opponents on account of owner Lamar Hunt's Arab oil interests. Mexican side Monterrey therefore stepped in for one game. Coventry won five of their six games, while the Washington Darts were awarded the International Cup after two wins and two draws against the foreign opposition. Washington's team included English defender Chris Dunleavy, who helped his team keep 12 clean sheets and was to be a key figure in another expansion team's success two years later.

Vic Rouse took over as head coach in Atlanta, where his team included Dave Metchick, the former Fulham, Orient, Peterborough and Queens Park Rangers midfielder, scorer of eight goals in twenty games. In Dallas, the Tornado had Englishman Ken Cooper in goal for the first of nine seasons with the team, playing behind Dick Hall, a defender with a handful of League games to his name at Bournemouth.

English-born Alan Rogers was back in the league as head coach of the Kansas City Spurs, having been in charge when the team had been in Chicago in 1967, while newcomers Rochester had NASL veteran Peter Short in defence alongside Scot Charlie Mitchell. Born in Paisley and signed by St Mirren, Mitchell had moved to America and joined the Lancers in 1967. The club's arrival in the NASL marked the start of his ten-year playing career in the league.

As Southern Division champions, Washington were heavily fancied to beat the Lancers, who topped the Northern Division despite winning only nine games. But it was Rochester who achieved a decisive 3–0 first-leg victory in the final, clinching the crown when Washington could win only 3–1 in their home leg.

The overall standard of play was considered to have increased and crowds had risen slightly to an average of 3,600, but it was in Mexico that the NASL had scored its most significant victory. Woosnam explains, 'We had set a goal to have eight teams in 1971 and we decided we had to go back into New York if we were going to have an impact. By this time I was vice-president of the US Soccer Federation [USSF] because that went with the role of commissioner. The people I met there said, "There are some people within Warner Brothers who have got a tremendous interest in soccer. Two brothers by the name of Ertegun." To make contact I decided I would go to Mexico for the last week of the World Cup.

'After the final I was trying to find Ron Greenwood, who was over there from England. I went to his hotel and said I was looking for Ron and they told me to try this big reception that was being put on by some guy from America. I went and knocked on the door and a little guy opened it. I said, "Hello. I'm looking for Ron Greenwood, my name is Phil Woosnam." He said, "Nice to meet you. I'm Nesuhi Ertegun." I laughed and said, "I have been waiting to meet you for six weeks." It was fortunate timing.'

Ertegun was executive vice-president of Atlantic Records, a subsidiary of Warner Communications. Coming from a Turkish background, he was a huge soccer fan and arranged to meet up with Woosnam when they returned to New York, along with his brother, Ahmet, and Steve Ross, the chairman of Warner.

The search for a major backer for a New York team had earlier led Woosnam to approach the broadcaster David Frost, whose interest in the sport was well known. Frost's advisers turned down a deal, but Woosnam's cocktail party encounter opened the mighty door of a media giant and on 10 December 1970, Woosnam found himself announcing the birth of the Warner-backed New York Cosmos. The first year of the new decade had begun with New York boasting the champions of gridiron and baseball, the Jets and the Mets, and now the year was ending with the birth of a franchise that would dominate its sport more completely than any of the other teams in town would manage throughout the '70s.

New York was only half of the NASL's big-city strategy for 1971. Canada's largest city had also been targeted and the Toronto Metros signed up to join the league. Woosnam announced, 'Stability of the league is now finally established and the addition of such great soccer centres as New York and Toronto is further indication of the progress the game has made at all levels.' The league did lose the Kansas City Spurs, but the addition of the Montreal Olympic increased the number of teams to eight and the NASL was able to command a franchise fee of $25,000 from each of the three new clubs.

Despite the money behind the club, the Cosmos team that took the field in 1971 had little of the glamour of its future sides. Composed largely of players from local amateur teams, the squad also included Englishman Barry Mahy, a former New York General, and player-coach Gordon Bradley, the former Carlisle midfielder who had played for the Generals in their final year, 1968, before spending a year under Gordon Jago in Baltimore. A promising junior with Sunderland, Bradley's career had been set back when, at the age of 16, he suffered a knee injury that kept him out of football for two years. His stint at Carlisle followed a brief spell at Bradford Park Avenue and he moved to Canada in 1963.

In Toronto, the choice as coach was 36-year-old Scot Graham Leggat, who had won 18 caps for his country and played more than 250 League games for Fulham after transferring from Aberdeen. Leggat, formerly youth-team coach at Aston Villa, was in the job market as part of the fallout from Tommy Docherty's sacking at Villa Park. 'I felt I was part of the Docherty set-up and was working on the same things as him, so I thought I should resign,' Leggat recalls. 'Phil Woosnam phoned me and said that Toronto were looking for a coach. I said at first that I was not really keen to move my family but Jack Daley, the general manager of Toronto, called me and said, "We have no team and we need you to build one. You can be player-coach." He asked me to send a résumé but there was a mail strike. So I said, "I can't send you anything but I can be in Toronto at 4 p.m. tomorrow."

'Two gentlemen showed me around, but at that time the team had no players, no field, just a couple of offices. And the first game was only eight weeks away! I said, "Let me think about it." I went home and said to my wife, "We shouldn't go, but I am going to go anyway."'

While the Cosmos might have had the money of Warner Communications behind them – even if they were not yet dipping into it – Leggat quickly discovered that there were very few dollars to throw around north of the Canadian border. 'I went to local practices and thought, "My goodness, how are we going to pick a team from here?" I managed to find a couple of players who looked like they might fit in and my assistant, Arthur Rodrigues, knew he could get players from Portugal. But I don't believe in having 11 veterans on your team.'

With no money to spend on established players and no desire to stock his team with Portuguese journeymen, Leggat turned to his contacts book. 'I phoned Aston Villa. I also phoned Bobby Robson, who I had played with at Fulham and was now manager at Ipswich, and I phoned Bert Head at Crystal Palace.'

Included in the handful of youth and reserve team players acquired from those sources were defender Neil Rioch, the brother of future Scotland player and Villa teammate Bruce, Glasgow-born full-back Brian Rowan, who would enjoy six seasons in the NASL, and a 15-year-old midfielder from Ipswich. 'I had been scouting amateurishly and I had seen Ipswich's youth team play Coventry. I liked the look of their right-half, Brian Talbot, and a lad called Bruce Tormley, who was Canadian. I asked Bobby Robson about it and said I would meet with their parents and let them know we would take good care of them. I said it would be great experience for them, that they would be playing against veterans and would come back better players. That was how we sold it.'

Talbot, who would go on to win England caps and FA Cup-winner's medals with Ipswich and Arsenal, celebrated his 16th birthday in Toronto, but Leggat admits, 'I actually felt a bit sorry for Brian and the young lads. The money was very, very poor because we had to pay to provide accommodation for all the guys from England. We were able to give them about $80 a week – a shoestring budget.'

Rioch recalls, 'I remember going over with Brian Talbot and we struck up a friendship straight away. We were housed in the Royal Oak Hotel, the finest hotel in Toronto, but only for about five days. Then it was the King Street West Motel. We really had to look after ourselves, do our own washing and ironing. But it was fine. There were about six of us who were full-time and it was a great experience for youngsters like us. We trained twice a day because we worked with Graham during the day and came back and trained with the part-time pros in the evening.'

Elsewhere in the league, Barry Lynch, a 20-year-old former Aston Villa apprentice, top-scored for Atlanta with eight goals, while West Ham full-back Clive Charles, one of the handful of black players in first-team squads in England's First Division, played a major role on the left flank of the Montreal defence. The Dallas Tornado added Tony McLoughlin, a 24-year-old Liverpudlian forward who had played 27 games in a two-year spell at Wrexham, and defender Tommy Youlden from Portsmouth. Ever-present in the Dallas midfield was Englishman Roy Turner, in his third season with the Tornado.

For once, the format of the regular season was unchanged. Teams again played twenty-four games, including four against overseas teams, one of whom was Hearts, runners-up in the previous season's Texaco Cup, who won four of their eight games on American soil. Changes were made to the play-offs, with the division runners-up included and sudden death extra-time introduced. That led to an epic semi-final confrontation between Rochester and Dallas.

Tornado coach Ron Newman recalls, 'We used to train in the evening because the players had jobs in the day. It used to get a bit dark and we could not afford to put lights on the field, so we went over to the local school, where they had big lights. We used to play under the light and to score you had to hit the light pole. We were like moths. The further away you got, the harder it was to see the pole so we all used to swarm round the light. Anyway, I had a problem with our Yugoslav goalie, Mirko Stojanovic, at training and I suspended him for the semi-final at Rochester, which was a great move considering my other keeper, Ken Cooper, had not long had knee surgery and hadn't played for two months! Kenny said, "I'll play." I said, "How can you play? You can hardly walk."'

Cooper, a former non-leaguer in England, talked his boss into letting him take part in what turned out to be the longest game in the sport's history. With the game tied at 1–1 after 90 minutes, Cooper continued hobbling around his six-yard box during period after period of extra-time. 'We had no shoot-outs at that time, so we kept playing until someone scored,' says Newman, whose team eventually lost in the sixth additional period when Brazilian Carlos Metidieri beat Cooper to end 176 minutes of action. 'It was the first game I had ever seen where both teams celebrated at the end.'

League commissioner Woosnam was present, but had missed the winning goal because he was on his way to the field to instruct the referees to end the contest if the period remained goalless. Dallas defender and assistant coach John Best adds, 'I remember having blisters on my feet and being absolutely exhausted. One of the thoughts I had during the game was that in America there were a lot of states where professional sports could not be played on a Sunday, so I was looking at the clock and thinking that we had better get the game over by midnight.'

Newman made up with Stojanovic in time for the second of the best-of-three series. 'He apologised and played brilliantly. But I learned a valuable lesson,' Newman admits. 'Never to back yourself into a corner.'

Dallas proceeded to win at home in the second game to set up a decider at Rochester, where it took another 148 minutes for the Tornado to win through to the final with goals from McLoughlin and English defender Bobby Moffat. Atlanta were the opponents in the title decider and the Chiefs won the first of another three-game series 2–1 with a decisive goal after 123 minutes. Dallas took the second game 4–1 at home and returned to Atlanta to take the lead after two minutes through another Englishman, Mike Renshaw. Moffat made it 2–0 just before half-time and the Dallas defence held firm for victory, although only 3,000 people had turned up to see the action.

The star of the Tornado's play-off run had been the eccentric McLoughlin, playing in his only NASL season. Best recalls, 'Ron and I had been talking in the off-season about how we needed a striker who was very good in the air, an old-fashioned English type of forward. We felt most teams would have difficulties with that because a lot of teams were not strong in the centre of defence. I was given a tip in England to watch Tony, who had been with Everton as a youngster and was playing in non-league for, I believe, Wigan. He was a real handful in the area so we offered him a contract. He scored in his first game and did well over here.

'But he was a handful off the field. How can I put this without getting into trouble? Let's say he marched to a different drummer. You have seen Liverpool fellows who are that way, very rough and ready. He was the only player I have ever known who taped his knuckles before the game. He had problems with the climate as well. He had a broken nose – it was somewhere around his left ear – and he had real problems. He had a lot of headaches and difficulty breathing during games. In the end he had surgery.'

Newman adds, 'Tony was a crazy man. I remember once we were at a big party at Lamar Hunt's dad's place. There was a TV reporter there who was helping us a lot. Tony was walking along the side of the pool with him when he nudged him into the water. The guy was about to go on the air. I have a feeling that incident didn't help his career, but I don't remember using it as a reason to get rid of him. Actually I can't even remember whether we didn't want him back the next year or if he just didn't come back.'

Atlanta's place in the final had been earned at the expense of New York. The Cosmos had limped to second place in the Northern Division, despite winning only nine of twenty-four games in a season during which they hardly lived up to attendance expectations at Yankee Stadium. Only 3,701 attended the season opener and only once did they attract more than 10,000 to a game.

New York's results, however, were still way ahead of Toronto's. Leggat's fears for his inexperienced side proved well-founded, as they won only five games. Indicative of the coach's problems was that he ended up playing in almost half the games himself. 'I had not played for three years and I was 37 but at times I was our best player, so I played in a few of the games,' he explains. 'One of my biggest pressures was to get the foreign players to accept the wages we had to pay and to convince them that withholding tax was the rule of the country. But when we went to Montreal some of the older players decided to go on strike because of the tax issue. We went there with 11 players and I was substitute for every position.'

The Metros' crowds, ranging from 2,000 to 12,000, also left something to be desired. 'The theory was that because Canada is made up of different nationalities, people would go and watch soccer,' says Leggat. 'But everyone in Canada compared what they saw with the best team they had seen back home. You may be a Scunthorpe fan but because you have seen Manchester United play you compared us to them.'

Crowds in Toronto were better than in some other cities in the NASL, however, and Leggat says, 'I remember playing at Yankee Stadium and in St Louis and if the crowd had held hands they would not have gone round the bottom ring of the stadium.' For someone who had played in internationals in front of 100,000 and been a First Division regular it was something of culture shock. 'Every game I thought, "What am I doing here?" But the kids were good kids. We had a kid called Angus Moffat who drove up from Detroit every game. We had a team that buzzed instead of strolling around like veterans would have done and that gave me satisfaction.'

☆

For once, the off-season between the 1971 and 1972 NASL seasons did not see any teams disbanding, although the Washington Darts, after only two years in the league, moved to Miami to become the Gatos – Spanish for 'cats'. Things were not exactly going smoothly, however, and in an attempt to stabilise the league, the season was reduced to 14 games. 'It was partly to reduce costs,' Woosnam explains, 'and also we weren't sure if we could attract people midweek.'

On the personnel front, Atlanta entered the year with many of the same players who had been lining up since 1969, although there was a significant addition in Paul Child, a 19-year-old striker who had been unable to force his way into the picture at Aston Villa. He scored eight goals in a season that was a preview of what was to come throughout his NASL career.

While Brian Talbot was returning for another season in Toronto, the Montreal Olympic – coached by Graham Adams, who had played for Plymouth 14 years earlier – brought over Graeme Souness, a dark-haired 19-year-old midfielder. The man whose skill and streak of menace would win worldwide renown in the heart of the Liverpool and Scotland midfields was still waiting for his opportunity at Tottenham, although he had not endeared himself to the London club when he disappeared back to Scotland because he was feeling homesick. Souness stayed to play ten games in Canada, scoring a couple of goals. Also in the Olympic line-up was centre-half Mike Dillon, a teammate in the Spurs reserve team who would return to the NASL as a member of higher-profile teams in later years. Dillon made his mark as a goalscorer, netting seven times in his ten games.

The two Canadian teams managed only four wins apiece and by the time Toronto were winning their third and fourth games in mid-season, Leggat was gone. 'The crunch came after we had played about six games,' he explains. 'We played a friendly against Werder Bremen and the day before the game the general manager, Jack Daley, said Arthur Rodrigues, my assistant, was complaining because I was not giving him anything to do. I said, "There is not much he can do." I was told they wanted him to take charge of the next day's game. I said, "I don't agree, but you are the boss." We were holding on until just before half-time, when our trainer came up to me and said my son had been rushed to hospital for an appendix operation. I said, "I am not in charge so I am going to the hospital." I rang the trainer after the game and he said we had lost 6–0. Arthur had substituted this player and that player.

The next day, Jack Daley called me into his office and said, "I am not at all satisfied with last night's game." I said, "Neither am I, but it was out of my hands. The players were confused about what they were supposed to do." He said, "From now I am going to fine players for playing badly." I said, "In that case you put on a tracksuit and I will stay in the office. My players will never shirk anything. Often the harder players try, the worse things get." I got up to leave and he said, "If you leave this office, you are fired." That was a red rag to a bull and I walked out. The papers were brilliant, they all wrote good things about me and in the next 10 days I had about 50 job offers.'

While Leggat was settling down to his new role in the public relations department of a local brewery, the New York Cosmos, relocated to Hofstra University on Long Island, were enjoying their first taste of NASL success by winning the Northern Division. Bradley and Mahy helped to anchor the defence, the only Brits in a line-up that had added a promising young American defender called Werner Roth and Scottish-born Canadian international midfielder John Kerr. Bermudan striker Randy Horton provided most of the goals.

Although they remained a predominantly American team, the St Louis Stars supplemented their American roster with two seasoned British defenders. Wilf Tranter, a former Brighton and Fulham defender, had played a dozen games for Baltimore in 1968, while full-back John Sewell had played in more than 400 League games for Charlton and Crystal Palace, where he had helped to earn the club promotion to Division One. The Stars were unbeaten until the sixth game and held on to win the Southern Division. Running them closest were the Dallas Tornado, whose defence of their title ended in the one-game semi-final tie against New York. The Stars booked their place in the final when Sewell scored one of the goals in a 2–0 win against Rochester.

The final was staged at the Cosmos' new home, before a crowd of 6,012. Goals by Horton and St Louis player-coach Kazimierz Frankiewicz had the game level until four minutes to play, when Czech international Josef Jelinek scored from the penalty spot. The New York Cosmos had won their first championship, and few in the United States had noticed. It would be very different when they won their second, five years later.

Attendance in league games was up by 39 per cent to 5,340 per game, although New York, despite their championship, could still only average 4,282. As usual, many overseas teams visited the US, with Dallas pulling in a 24,742 crowd at Texas Stadium for their scoreless draw against Moscow Dynamo. The attendance figure was another step forward for the NASL, although coach Ron Newman admits, 'We cheated a little bit on some of the crowds. For some games we would invite all the local kids' teams to the game, let them wear their uniforms and carry team banners round the field. Then we counted them in the crowd.'

There had been a significant day midway through the NASL season when, on 26 June 1972, the league introduced its new offside law. A line was painted across the field in each half, 35 yards from the goal line, and it was declared that players could not be offside unless they had crossed that line. In the rest of the world, of course, players could be offside once they crossed into the opponents' half, but the NASL saw its version of the rule as a way to encourage more attacking football. Even though the league initially had permission from FIFA to conduct the experiment, it was one of the rules that would most upset the purists in years to come. It was hardly an overnight success, with the first weekend after the introduction of the rule producing only three goals in three games. But the 35-yard line, which helped to give the NASL's style of play a unique identity, was here to stay.

5. ☆ Southport's Mighty Atoms

The eyes of British sport were on Southport in the spring of 1973 as racehorse trainer Ginger McCain made headlines by preparing fancied Grand National runner Red Rum along the beaches of the Lancashire coastal town. Unknown to most, a new NASL club was looking in the same direction in search of a team that could win them the championship. McCain's methods paid off when Red Rum got his nose to the line ahead of Crisp at Aintree. And so would those of Al Miller, head coach of the Philadelphia Atoms.

Lamar Hunt, owner of the Dallas Tornado and the NFL's Kansas City Chiefs, had set the story off on its unlikely course to the English north-west when he was in Los Angeles in January for the Super Bowl. Hunt heard that Tom McCloskey, a success in the construction industry and owner of a minor league ice hockey team, was looking for nine seats for the game. Hunt came up with the tickets, adding, 'How would you like to have a soccer franchise in Philadelphia?' McCloskey, eager to see the Washington Redskins and Miami Dolphins do battle, took the hint and, for a $25,000 fee, became the NASL's newest owner. The team's name was selected in a competition in the Philadelphia media, the prize for which was a trip to see Sunderland play Leeds in the FA Cup final at Wembley.

Al Miller, coach at Hartwick College in New York, was chosen to take charge of the team, the job interview having included an impromptu soccer game between McCloskey and Miller's son in which the owner broke a window in Miller's house. Miller put aside his scepticism about the NASL and accepted the job, with the brief to recruit as many good American players as possible.

The 1972 season had seen the introduction of an NASL college draft, similar to that used by all the major American sports leagues, whose teams stocked their squads by taking turns to select the best players coming out of the college sports system. But whereas a gridiron star at the University of Notre Dame was a good bet to succeed in the NFL, even the best college soccer talent was hardly likely to pose a threat to the European professionals inhabiting NASL rosters. With his group of Americans assembled, including goalkeeper Bob Rigby, promising forward Bobby Smith and Casey Bahr, the son of one of America's 1950 World Cup heroes, Miller set off for pre-season training in England.

The destination was Lilleshall, where Miller hoped to impress his team with top-rate facilities in a real football country. He also took the opportunity to scout for British players to pad out his team. He wanted players with speed and alertness to match the style of play he envisaged for his side, although the men he came back with were hardly names to send shivers down opponents' spines. It was Southport, the new Division Four champions, to whom he turned to borrow a trio of players. Defender Chris Dunleavy had been a member of the Washington Darts in 1970, while forward Andy Provan had made a career out of lower-division football at teams like York, Chester and Wrexham and had just notched 13 goals in Southport's title-winning season. Centre-forward Jim Fryatt, the club's top scorer with 21 goals, had enjoyed a nine-team career that had produced 188 League goals. He had earned a place in the record books in 1964 when, playing for Bradford Park Avenue, he scored a goal timed at four seconds against Tranmere.

Joining the Southport contingent was Liverpool full-back Roy Evans, whose eight-year career at Anfield had seen him play only nine League games. 'While they were talking to Southport they got hold of my name and were told by Liverpool that I might be available on loan for three months,' says Evans. 'I was not playing that many games in the first team and I had just got married, so this was a chance for a honeymoon as well.'

The team enjoyed good coverage from Philadelphia newspapers becoming jaded by covering under-performing major sports teams. Following a parade of 3,000 children in full soccer kit, the Atoms kicked off their home programme with a 1–0 win in front of 21,700 fans. Their opponents were the St Louis Stars, which meant that 12 of the 22 starting players were Americans, a ratio previously unheard of in the NASL. The other seven teams in the league had only 19 Americans in total. The Atoms quickly established themselves as the team to beat with a 12-game undefeated run. A back four of converted striker Smith, Dunleavy, former Aston Villa and Lincoln player Derek Trevis and Evans won the nickname of the 'No Goal Patrol' and the Atoms conceded only 14 goals in 19 games.

Evans recalls that rookie professional coach Miller was happy to rely heavily on his English players. 'The big thing about Al was his enthusiasm, which is always a great thing if you can get it over to the players. The English lads had a reasonable amount of experience and he was prepared to listen to us. He was his own man and did his own thing, but he was happy to ask us what we thought and listen to us. We were a very close team. The American players were all willing to learn and, as you would expect, were all great athletes. There was a good balance in the team.'

It was the forward players who captured the imagination, none more so than Provan. At 5 ft 5 in. and only 10 stone he earned the nickname 'The Flea' because of his size and ability to jump and win balls that seemed beyond him. He finished as top scorer with 11 goals, winning over the fans as early as his second game. In a town where the love of a good fight is legendary, Provan took exception to the way 6 ft 2 in. New York Cosmos forward Randy Horton landed on top of him after they challenged for a high ball. Provan jumped angrily to his feet and began shaking his fist in the bearded face of Horton, who had been the NASL's Most Valuable Player in 1972. Then he slapped Horton, sparking a fight that ended with both men being sent off. A legend was born.

Meanwhile Fryatt, powerful in the air, proved to be the perfect foil and scored seven goals himself. 'Jim and Andy were the ideal partnership,' says Evans. 'Jim was the big centre-forward who could get hold of the ball, while Andy had decent pace and good goalscoring ability. They were both skilful and they were so different in size that they became a novelty as well to the Americans.'

The Atoms' success extended to the gate, where they set a league record by averaging 11,382, contributing to an increase of 18 per cent around the league. By the end of the season, Philadelphia, in their distinctive white shirts with the word 'Atoms' inside two blue horizontal stripes, had lost only two games, winning nine and drawing eight, and had won their division by thirteen points from the Cosmos. In the semi-finals, against the Toronto Metros, Fryatt and Provan each scored goals as the Atoms delighted a crowd of 18,766 by winning 3–0. The fans even saw them off to the NASL final with a rousing rendition of 'Auld Lang Syne'.

☆

The league's search for new foreign players had brought reports early in 1973 of a bid by the New York Cosmos to sign George Best, who had fallen out yet again with Manchester United. Suspended for two weeks after skipping training late in 1972, Best was placed on the transfer list at £300,000 by manager Frank O'Farrell. The softly spoken Irishman was under considerable pressure in his second season in charge of a fading United team, pressure that increased when former manager Sir Matt Busby, still the dominant figure at Old Trafford, agreed to take Best off the list several days later. A 5–0 defeat against Crystal Palace spelled the end for O'Farrell and the team was placed temporarily in the care of European Cup-winners Paddy Crerand and Bill Foulkes. Best decided not to hang around to see who the next man in charge would be, announcing his intention to quit the club.

It did not take long for the news to reach America and Clive Toye, now installed as general manager of the Cosmos, was soon telling reporters that coach Gordon Bradley was visiting England to talk to Best and discuss a contract worth £40,000 a season. Bradley explains, 'George was still a Manchester United player so I went over to see him. I spent some time with Paddy Crerand and he said, "If you get George he will set the field alight." George came over to New York and he spent a couple of weeks with me at my home on Long Island. You could see he was interested. But in the end he never said anything. He just went. We found out he had gone to Spain, where he had a bar. I felt I should have gone out there and got on to him. Paddy was very upset and apologetic about the whole thing. It would have been great.'

Best would admit years later in his book, *Blessed*, that he was scared away by the 'madness' of New York. One United player on his way to the States, however, was centre-half David Sadler, who signed for Miami, now known as the Toros. Capped four times by England and one of the men who just missed out on a place in the final squad of 22 for the Mexico World Cup, Sadler had played 266 games as the successor to Foulkes in the United defence. Playing alongside Sadler, although for only seven games, was Willie Henderson, capped 29 times by Scotland during his Rangers career and coming off his first season in English football with Sheffield Wednesday.

At the Dallas Tornado, Ron Newman's side was almost entirely made up of British professionals, with the exception of a strike force of Yugoslav Ilija Mitic, scorer of 12 goals, and American Kyle Rote Jr. As Dallas compiled the best record in the league, winning eleven and drawing five of their nineteen games, Rote captured the headlines by becoming the first – and only – home player to win the NASL's individual scoring championship. Rote had been something of a project for Newman after being the Tornado's selection in the NASL's inaugural draft early in 1972. 'I had never even heard of a draft,' Newman remembers. 'Someone came in and was talking about a draft and I said, "Well, shut the door then. That will get rid of it." I couldn't see the point of a draft at first because there was virtually no one playing in college at that time.'

Newman, however, recognised the marketability of a young man whose father, Kyle Senior, had been a famous player for the NFL's New York Giants throughout the '50s, revelling in the nickname 'The Mighty Mustang'. 'I thought it would be good PR if I picked him because of his dad. Kyle was a great athlete, but he didn't have the fine touch he would have had if he had played at a young age. We promoted the crap out of him because we needed an American hero. He didn't really play in his first season, but in 1973 I put him in and we told him to go for everything in the box because he could jump so high. We scored a bunch of goals when he jumped and won the ball or it hit him on the shoulder or he just put the defender off.'

The individual scoring title was based on awarding two points for every goal scored and one point for an assist and Newman could see the value of having an American player challenging for that honour. 'I told our players, "Whenever we score, go to Kyle and pat him on the back so they will think he had an assist." We got a few like that. Towards the end of the season he was only a few points away from being the top points scorer and in the last game we got a penalty against the New York Cosmos. Ilija put it down to take it like he normally did, but I ran over to him and said, "Let Kyle take it. If he scores he gets the individual championship." Up goes Kyle and he whomps it right down the middle. The keeper took off, but if he had stayed where he was it would have smacked him in the nose. It meant Kyle was top scorer and that was terrific for the league.'

It was Rote who headed the only goal in the semi-final victory against the Cosmos, who had qualified for the semi-finals as the division runner-up with the best record. With their superior regular season record, Dallas earned the right of playing host for the final against Philadelphia, while Tornado general manager Joe Echelle was able to name the date for the game. His selection, 25 August, was the day that the Atoms' two scoring stars, Provan and Fryatt, were due to report to Southport for the opening game of the Division Three season against Cambridge United.

However, defender Dunleavy – named in the league's all-star team, along with Fryatt, Provan, David Sadler, Dallas defender John Best and goalkeeper Ken Cooper – was suspended for Southport's game, which meant he stayed for the final. That infuriated Dallas coach Newman. 'We thought that was illegal. We felt if he was banned on one day in one place he should not be able to play somewhere else. We went to Phil Woosnam about it but he didn't want to get caught up in it.'

Dallas also lost key players, forwards Richie Reynolds and Nick Jennings and full-back John Collins, who were due on the field for Portsmouth against Middlesbrough. With his Atoms strike force absent, Miller fielded six native-born Americans in his starting line-up, including defender Bill Straub, who had not played since being signed from Montreal during the season, as an emergency centre-forward.

From the kick-off, it was the Atoms who adjusted better to their enforced changes. In front of a crowd of 18,824, they took control of the game and spent most of the first half in Dallas territory. Rigby had little to do in the Philadelphia goal, while Dunleavy smothered Rote. 'Chris was a really steady player,' says Evans. 'He was very reliable and had the kind of experience the team was based upon. The whole team did themselves proud. It was about 100 degrees and that heat made it tough for an energetic team like us.'

With 20 minutes played in the second half, Dallas defender John Best attempted to deal with a dangerous-looking Atoms attack and diverted the ball into his own net. Five minutes from the end, makeshift striker Straub scored with a header to clinch a 2–0 victory. Best recalls, 'It turned out that it was going to be my last game because I had a bad hip and I wanted to get into coaching. Kenny Cooper used to tease me because he was at a game at Blackpool when I was playing for Liverpool reserves and he saw me score an own goal. After that game in Texas he told one of the reporters I was one of the most honest players he had ever met because after the Blackpool game I'd said that if ever I scored another own goal I would quit.'

As the first team to win a championship in their inaugural year in any professional American league – and one that did it with several important American players – the Atoms had a bigger impact than any previous NASL champions. Goalkeeper Bob Rigby made the cover of *Sports Illustrated*, and the magazine's headlines claimed, 'Soccer Goes American'. The attention the sport was suddenly receiving saw Kyle Rote selected for the American version of 'Superstars'. While British television audiences were watching hurdler David Hemery and judo's Brian Jacks beating fellow sportsmen at everything from cycling to canoeing, US viewers would see Rote dominate the event in the US. Newman says, 'He won it three times, until eventually they asked him not to come back. They wanted one of their big football or basketball stars to win it.'

Rote's career would never be the same, as the Tornado and the NASL used his new-found fame to promote the sport even more heavily. English midfielder David Chadwick, who joined him as a teammate the following season, recalls, 'Kyle was outstanding. He knew he was not technically the best and he knew a lot of American kids were riding on his success, so he worked hard. After training he would stay out there for another hour and do more work.'

While Rote's career would fail to reach such heights again as he attempted to balance playing with promotional work, scoring only fifteen goals in the next three seasons, his success in 1973 helped put soccer in position for its next big step towards the west. The development of the American players, however, would not advance at the same pace as the league itself. Teams would continue to look abroad for their professionals and the local talent would never again play such a significant part in any season. The new wave of imports was on its way, with the British to the fore.

6. ☆ Way Out West

The west coast had not seen NASL football since 1968, but the relative stability achieved by the league left team owners in no doubt that the time was right to rectify that situation. 'There was a lot of pressure to get out to the west,' says commissioner Phil Woosnam. 'The east-coast owners were saying that if we didn't become fully national they were gone.'

As usual it was left to Woosnam to come up with the teams. 'Much of my time was spent on expansion and I would always be working on certain cities. My approach was usually to go in and talk to the media and ask if they knew anyone who had an interest in owning a soccer franchise. I would then follow up any leads. I had a pretty good presentation ready, and having Warner Communications in there as owners was a big help in persuading people. Lamar Hunt was a great closer of deals. When I had found potential owners and got things to the key moment, he would jump on a plane and the last push was down to him. It was a combination of his reputation in sports and his personality. Lamar was a very straightforward guy and people trusted him. We told clubs that their payback would come over a long period of time. We felt we were coming along nicely.'

By the end of the 1973 season, the mood in the country had been lightened by the end of America's involvement in Vietnam, attention in Washington DC turning instead to the riddle of the break-in at Democratic Party offices in the Watergate complex. Woosnam's own political campaigning had produced new NASL ownership groups in Vancouver, Seattle and Los Angeles. All three franchises, however, insisted on a fourth western team in order to keep travel costs down. In the hope of getting a club into San Francisco, Woosnam spoke to Lica Corp.'s founder, Milan Mandaric.

But, as Woosnam explains, 'Milan said, "I won't go in there. I can't make it work there. The only way I can succeed is to go out into the suburbs, where the sport has a following. Let's go to San Jose." So I said, "OK, we'll keep in touch, but I am going to try San Diego." We went right to the deadline and could not get a deal done in San Diego, so we had no choice and we agreed to San Jose. And Milan was right. San Jose became a power.'

Four other teams were added, in Denver, Boston, Washington and Baltimore, with the new teams each paying a franchise fee of $75,000. Even with the loss of Montreal and the Atlanta Apollos, as the former Chiefs had been known in 1973, it meant the NASL was now a 15-team league spanning the country.

The league was split into four divisions, with each team playing 20 games. In the Eastern Division, the defending champions, Philadelphia Atoms, were kept waiting for Southport to give their approval for Andy Provan and Jim Fryatt to return to America, but Provan heralded his comeback by scoring four goals in the first half of a 5–1 win in the season opener against Washington before adding two in a 3–2 win against the Baltimore Comets. Fryatt weighed in with a goal in each of the first four games, all of which were won. But after winning five of their first six games, the Atoms managed only four more victories all season and finished out of the play-offs. One of those wins came via the NASL's newly introduced penalty shoot-out system. Like baseball, gridiron and basketball, soccer was doing away with drawn games. From now on, matches ending level would go straight to penalties, although the winning team would receive only three points instead of six. The losing team would get nothing, apart from whatever bonus points they picked up for goals scored.

Elsewhere in the Eastern Division, Baltimore, returning to Memorial Stadium, were coached by Doug Millward, who had been in charge of the Baltimore Bays back in the NPSL days of 1967. Up front was Frank Large, a 33-year-old centre-forward whose 15-year Football League career had taken him from Halifax to Chesterfield via ten transfers, including three spells at Northampton. His nine regular season goals for the Comets saw him finish as the team's second-leading scorer behind Norwich City's Peter Silvester, eight years his junior. Silvester's 14-goal NASL tally would be the second-highest in the league, as was his individual points total of 32, and saw him voted the league's Most Valuable Player. Baltimore's British contingent also included full-back Geoff Butler and former England youth winger Terry Anderson, both of whom had played in Norwich's League Cup final loss to Tottenham a year earlier.

Despite winning ten games in regulation time, more than any other team in their division, the Comets had to settle for second place behind the Miami Toros, led for the second season by Scotsman John Young, named as Coach of the Year. The Toros proved themselves the kings of the new penalty shoot-out, winning on all six occasions that their games finished level. Bringing up the rear in the division were the Washington Diplomats, whose coach was the former Manchester United and Baltimore Bays forward Dennis Viollet. Washington's team featured Alan Spavin, who had played more than 400 games in midfield for Preston, and Clive Clark, the former Queens Park Rangers and long-time West Bromwich Albion outside left.

The Boston Minutemen joined Toronto, New York and Rochester in the Northern Division. Coached by Austrian Hubert Vogelsinger, Boston's Football League imports included former West Ham striker Ade Coker, a forward from Lagos in Nigeria. Coker had exploded into the First Division on the final day of October 1971, when, as a 17 year old, he scored a debut goal after only seven minutes at Crystal Palace. His broad smile lit up London's television screens when the game was shown the next day and Coker, who had moved to England with his parents at the age of 11, was inevitably bracketed with West Ham's powerful Bermudan centre-forward Clyde Best, who had been the First Division's only regular black goalscorer since winning a place in the Hammers' team during the 1969–70 season. Although both men would find their way to America, Coker's Football League career never followed Best's path of success and by the time he arrived in Boston he had played only nine league games for West Ham.

The Boston locker room also featured veteran Hull goalkeeper Ian McKechnie and former Sheffield United defender Frank Barlow. The much-travelled former England centre-forward Tony Hateley even played in three games early in the season. Boston would finish on top of the division, with Coker weighing in with seven goals and John Coyne, who had come from Hartlepool, via a handful of games for Dallas, scoring eight.

Dallas and the St Louis Stars were joined in the Northern Division by the Denver Dynamo, who named Englishman Ken Bracewell, a seven-year NASL veteran with Toronto and Atlanta, as player-coach. Former full-back Bracewell, born in Lancashire, had earned a reputation for his fierce shooting as he journeyed around Burnley, Tranmere, Lincoln, Margate, Bury, Rochdale and Canadian team Toronto Italia. To spearhead the attack, Denver signed the distinctively bald centre-forward Andy Lochhead, whose Football League career had produced close to 150 goals for Burnley,

Leicester and Aston Villa. Indicative of Denver's problems was that Lochhead found the net only once in 16 games and, with only five victories, the Dynamo trailed a long way behind division winners Dallas.

In the all-new Western Division, the Los Angeles Aztecs stocked their team with players from Central and South America, while the San Jose Earthquakes' dominant overseas group was from Yugoslavia, not surprisingly given their owner and Yugoslav coach, Momcilo 'Gabbo' Gavric. But also signing for the Earthquakes was 28-year-old English left-back Laurie Calloway, whose route from Shrewsbury Town to California demonstrated a somewhat haphazard method of recruiting players from Europe.

Calloway, who had begun his career as a Wolves apprentice and played for four other teams before Shrewsbury, recalls, 'I had written to Phil Woosnam in 1973 about the possibility of going over. A good friend of mine, Jim Fryatt, had done well at Philadelphia and told me what a great time he had had. I wrote the letter and never heard a thing. Some time later, I was contacted by Hubert Vogelsinger and he said he was coming over to see some players. He was going to be bringing players together for a trial before taking the 18 best back to the US. I told him he could see me play for Shrewsbury against Charlton the week he was going to be there.

'It was a rainy night and, being left-back, I was sliding into tackles. He saw me afterwards and said he was a bit concerned about the way I played because of the Astroturf they would be playing on in the NASL. I said, "I have been playing professionally for 13 years, so I can adjust." I was concerned at him being that naive. Anyway, he said he liked my aggressiveness and to come to his training camp at Walsall. I got a couple of days off from the Shrewsbury manager, Alan Durban, but I didn't feel comfortable about my chances because he was bringing in 40 guys and, based on his comments, I was concerned.

'Then I got another call from San Francisco. It was Milan Mandaric, who said he'd been given my letter by Phil Woosnam. He said he was putting an expansion together in San Francisco – he didn't mention San Jose! "I am looking for a left-back," he said. "Can I see you play in the next few days?" I explained we were about to play Hereford home and away. "I am coming to London," he said. "Can I fly from London to Hereford?" I said, "You can, but there'll be nowhere to land." So he turned up in Hereford in a limo instead. I had a good game and he offered me a deal. I went to the Boston camp a few days later and told Vogelsinger I had a guaranteed offer from San Jose. He said he didn't want to let me go but he thought about it over breakfast and changed his mind.'

Calloway's only English companion was Paul Child, who had scored 16 goals in the previous two seasons for Atlanta. 'I came back to England after Atlanta folded and I was in Birmingham for a month,' recalls the former Aston Villa reserve. 'The whole time I was being bugged by San Jose, who had picked up the rights to me after the Chiefs folded. I was not sure what was going to happen with the league and I wondered if I was going to be out of a job again if I went back. But living with my wife and our new baby at the in-laws motivated me to go back and give it another try.'

Surrounding Calloway and Child were the Yugoslavs, players from Haiti and Poland, and a group of Americans who included Glasgow-born Johnny Moore. Calloway adds, 'We did have some factions. But you have that in any team. In England now there are a lot of people in the same team who don't like each other. And in those days, even if you had all English and Scots in your team it was something if you had a week without a tussle.'

At Western Division rivals Seattle Sounders, John Best had graduated from Dallas to land the coaching job, setting himself a three-year timetable for success. 'In that time span you should be able to build a competitive team,' he explains. 'You may get lucky and have some good things happen on the field early but I didn't expect to win the championship in the first year. It is not always healthy for that to happen anyway. Maybe then there is a temptation to grow too quickly, without establishing the organisation.'

Having interviewed with Los Angeles and Denver, Best was impressed by Seattle's 'civic-minded' owners and accepted their offer to build the Sounders team. 'I basically went to England and Holland for the nucleus of the players. I knew managers and ex-players and I would go and speak to them, tell them what I was looking for and see if they knew players who might fit those profiles. Then I would watch them as many times as I could and talk to other teams' scouts. I didn't necessarily have the perfect team, but it was a good solid club.'

Best's most significant signing was former Everton and Southampton wing-half Jimmy Gabriel, a fiery red-haired Scot who had proved over the years that he was unafraid of sticking up to the likes of Billy Bremner and Tommy Smith in the heat of battle. Gabriel had gone on to have spells at Bournemouth, Swindon and Brentford, pushing him past 500 League games, and by 1974 was thinking of life after his playing career. 'John Best had been in the Liverpool reserve team when I was at Everton but I didn't really know him,' he remembers. 'But when he came over and asked me if I would go over as assistant coach I trusted him right away. He laid out in plain and simple terms what he wanted and what he was offering and I was looking for the opportunity to coach. It sounded like a good deal to go over for a few months to coach and continue playing.'

Best says, 'Jimmy was the classic example of what I was looking for. I didn't just want a team that was made up of skilful players, but more down-to-earth guys. A typical English club, if you like, in terms of how they played and the determination and discipline they brought to the field.'

Among the rest of the large British group in the squad, Hartlepool goalkeeper Barry Watling arrived with a rather less impressive résumé than Gabriel, but proceeded to lead the league in the goalkeeping statistics by conceding only 0.8 goals per game. John Rowlands, another Liverpudlian who had skipped around eight lower-division teams, was the Sounders' top scorer with ten goals and eight assists.

The Western Division was completed by the Vancouver Whitecaps, whose squad included 34-year-old Scottish midfielder Willie Stevenson, the former Liverpool and Stoke veteran who won a winner's medal in the 1965 FA Cup final. The action out west began with a crazy game in Los Angeles between the Aztecs and the Sounders. Gabriel explains, 'Every time the ball went out of play they stopped the clock, like they do in American football. So instead of playing 90 minutes we played for about two hours. It nearly killed half the team. We said, "We can't be playing like that every week," but they got it right after that.'

That game was the first of the Aztecs' 13 wins, a total that saw them finish with a league-best 110 points. At one point they won a league-record eight straight games and finished seven points ahead of the Earthquakes, for whom Child scored fifteen goals and added six assists to win the individual scoring award with thirty-six points. Child scored seven goals in the last seven games of the season and the Earthquakes put together a late-season burst of five wins to send them into a play-off game at Dallas full of confidence.

'It was one of those seasons when everything was going right,' recalls Child. 'There were no individuals. We won as a team and lost as a team. We thought we would do very well in the play-offs. But Ron Newman at Dallas was a damn good coach and he had some very good players.' They proved too good for the Earthquakes, who were beaten 3–0, Renshaw scoring twice. Child continues, 'We played on Astroturf and they were very good on it.

All you seem to do on Astroturf is chase the ball and unless you play on it regularly you are not used to the bounces or the timing of the ball. A big part of my game was getting on the end of through balls and I just remember chasing the damn thing out of bounds the whole time.'

Dallas were beaten in the semi-finals by Miami, who lined up in their own Orange Bowl stadium against Los Angeles in the championship game. CBS carried the game live and, even though it received disappointing ratings, the few lucky viewers and 15,507 in the stadium enjoyed a dramatic contest, the Aztecs drawing level at 3–3 with two minutes remaining. Ironically, the Toros, so successful in penalty shoot-outs during the season, missed twice from the spot to allow Los Angeles to take the title.

NASL attendances had increased by 24 per cent in 1974, the success of many of the new teams paving the way for more growth the following year. San Jose averaged 16,576 fans in Spartan Stadium and Calloway recalls, 'The public made us feel so welcome. California was conducive to all the events they laid on for us, like barbecues and picnics, and we developed a great relationship. We had players who were good at all the public relations stuff – school appearances, speaking at Rotary Clubs or whatever. There were a couple of bad eggs. For example, Ilija Mitic would score goals, but caused a few dust-ups because he was a miserable sod. But the guys accepted that because he got goals.'

Child adds, 'Pretty much all the guys at San Jose had something to give and worked to promote the team. They weren't perfect players, but they didn't have any chips on shoulders. The club was coming out with all the razzmatazz, like a mascot called Crazy George who would come in on a camel or a racing car.'

In Seattle, the Sounders were the victims of being in a highly competitive division, finishing only third in spite of winning 13 games. But with the NFL's Seahawks and baseball's Mariners not yet in town, the team had been given a rapturous welcome when they made their home debut against Denver at the tiny Memorial Stadium. 'We didn't expect big crowds to start with,' says Gabriel. 'The stadium only held about 12,000, but for the first game it was more or less full. When we came out, the crowd stood up and cheered like you have never heard. Our side was made up mostly of guys from the lower divisions and they had never heard a crowd like that. Every time we touched the ball they were cheering and if someone headed the ball, well, it was the most wonderful thing they had ever seen. The feedback from the crowd lifted us up and we rose to it. We won that game 4–0, started to sell out the games and they had to put extra bleacher seats in there.'

According to Best, 'the first year in Seattle was magical'. He adds, 'At the end of the season we were out of the play-offs, but our final game against Vancouver sold out, even though it was a lame duck game. At the end, we had a whole pile of red roses in the centre of the field and the players ran up into the stands and gave each woman a rose and said thanks for a great season. There were tears in people's eyes and my mail came in by the sackful. Hal Childs, our PR director, called it "Camelot" and that caught on big-time. The press wrote about "Camelot Day" all the time.'

The experience of the season persuaded Gabriel that Seattle was where he wanted to make his home. 'The club asked me to work with some of the players in the off-season, going round to schools and showing the kids how to play the game. I had the chance to be the full-time assistant head coach and to go across to England with John Best to get some new players. I'd had some coaching and playing offers in England, but I liked Seattle so much I decided to stay. It was largely because of the positive nature of the fans. Even recently, I was at an international in Seattle and almost all of the 40,000 crowd seemed to be old Sounders fans. I met so many people that day who remembered all the way back or told me their kids had been at a school when we went round teaching them how to play soccer.'

7. ☆ Welcome to Soccer City, USA

One was the best player the world had ever seen, scorer of more than 1,000 goals, star of World Cups, a name known around the globe. The other had not managed to play a single game in the Football League, had spent four years applying his relatively limited talent in transatlantic obscurity and was anonymous even in his hometown of Tipton in the West Midlands. Yet despite their vastly differing football pedigrees, Pelé, the brilliant Brazilian, and Mick Hoban, the unknown Englishman, would each play their part in the storylines that were to make the 1975 season one of the NASL's most intriguing and important.

The city of Portland, about 460 miles north of San Francisco in the state of Oregon, had enjoyed only limited experience of professional sport. A clean, green city, its people were more used to pursuing their own vigorous outdoor activities than paying to watch others perform on their behalf. Basketball's Portland Trailblazers and American football's Portland Storm, part of the upstart and ill-fated World Football League, had attempted to provide a vehicle for an outpouring of civic pride. Neither had delivered, the Trailblazers suffering the usual teething problems of a franchise still only five years old – although their first NBA championship was only two years away – while the Storm and the WFL, which arrived on the scene in 1974, would fold before completing a second season.

A former Storm employee, Don Paul, an NFL player for the Los Angeles Rams in the '50s, had become disillusioned so quickly that he quit his job and went to visit his mother in Tacoma, Washington. While there, a friend had taken him to a Seattle Sounders match and he rushed back to Portland to tell corporation lawyer John Gilbertson, 'I have seen the future of pro sports and it works.' Attracted by the NASL's asking price of $100,000 for a franchise – the WFL had demanded $500,000 for the Storm – the duo set up Oregon Soccer Inc. With a deadline of 17 January to produce $200,000 for operating expenses, they made NASL commissioner Phil Woosnam sweat before he could announce the league's 20th team. 'I had an hour to go on the last day before the bank closed at five,' said Paul. 'I called a friend and told him I needed a cheque for $30,000. It was raining and I couldn't get a cab. I ran all the way to his office, grabbed the cheque and ran to the bank just before the deadline.' Portland, a city known for its lumber industry, had its Timbers.

Portland was one of five new NASL cities, including Chicago, which was being revisited following the demise of the Mustangs seven years earlier. The success of the previous season's expansion had convinced Woosnam of the viability of adding even more teams and he had identified 24 as his 'magic number' for achieving major league status. This round of expansion would leave him only four short of his target. There were clearly still problems in Baltimore, Toronto and Denver, but nothing could dissuade Woosnam from talking the owners into five new franchises for the 1975 season – the Tampa Bay Rowdies, Chicago Sting, San Antonio Thunder, Hartford Bi-Centennials and the Timbers.

As the season approached, Toronto solidified its precarious existence by merging with Canadian National Soccer League power Toronto Croatia. They would field a mostly Yugoslavian side and defy league policy about ethnic nicknames by calling themselves Toronto Metros-Croatia. In Portland, meanwhile, the name may have been a happy fit but with only six weeks left before the season kicked off, the team still had no coach or players. It was Woosnam's old Villa and Atlanta pal Vic Crowe who landed the job, although Woosnam stresses, 'It was purely the Timbers' decision. If someone asked me to try to get a coach I would do so, but I didn't force anyone to take anybody. I didn't go around with a list of names in my pocket.'

Following the announcement of his appointment, Crowe jetted back to England in search of a team. It was a race against the clock, although taking over a club at a time of need was not exactly new to the quietly spoken Welshman. Following his season in charge of the Atlanta Chiefs, Crowe had been called upon to stabilise Aston Villa, the team he once captained, following the turbulent reign of Tommy Docherty.

In his book, *Deadly*, Villa chairman Doug Ellis reveals how Crowe had talked himself into the job at Villa. 'There had never been any intention of offering it to Vic Crowe, who, in personality and image, was the exact opposite to the Doc. I travelled to Manchester with Vic to watch a player. During what proved to be an enlightening drive I got to talk to him seriously, at length, perhaps for the first time and as we chatted, that scouting trip became a successful job interview. Long before we arrived back I realised that this Welsh-born true Brummie was Aston Villa to the core, a very serious-minded professional and a man with an absolute desire to see Aston Villa on top of the football world.'

Villa were already bound for the Third Division when Crowe had taken charge during the 1969–70 season, but in his first full campaign he led Villa to a place in the League Cup final against Tottenham, claiming the scalp of Manchester United in the semi-finals before losing 2–0 to the Londoners at Wembley. Promotion followed a year later, but with the First Division still out of reach, Crowe was sacked by Ellis at the end of the 1973–74 season.

By the beginning of April 1975, with the NASL season opener now only days away, Crowe's organisational and recruiting skills were being fully tested. The Timbers' locker room still had no names above the players' changing spaces. According to Don Paul, 'I kept calling Vic in England and telling him, "We must have some players here!"'

Which is where Hoban came in. An articulate, 23-year-old centre-back, Hoban had played for Atlanta for three seasons and Denver for one and had long since given up his ambitions of a Football League career. 'I was with Villa as a kid and played back and forth between there and the States,' he recalls. 'I was substitute in Division Three a couple of times but by the end of my second season in America I realised I was going to be farmed out to a lower league by Villa. George Curtis, Freddie Turnbull, Brian Tiler and Neil Rioch were the regular crew in central defence. I had stayed on at school to take my A levels because my dad wanted me to get some education and I didn't feel I was as good as the other young defenders at the club, like John Gidman and Bobby McDonald. I had liked the US from the day I got there and the Chiefs offered me a job as a soccer development officer.

'By the spring of 1975 I was back in England working at the West Bromwich post office when I got a call from Vic to say he had taken the job in Portland. He said, "I need you to do the job on the ground for me while I get the rest of the team together. By the way, you will play as well." I think even when I first went to Villa there was an acknowledgement that "we can get more out of this kid" and that was always the case with Vic. As a player I took the preliminary coaching badge at 18. It was a wonderful programme offered to the forty pros at Villa, but only three or four took it.

'I learned a lot about coaching in America. The team in Atlanta was owned first by the Braves baseball team and then by the multi-sport Omni Corporation. I worked in the building where other sports, like basketball, were staged and saw all the promotions and marketing. It intrigued me. I was captain of the team at the age of 20 and I had a business card that said I was the business manager. I was responsible for booking airline tickets, filing match reports to Atlanta newspapers and booking half-time and pre-game entertainment.'

The Timbers set their season ticket price at $5 and Hoban was suddenly in every newspaper and radio station selling them. 'For several weeks I was almost single-handedly trying to saturate the city, saying, "This is what is coming." I was explaining rules and getting questions like, "How many on a team? Do you play with sticks?" It was like someone clearing the ground in advance for a politician. I was relieved when the rest of the players got off the plane!'

There were only ten days left before kick-off when Crowe arrived back in Oregon. Five days later nine weary Football League veterans trooped off a ten-hour flight from London; three more followed three days later. Crowe brought his players together to train for an opening game that was now only two days away. What stood before him was a squad made up mostly of professionals from the West Midlands, including some tried and tested veterans from Villa and up-and-coming younger players from Wolves.

At 31, goalkeeper Graham Brown had played close to 200 League games for Mansfield and Doncaster. In front of him at full-back were Ray Martin, the former Birmingham City skipper, and ex-Atlanta Chief Barrie Lynch. Hoban and Graham Day, from Bristol Rovers, marshalled the centre of defence, while the midfield was anchored by Crowe's on-field lieutenant, Brian Godfrey, who had captained Villa to their Wembley appearance four years earlier. Godfrey made up in knowledge what he lacked in pace and was a valuable organiser and coaxer. Also in midfield were Port Vale's Tom McLaren, 21-year-old Wolves player Barry Powell, who had appeared in his club's League Cup final victory over Manchester City in 1974, and Tony Betts, Villa's former England youth international. Willie Anderson, on loan from Cardiff, had been a member of the Villa League Cup final team under Crowe. Dark and handsome, skilful on the ball, Anderson had a reputation for relaxing in the changing-room after the game by smoking a cigar.

Wolves' bearded centre-forward Peter Withe was the spearhead of the attack. For Liverpool-born Withe, a 23-year-old reserve team player at Molineux, the NASL season would be a springboard to moves to Birmingham, Nottingham Forest, Newcastle and Aston Villa, winning 11 England caps and two League Championships along the way and scoring the winning goal in Villa's 1982 European Cup-final triumph.

'I had played in South Africa and I asked Bill McGarry if I could go back there that summer,' he explains. 'I was young and enthusiastic and had got into the game late and I just wanted to continue playing, but he didn't want me to go. I thought maybe that meant he wanted me to be more involved in the first team. Then Vic asked Bill if he could take me to Portland and he let me go.'

Joining the future England man were two of his colleagues in the Wolves second team, Jimmy Kelly, a promising young winger from Northern Ireland, and Chris Dangerfield, a former England youth international. With Derek Dougan, John Richards and Alan Sunderland occupying the striking positions in McGarry's first-team squad, the Timbers offered a chance for the three young forwards to gain some competitive experience.

Dangerfield, who would join the band of English players that stayed to enjoy long NASL careers, says, 'There were 44 professionals at Wolves at that time. I felt I should be given the opportunity to play for the first team but I wasn't going to get a game and Vic told me this would be a chance to get some experience. The money was secondary. My position at Wolves hadn't been helped by a blow-up I had with Bill McGarry over Steve Daley. He borrowed my car, had no insurance and had a bust-up in it. I think McGarry felt I was responsible and wanted to get me out of the way.'

Dangerfield recalls the mood surrounding the Timbers' camp as they prepared hurriedly for their opening game. 'Vic and Leo Crowther, his assistant, did a great job of selecting players and getting them to meld together at short notice. To be honest, it was a lot of fun; this feeling that we would sink or swim together. It was a good mix of young guys and veterans. Many were guys I watched when I was going down to Villa as a fan.'

Withe recalls his first Timbers training session. 'Most people out there had never seen soccer before in their lives and we felt we were going on a bit of a mission. There was a camera crew watching us train and they were bored to tears. I heard one of them say, "What are we doing here looking at these limeys?" I asked Kelly and Anderson to cross a few balls into the middle and I headed the ball into the net. The guy almost dropped his camera. "Did you see that?" he said. I was the first person they had ever seen do something like that and they ended up nicknaming me "The Wizard of Nod" and the "Mad Header".'

The day of the Timbers' season opener against Seattle brought incessant rain and, with one hour to go before kick-off, there were no more than 500 fans dotted around Civic Stadium. But with Don Paul outside apologising for the shortage of ticket sellers, there were plenty trying to find their way in and when the teams lined up to start the game on the slick artificial turf there were 8,131 inside the ground. There was no fairy-tale ending, with Portland going down 1–0, but the fans braved the rain until the end. 'They took us to their hearts,' says Dangerfield. 'It rained very heavily on that night and the baseball diamond that was part of the field was uncovered. It meant the playing surface was a mix of mud and Astroturf. Third base was in the middle of the six-yard box so you would have guys trying to kick the ball out of the box in knee-high mud, while the rest of the field was rock hard. But the people showed a lot of enthusiasm. We were lucky to get into a city that was really trying to find something sports-wise that was a winner.'

The fans' reward came in the next game when Withe scored the only goal against Toronto. Taking their lead from the big forward's enthusiastic celebration, the crowd came to life and the Timbers' bandwagon was rolling. Hoban explains, 'With the promotional skill of Don Paul, who was like Barnum and Bailey, and Vic's support, the club did some wonderful stuff. There was a deep sense of community among the fans and the players.'

During the season, Kelly summed up the difference that playing in America could make to a lot of reserved, media-shy British players. 'I was self-conscious and I had no confidence in meeting other people. I didn't even give a speech at my brother's wedding, and I was best man. Now I give talks and I look forward to meeting people. I've got more assurance and I think my game is better because of that.'

Withe continues, 'I looked upon myself as an entertainer and showman more than just a footballer, and so did a lot of our players. Also, it was evident to people that their Johnny, who was 5 ft 7 in., could play this game. You didn't need to be 6 ft 2 in., 220 lb and able to run 100 yards in 10 seconds.'

After a loss in their third game at Denver, the Timbers embarked on a four-game winning streak, which included an overtime victory against Rochester. The NASL had again changed the rules for drawn games, playing sudden-death football over two periods of seven and a half minutes each before going to penalty kicks if neither team had broken through. Against the Lancers, the game was won 3–2 when Withe headed down into the path of Anderson, who fought off the attention of two defenders, controlled the ball, took it round the keeper and scored with the side of his foot. It was the first of Portland's five overtime victories.

When the Timbers played Dallas on 18 June, beginning a seven-game winning run, the crowd had grown to almost 15,000. One banner read 'Jimmy Kelly for Mayor' and the winger obliged his fans by scoring in a 3–0 victory. A couple of weeks later more than 18,000 saw Dangerfield grab the winner in a 2–1 success against Vancouver, with Paul having proclaimed at half-time, 'Welcome to Soccer City, USA'.

The first sell-out was achieved against Seattle, the team from the next state. A crowd of 27,310 saw the Sounders take the lead after half an hour but within three minutes Kelly had set up Withe for the equaliser. The duo repeated the trick in the second half and the game was won. After the game, Crowe told his players to get back out and perform a lap of honour, which took 20 minutes to complete as half the crowd, it seemed, came out to join them. Scarcely a single Timbers shirt made it back to the dressing-room as the fans grabbed their souvenirs.

Portland had enjoyed a stretch of 15 wins in 17 games by the end of the season and were nine points clear of Seattle at the head of the division. Crowe's team, one of the youngest in the league with an average age of 24, had achieved their success by utilising a fast-paced English style of play. Dangerfield explains, 'It is an overused word but it was the concept of the "team" that really made us. We had players who would work hard for each other. Peter Withe was an unbelievable athlete who had the ability to hold the ball up front and take pressure off you. You knew you could always find him. Anderson and Kelly were wingers who could get behind players and could give you width, and we had a big, wide pitch that suited us.'

Withe adds, 'Vic had a plan in his mind, knew the system he wanted to play. He knew he had some fit players because we had all just come off an English season and he blended us into the team. We ended up playing a system that had Anderson and Kelly on the wings and me down the middle. We always kept the same shape. And Vic trained the arse off us. Whatever he threw at us, we did. We enjoyed all the running.'

By scoring 16 goals in the regular season, Withe caught the attention of several English clubs and earned himself a transfer to Birmingham City. 'Two teams tried to sign me while I was in Portland,' he explains. 'Peter Taylor wanted me to go to Brighton and then Birmingham came in for me. Freddie Goodwin flew out to America to watch me and I signed when I was in the US. Playing for Portland had given me the opportunity to prove what I could do.'

In the play-offs, Portland were at home to their old rivals from Seattle in the quarter-finals. The club installed additional seating to take the Civic Stadium capacity up above 30,000 and Hoban recalls, 'We walked the stadium before the game, shaking hands with everyone.'

The Sounders would be no pushover, having won only one game fewer than the Timbers in the regular season. Chelsea forward Tommy Baldwin and Wales and Tottenham central defender Mike England, a veteran of 44 games for his country, were among Seattle's new additions for the season, along with Wrexham's Arfon Griffiths. England, a future Wales manager, had earned a place on the NASL All-Star team and, according to teammate and assistant coach Jimmy Gabriel, was revelling in the American scene. Already 33 when he arrived in the States, England would play for five NASL seasons, winning individual recognition in four of them.

'Mike was another who came over thinking, "I am only going to spend a season here and then that's it,"' says Gabriel. 'But we played on Astroturf and if you are player of Mike's calibre your technique works so well on it. I felt the surface helped the older guys. Instead of running in mud we were bouncing off the hard surfaces and it meant our legs didn't get wasted. The first thing you feel when you are getting older is playing in mud; it drags your energy. Having the ability to manage the surface, like Mike did, meant he could keep playing for so long.'

Sounders coach John Best had been alerted to the possibility of signing England when he struggled to maintain his place in the first team at Tottenham, the club he joined from Blackburn and had helped to FA Cup, League Cup and UEFA Cup triumphs. 'I saw that Mike had some problems and disagreements at Spurs so I thought, "Jeepers, that might fit just great." He was the sort of player I tried to go for. He was not as quick as he once was but he was totally dominant in the air and had great touch on the ball. He used his experience and maturity in positioning and was an absolutely dominant player.'

The veteran England against the young, raw talent of Withe promised to be one of the key battles in a game in which regional pride, as well as a place in the semi-finals, was at stake. Gabriel explains, 'Portland were huge rivals. We had beaten them in their first ever game, even though we had just defended well and stolen a win. When we played them in Seattle we beat them again, 3–2 in overtime, so they definitely had a score to settle. Portland were a strong team, even though they were in their first season. It was possible in those days to open a franchise, go over to England and get a very good team straight away.'

Best recalls, 'They had the teams walk out with the coaches in front, like at Wembley. The place was absolutely jammed and people were in trees outside and on the rooftops. Excitement and tension caused me to think, "Oh boy. Now we are really on our way."'

John Rowlands, who had finished the season as Seattle's top scorer with nine goals, gave the Sounders the lead, only for Powell to equalise. Coaches Crowe and Best shouted in vain to have their instructions heard over the deafening noise of a 31,523 crowd as a fraught battle went into extra-time. After six minutes of sudden-death play the game was decided when a quickly taken Portland corner found the Seattle defenders out of position. A dipping cross reached the penalty area and Timbers substitute Tony Betts rose to make contact with his blond head and send Portland to the semi-finals. A disappointed Best said, 'He fell over and the ball hit him on the head and it went in.' Once again, the Timbers fans came down from the stands during the players' victory lap, risking injury by dropping over a 20-foot wall to get to the field. Outside the stadium, the streets quickly became packed with cars and fans making their way to the post-game party at the nearby Benson Hotel.

Meanwhile, Gabriel, a fierce competitor, took the defeat as hard as any in his professional experience, even after a career that had brought him Scotland caps and winners' medals in the Football League and FA Cup. 'My attitude was that you were a professional and you were taught to win. It hurt. Maybe it was easier for some of the players because they would go back to England and carry on playing, but for me it was the last game of the season.'

The fact that the Timbers' campaign was continuing caused some problems, as Withe recounts. 'Freddie Goodwin wanted me back for the start of Birmingham's season, Barry Powell was signing for Coventry and Graham Day was wanted back by Mansfield. The clubs were screaming and hollering for us to go back, but Phil Woosnam said every player must honour his NASL contract. We got together as players and said, "We know they are shouting for us to go back, but we want to stay here because we can win this."'

The next opponents in the Timbers' quest to fulfil that prophecy were the St Louis Stars, whose coach John Sewell had added some familiar Football League names to a predominantly American squad for the 1975 season and had been rewarded with the Central Divison title and the Coach of the Year award. Goalkeeper Peter Bonetti, who had lost out to Welsh international John Phillips as the number-one keeper at relegation-bound Chelsea, arrived determined to prove that he still possessed many of the qualities that had made him one of England's leading goalkeepers over the previous ten years. Bonetti performed well enough to complete the journey from the Stamford Bridge reserve side to the NASL All-Star team. Veteran Millwall defender Dennis Burnett also played an important role, while Hull City striker John Hawley, later to join Leeds, Sunderland and Arsenal, contributed 11 goals in 20 games. It was Hawley who scored for the Stars in their 1–1 draw against the Los Angeles Aztecs in the quarter-finals, a game they eventually won in a penalty shoot-out.

The frenzy among the fans in Portland continued throughout the five days that separated the two play-off games. On the eve of the semi-final some began queueing outside the stadium, prepared to wait all night to take their places in a crowd of 33,503. A goal from the prolific Withe rewarded them for their patience and sent the Timbers into the Soccer Bowl, as the NASL final had been renamed. With the game to be played in San Jose one week later, the fans said farewell to their team one last time after a season that had seen their club progress from an idea in Don Paul's head and a list of names in Vic Crowe's pocket to a team that had captured its public's imagination and attracted fans to NASL games in record numbers.

Hoban concludes, 'When we see guys nearly 30 years on from that year, we still say what a wonderful summer it was.' But, as important as the events were in Oregon, the biggest story of 1975 was developing thousands of miles east in New York. Pelé had come to play.

8. ☆ Coming to America

In October 1974, Pelé had waved an emotional farewell to football. After only 21 minutes of Santos's home game against Ponte Preta he sank to his knees and, with tears streaming down his cheeks, bowed to kiss the grass. He rose to his feet, trotted around the field and, after 1,254 games and 1,216 goals, including 96 in 111 internationals, disappeared down the tunnel for what seemed like the last time. It was a day the NASL had been waiting for.

'It all goes back to 1971 when we expanded into New York,' explains Phil Woosnam. 'We said that in the long term we had to attract the great players and get two or three years out of them. Chelsea asked the US Soccer Federation secretary Kurt Lamm if he could set something up for them while England was snowed up. They ended up playing Santos in Jamaica and I said to Kurt, "Do you think we have a shot at meeting Pelé?" Before going down there I went to Coca-Cola and said, "We are having a meeting with Pelé. How about making him a worldwide spokesman?" They said it sounded interesting.

'So Kurt, Clive Toye of the Cosmos and I met Pelé and his adviser, Professor Julio Mazzei. We sat around the pool talking and I said, "We have come for one reason. When you retire, before you retire completely, would you consider coming to America for two or three years?" He said, "Yes, sure." So I thought that maybe it would happen, maybe it wouldn't, but at least we had sown the seed. "And one other thing," I said. "Do you have any interest if I can fix up for you to be a spokesman for Coca-Cola in a worldwide sponsorship?" I needed him to think that those guys from the NASL had done something for him. I came back and told Coke we had spoken to Pelé, but my guy there hadn't been able to get it sold to the rest of his company. We were moving offices from Atlanta to

New York, so the first thing I did when I got to New York was find Pepsi's number, find out who was handling their sports sponsorships and it was a done deal. All of a sudden Pelé was their worldwide ambassador. That was the end of my involvement and I said to Clive, "When you feel the time is right, go and see if you can do it."'

After winning the NASL crown in 1972, the Cosmos had performed unspectacularly and by the beginning of the 1975 season were playing in front of crowds of fewer than 10,000 in Downing Stadium, Randall's Island. Gordon Bradley, entering his fifth season as coach, recalls, 'Because we were owned by a gigantic organisation like Warner, we took the initiative to ask the powers that be if we could spend more money to get Pelé, and they allowed us to do it.'

Toye continues, 'I had pestered Pelé constantly after that first meeting. I did not want anything else to attract him and I met him on every possible occasion in more countries than I can remember. After he had been retired about four or five months, the itch to play again had plainly set in. Juventus and Real Madrid were sniffing around as well, but I told him, "If you go there, all you can win is a championship. In America, you can win a country."'

The Cosmos became more optimistic about getting their man when it emerged that Pelé's estimated £1.5 million-worth of business interests in Brazil had been hugely diminished by the bad advice, and worse, of his advisers. Bradley explains, 'Everything seemed to come right for us to get him. We took an entourage from Warner to see him. He passed everything on to Professor Mazzei, who thought it would be a good idea for Pelé to be part of the league. Pelé liked the idea of who we wanted to be and where we were going and knew he would be with a tremendous organisation. There was a good rapport from the start.'

So it was that on 3 June, Toye announced that Pelé, star of two World Cup finals, had signed a three-year deal with the New York Cosmos. Speculation focused on how much the 33 year old would receive for a contract that also called for him to promote Warner Communications. An amount of $4.7 million, plus private yachts and planes, was reported, but Toye says, 'We paid him a total of $2.8 million for three years as a player and ten years of marketing rights. I found out later that Real Madrid had offered roughly the same.' It bought the NASL the credibility the league had been seeking for eight years.

Pelé, who hailed from the poverty-stricken mining village of Trés Coracoes, had first made his mark on the world game as an outrageously talented 17 year old, helping Brazil lift the 1958

World Cup in Sweden. Injury meant he played only one complete game as Brazil successfully defended their title in Chile in 1962 and he limped out once again after being subjected to brutal treatment as his country lost its crown in England in 1966. The 1970 finals in Mexico belonged to Brazil and, most notably, Pelé. His goals and near misses (who can forget his lob from the halfway line against Czechoslovakia or his dummy against Uruguay?) shaped the most memorable of all World Cup tournaments. Now he was coming to America. Bradley recalls, 'Once Pelé arrived, he drew in all kinds of people. Celebrities from all over the world, people like Muhammad Ali, came to watch him.'

Woosnam adds, 'Now no one could refuse to come and play in the NASL because they thought it wasn't good enough. It was good enough for Pelé. We really needed this in New York because the media were killing us and didn't think we would succeed. Suddenly Pelé walked through the door and the whole attitude to the sport in this country changed overnight. That was the most critical moment in the history of soccer in the USA. All of a sudden, the youth organisations started playing. It was the turning point. And it meant that as he went around the country we had great attendances.'

Given the obvious benefits to the NASL as well as the Cosmos, it was natural that Woosnam should have to contend with accusations that the league had contributed to the cost of such a coup. 'I know a lot of other people thought we had helped out and didn't like it, but it was purely club money,' he insists. 'Unless someone did something behind my back.'

Toye adds, 'I had to go to a league meeting and present a case for allowing us to pay above the maximum wage for Pelé. The teams voted for it unanimously because of who it was.'

However, future Cosmos head coach Ken Furphy says that the NASL took steps to ensure that the club was rewarded for their investment. 'He was the highest-paid sportsman in any sport in America at that time. The league agreed that, wherever he went, we got 50 per cent of whatever gate the team drew in excess of their average. It was to help pay for him.'

John Best, coach of the Seattle Sounders, remembers, 'The reaction from most other teams was one of excitement. For him to pitch his tent in America was obviously going to bring more awareness of the game and I don't feel his signing was regretted by anyone. With the help of Pelé, people in other countries were more aware of the league and it made it easier to talk to some of the other well-known players.'

For the players around the league, the ripple effect of Pelé's arrival was to reach both the big fish and the tiddler. Portland Timbers defender Mick Hoban recalls, 'Pelé's salary raised the bar and his presence attracted players of different quality to those who were going to America in the early days. For me, and others like me, the greatest pleasure now is looking back and saying that I played against some of the world greats.'

Pelé would be followed to the NASL by a veritable 'Who's Who' of world football, from Franz Beckenbauer and Gerd Müller to Johan Cruyff and Johan Neeskens, along with some of the leading British stars. Says Hoban, 'Suddenly every team had a famous player. There was always a story coming to town to use as a hook. And there were good journeymen professionals behind them.'

Woosnam believes that the Pelé gamble would not have paid off so handsomely if the man himself had not been such a willing ambassador. 'His personality was something else. He always had a smile on his face and did a great job with the media, who loved him. The biggest problem was to get him anywhere on time.'

Toye adds, 'Pelé had no airs and graces. Of course he had a security guy and had his calls screened and he knew how important he was, but when he first stepped into the locker room he went round to each player and gave him a handshake and a hug. Sometimes he would tell me I worked him too hard. We would arrive somewhere and I would present him with a list of about seven appearances, but I knew I would end up with the two or three I really wanted. In the beginning, the other players didn't want to play with him. They wanted to sit on the bench and watch him play. They were in awe of him.'

One-time New York Cosmos captain Keith Eddy recalls witnessing Pelé's public relations skills at the team's weekly press conferences. The former Watford and Sheffield United defender says, 'Pelé was a diplomat and a politician. He always said the right things. Before every game, he and I met the press. He was there because of who he was and I was there simply because I was the Cosmos captain. Of course, nobody ever wanted to ask me a question, so everything was directed at him. His English was as good as mine, but every time someone asked a question that was a little controversial, he would say, "Sorry, my English is not quite good enough. Let Keith answer that question."'

Pelé missed the first nine games of the 1975 season and would also be absent for the final four. Yet the foundation had been laid for future years. In their final home match before Pelé's debut, the Cosmos attracted only 5,227 for a contest against the Hartford Bi-Centennials. The figure jumped to 22,500 when the club's new signing took the field against Toronto. The effect was the same on the road. Fewer than 5,000 Toronto fans had turned up when their team faced New York in May, but when the Cosmos returned with Pelé two months later almost 22,000 ventured out. The Washington Diplomats went from a crowd of 35,620 for the Cosmos game to 2,140 against Philadelphia three days later, although a 9–2 thrashing at the hands of New York had done nothing to encourage fans to return.

But while the crowds were flocking to see the Cosmos, results on the field were disappointing. The New York team of 1975 consisted largely of South American players, one of the exceptions being Mike Dillon, the former Tottenham reserve centre-half who had played for Montreal in 1972. For the last few games of the season, he acquired an English teammate in Tommy Ord, signed from Rochester, for whom he had scored 14 goals. Ord, who played three games for Chelsea in 1972–73 after joining from non-League Erith and Belvedere, first played in the NASL for Montreal in 1973. A late-season replacement for Pelé, Ord got both goals in a 2–0 win on his debut against the Lancers, but defeats in the next two games, including a 5–0 thrashing at Boston, ended New York's hopes of a play-off place.

While Pelé had been considering life in the Big Apple, another renowned star of the world game was already on his way to America, although Eusebio's signing for the Boston Minutemen had only a minimal impact. The Portuguese striker had been top scorer in the 1966 World Cup finals and spearhead of a powerful Benfica side throughout that decade, but with a series of knee injuries behind him he played only seven games for a Boston team that finished on top of the league's Northern Division. He was overshadowed by Ade Coker, top scorer once more with ten goals, and Geoff Davies, on loan from Wrexham, who added six.

In the Central Division, the new Chicago Sting franchise had former Manchester United centre-half Bill Foulkes as their coach. To provide the flair going forward, Foulkes brought in another former Old Trafford figure, Ian Storey-Moore, a quick and skilful forward with an eye for the goal, whose career had been plagued by a series of injuries. He had scored 105 goals for Nottingham Forest but had been limited to just 1 England cap before United pulled off one of the biggest and most controversial moves of the 1971–72 English season, snatching him from under Derby's noses after Brian Clough had even introduced him to the Baseball Ground fans. Storey-Moore played only 39 League matches at

United and had spent a year out of football before joining Chicago, for whom he played ten consecutive games in the first half of the season before making only four appearances as substitute in the second half of the year.

The Sting, however, were well catered for up front by future United player Gordon Hill. Only 21, Hill, an explosive left-winger, joined on loan from Millwall and was one of the players of the season, scoring sixteen goals and adding seven assists. By November of 1975, Hill, his reputation flourishing, was on his way to Old Trafford in a £70,000 transfer, helping Tommy Docherty's team rebuild their tarnished image with an exciting brand of football that took them to a place in the FA Cup final and third position in the First Division. Eddie May, the veteran Wrexham central defender, was second-leading scorer for Chicago with seven goals.

The Denver Dynamo brought in former Miami Toros coach John Young as part of their makeover. On the field, 31-year-old Southampton midfielder Hugh Fisher provided his renowned competitive streak, while nomadic defender Peter Short joined a team otherwise made up of little-known Brits, Americans and South Africans, whose number included former Atlanta striker Kaizer Motaung.

Denver won fewer than half their games and finished with an identical record to the Dallas Tornado, who finished the season by parting with their former championship-winning coach, Ron Newman. 'We had a lot of injuries,' he says. 'Lamar Hunt was a stickler for keeping the roster to 17 players. He said you didn't need more. But you did if you got injuries in the same position. We fought over the fact that I could not bring in extra players and in the end I was fired. Lamar said, "We are going to find the best coach in the world." I said, "You have just fired him."' Newman, however, would be back.

One of the year's most interesting signings was Jimmy Johnstone, a hero to Celtic and Scotland fans, who turned up at the San Jose Earthquakes. The little flame-haired winger was one of the famous 'Lisbon Lions', the team that had become the first British club to win the European Cup when they beat Inter Milan in 1967. Still not 31, 'Jinky' was recruited to provide the service for English forward Paul Child. However, Johnstone's run of ten games in the second half of the season included a seven-game losing streak. Child, whose four goals represented his least successful NASL season, failed to score a single goal alongside the ex-Celtic man.

Child recalls with a chuckle, 'They brought Jimmy in for his first game in a white Rolls Royce. He was very, very average. He was a great talent and at times he could do things that mesmerised us. Being so small and fragile, you wondered how he got away with it all his life. He was so quick he could fake you out. But he came in during a very frustrating year and he was obviously on his way out.' According to teammates, Johnstone was not the most diligent attendee when it came to training sessions, and defender Laurie Calloway says, 'There were times when you saw the magic, but there was only one game when he did it the whole time and then he absolutely terrorised the full-back.'

☆

While Portland's British legion was ruling in the west in 1975, it was another expansion team built on Football League foundations that was emerging as the NASL's challenger from the east. The Tampa Bay Rowdies' first attempt to grab national attention was thwarted when Buffalo Braves basketball star Randy Smith, who had played soccer at college, was prevented by his employers from spending the summer kicking a football. But there was no gimmickry involved as coach Eddie Firmani made the rounds of London's clubs to construct his team.

Born in Cape Town, South Africa, Firmani was taken to London by Charlton Athletic after being spotted in a junior game. A skilful inside-forward, his 51 goals for Charlton captured the attention of several clubs in Italy and in 1955 he moved to Sampdoria. Thanks to his Italian background he was selected to play for his new country and he was involved in further transfers to Inter Milan and Genoa before returning to Charlton. After one season at Southend, he was back at The Valley to begin his managerial career, where he spent three seasons in charge.

The defence Firmani built for the Rowdies included former Orient centre-half Malcolm Linton and long-serving Chelsea utility man John Boyle, languishing at Orient after ten years at Stamford Bridge. Further forward, John Sissons, the former Chelsea and West Ham winger, and Stewart Scullion, ex-Watford and Sheffield United, were the men who would support Clyde Best, the Bermudan striker signed from West Ham, and Derek Smethurst, a South African who had played for Chelsea and Millwall. Signed as a job lot was a trio of players that Crystal Palace manager Malcolm Allison had released on loan: goalkeeper Paul Hammond, former Stoke centre-half Stewart Jump and 20-year-old midfielder Mark Lindsay.

Jump recalls, 'Eddie Firmani came over looking for players and spoke to Malcolm about us. The three of us did meet together but

I don't think it was a question of all going or no one going. Eddie sold it well and Tampa looked like a nice place. I felt the game in England was becoming a bit of a grind and a slog, and not as enjoyable as when I first started.'

Jump and his teammates responded to the more relaxed atmosphere of playing in the Florida sunshine. Lindsay explains, 'It was a real adventure for a 20 year old. At that time, Florida was a dream trip because not many people from England were going there. There was no other sports franchise in Tampa so we were in the media a lot – on the front pages of the sports section and on TV. I even did my own radio show once a month.'

There was, of course, the usual payback. 'When I got to Tampa I discovered that the PR was much more intense than we were told,' says Lindsay. 'We were going to schools after training in mid-afternoon and for the most part it was 95 degrees. And in the evenings we coached the parents.'

Hammond admits, however, that it was not all work. 'Because most of us were English it was like a social club. We treated it as a bit of a holiday. We were typical Brits and went out partying.' The partying proved to be a boon to the local licensed trade, as Lindsay recalls. 'I met a guy after I finished playing who said he used to own a bar in Tampa. He said, "I was dying there until one day in the middle of summer, when in came 20 foreigners." We used to go down there two or three nights a week. That infusion of money helped him make the bar a success.'

Firmani's interest, of course, was in making sure his players were contributing to the health of the Rowdies' Eastern Division challenge rather than the wealth of the local hostelries. 'Eddie was very intense, a very proud man,' Lindsay explains. 'His approach was, "We don't have to worry about anybody else if we go out with the right attitude." It was so easy to lose your focus out there when you were being invited out to barbecues and God knows what. There were people offering you drinks the night before a game. Eddie would remind us, "We need to go to bed early tonight." Some of the lads said, "Bollocks," and were still going out. Eddie's attitude was just to go for the jugular. There were not a great deal of tactics, but everybody knew their job.'

Jump adds, 'I think perhaps we were treated differently as players than we would have been at home. There was not as much pressure. Eddie let you go out and play and, of course, winning relieves the pressure. There were no big egos, everyone wanted to play and promote the game.'

Lindsay continues, 'We would go 1–0 up and other teams would self-destruct. They were fighting on the field; they didn't have the cohesiveness we had. One of the things that helped us was that teams would go to Miami to play on a Friday, have a tough time in 90 degrees and get injured, and then they would come and play us on the Sunday when they were still tired.'

The Rowdies never looked back after Smethurst scored an overtime winner to beat Rochester in the franchise's inaugural match – in which Firmani appeared as a substitute while he awaited the arrival of many of his squad from England. They won 15 of the next 18 games and the division title was already secured when they lost their last three regular season matches.

The main source of goals was the tall, dark-haired Smethurst, whose move to Tampa had been an escape from four frustrating years at Millwall. Although he appeared as a substitute in Chelsea's Cup-Winners' Cup final victory against Real Madrid in Athens in 1971, Smethurst played in only 14 League games in almost three years at Stamford Bridge. He transferred to Millwall for £33,000 in search of first-team football, but admits, 'Millwall was a shock to my character. People there wanted you to kick guys into the stadium. You could nutmeg a guy, sell a dummy, curl the ball round two players, smack it into the net and you'd get a little round of applause. If you whacked a guy into the stands like Harry Cripps used to, they would cheer you off the pitch.'

Smethurst's return from his Millwall career was a disappointing nine goals in sixty-six league games, but he explains, 'Benny Fenton, the manager, wanted me to become a midfielder and then I was out for a long time because I had torn a thigh muscle. I did it on a Saturday but they made me play in the League Cup a couple of days later. I took three or four steps and tore it again. Eddie Firmani had seen me play at Chelsea and knew I was being played out of position. Gordon Jago, who was the new manager, said he would let me go for free to America, but if I stayed in England he would ask £80,000 for me. Eddie asked me to go and told me what was involved financially and I jumped at it. It took me two seconds to decide. I knew if I went I could get fit. It was warm weather, Bermuda grass and I knew Stoke and Nottingham Forest wanted me, but didn't want to touch an injured player. I thought it would be three months at Tampa Bay and then I was coming back.

'I didn't feel I had failed in England. I felt people knew I could play and I saw it as a chance to prolong my career and produce. And in Tampa we drew an average of 12,000 in our first year. Millwall couldn't do that at that time. When I saw the excitement I could see that the opportunities for me, both in playing and after, were 100 times more than in Britain and South Africa. Rodney Marsh hit it right on the head when he talked about English football being grey. The ball players weren't honoured in those days. George Best should have played seventeen years in the Football League instead of seven. I felt he was drinking because of the pressure of not being accepted. That was a hard thing to overcome and it made me think, "Why don't they honour their players?" And I remember getting taxed at 35 per cent in England!'

Smethurst proved emphatically that, at the age of 27, he was far from being a spent force. His tally of 18 goals was the second-highest in the league and included 12 in the final 10 games. 'I was knocking in goals left, right and centre. What helped me was playing up front with Clyde Best. He knew when to hold it up and when to release me so I could get into the space and finish. We got on immediately.'

Lindsay adds, 'Derek had the ability to get across people and get his head in the right place. He scored a lot of goals at the near post with his head. Later, Rodney Marsh said he was one of purest strikers of the ball he had ever seen. His volleys rarely missed the target. We had games we should have lost, but he would pop up in the last 30 seconds and score.'

The Rowdies showed their defensive capabilities as well as their forward power during their play-off run, which began with a 1–0 home victory against Toronto, Best scoring the goal. Miami, who had disposed of Boston, were the visitors to Tampa Stadium for the semi-finals. Lindsay explains, 'One of the first games we played was down in Miami and I got sent off with one of their guys for a scuffle. The next game against them was five days later. There was a big press conference and one of their guys said there was going to be blood. Our crowd for that game went up by about 6,000 and they beat us. So there was a lot of publicity about the play-off game and in the end we gave them a right good pasting.'

Tampa Bay's 3–0 win, in which Boyle, Scullion and Smethurst found the net, set up a trip to San Jose to face the Portland Timbers for the NASL championship. The choice of venue did not sit well with Portland, who had been involved in an unpleasant game at Spartan Stadium earlier in the season. Timbers striker Peter Withe explains, 'There was a loose ball and I went through on their player and he went down injured. One of their supporters ran on the pitch and had a swipe at me. I remember out of the corner of my eye seeing him throwing a punch and as he came through I pushed him and he went down over my leg. We ended up winning the game in overtime, and then we were locked in the dressing-room with all these fans screaming at us. It turned out the guy was the mascot's brother. This mascot, Crazy George, was the mascot for the final as well and he was trying to bait the crowd.'

Tampa Bay's Lindsay agrees that it was an unsuitable venue for the championship decider. 'The ground was rock hard. The field was tight and there was dust everywhere. They should have played the game somewhere else. It was a very scrappy game and I cringe a bit now when I look at it on tape.'

Even though his team had not reached the final, the NASL's newest and biggest star, Pelé, took his seat among the 17,009 crowd and, once blues singer Lou Rawls had performed the national anthem, the action began. The Timbers' fears that the narrow field would deny them attacking options were quickly proved correct. Withe says, 'It was only a 55-yard pitch and it nullified the wing threat of Jimmy Kelly and Willie Anderson. On the bigger pitches we had played on we were a superior team, but we could not get into position down the flanks to get crosses in, which was our strength. It was a lot easier for them. It was disappointing because we had done so well during the season.'

The Timbers, pre-game favourites, found it difficult to break down the stubborn Rowdies defence and in the second half the Rowdies' Haitian substitute Arsene Auguste broke the deadlock when he slammed home a shot from 30 yards. Then Best, the man his teammates called 'Big Daddy', added a decisive second goal. The Rowdies held out for victory, keeping the Timbers scoreless for only the second time since their hastily arranged opening game of the campaign.

One of the keys had been Jump's success in his duel against Withe. 'They were a very English-style team,' says the defender. 'It suited me to be marking a big centre-forward and defensively we did well. They didn't make too many chances. At the end of the game someone came up to me and said I was going to get a trophy for being the MVP. I said, "What's that?" I didn't know MVP meant Most Valuable Player.'

In truth, the NASL's most valuable asset had been watching from the stands. But his time would come. Eventually.

9. ☆ George and Rod's Excellent Adventure

Phil Woosnam's words sum up the feeling around the NASL in the winter of 1975–76: 'If Pelé could do it, anyone could.' While Liverpool were marching towards their first League Championship under Bob Paisley, the NASL commissioner watched some of the biggest names in English football find their way onto the shopping lists of clubs eager to buy the instant credibility enjoyed by Pelé's New York Cosmos.

By the time the 1976 NASL season kicked off, England World Cup stars Bobby Moore and Geoff Hurst had signed for the San Antonio Thunder and Seattle Sounders respectively. Both were huge names, big coups for their teams, but the league's critics could point out that both were a decade removed from their finest hour. No one, however, could argue with the validity of George Best and Rodney Marsh. No players had captivated English crowds in the manner of those two in the previous ten years.

Both had very publicly become disillusioned with football in England. Best had walked out on Manchester United for the final time during the 1973–74 season, while Marsh, one of that talented group – along with Alan Hudson, Stan Bowles and Charlie George – whose face and feet never quite seemed to fit into Alf Ramsey's rigid England set-up, had fallen out with Manchester City manager Tony Book. He found himself on the transfer list and banished to train with the youth team. Marsh and Best, though, were still at an age where their skills were expected to be intact, Best only 29 and Marsh 31. Both were intrigued by the prospect of a new beginning in a country whose soccer was crying out for entertainers of their calibre.

The approach to Marsh had come in January 1976, several weeks after he last kicked a ball for City. Marsh's former agent, Ken Adam, remembers, 'I was friends with the photographer Terry O'Neill, who did the Elton John album covers. Elton wanted to get involved in football in America and John Reid, his manager, asked Terry to talk to me to see if I could fix up for Elton to get involved in the Los Angeles club. I knew the club owner, John Chaffetz, and we fixed it all up. Rodney fancied coming to the US and Elton thought it would be great to have him in LA. John Reid arranged for Rodney and me to visit Los Angeles and they took us to Elton's concert at Dodger Stadium, the works.

'While we were out there I was called by a man by the name of Theodore Beauclerc Rogers the Fourth – Beau Rogers. He was the general manager and co-owner of the Rowdies and said, "Would you be interested in taking a look at Tampa?" We had no idea where it even was. But we flew there and there was a crowd of people waiting for Rodney at the airport, like The Beatles had turned up. Beau Rogers had arranged it all. Rodney fell in love with the place and decided to go there instead of LA.'

The product of a harsh upbringing in London's East End, Marsh had found his escape route from poverty on the football field, eventually signing for Fulham. In March 1966, he was sold for a bargain £15,000 to Queens Park Rangers. It meant a drop of two divisions, but it was at Loftus Road that the legend of Rodney Marsh was born as he led the Third Division side to one of the great Wembley upsets when they beat First Division West Bromwich 3–2 in the final of the 1967 League Cup. Marsh, who scored twice to bring Rangers back from two goals down, had established himself as the south's answer to George Best, full of versatility and flair for the extravagant.

After successive Marsh-inspired promotion campaigns, Rangers experienced one ill-fated First Division season in 1968–69, their star player being forced to miss the early months of the battle through injury. By the closing weeks of the 1971–72 season, QPR's latest attempt to return to the top flight had petered out and Marsh was allowed to join Manchester City for £200,000. A regular in the England squad, if not the starting line-up, Marsh posed an immediate problem for City manager Malcolm Allison: how to work his new signing into a system in which Colin Bell, Francis Lee, Mike Summerbee and Wyn Davies were spearheading City's challenge in an exciting four-way race for the title. With the line-up chopping and changing to accommodate Marsh, who scored four goals in eight appearances, City's championship train came spectacularly off the rails as they won only three of their final eight games.

It was a sign of things to come in a City career that brought no tangible rewards. There was a shot at winning a second League Cup-winner's medal in 1974, but a 2–1 Wembley defeat by Wolves put paid to that. And when City won the 1976 final against Newcastle, Marsh was out of the picture, his bags packed for Florida.

The response to his decision to join the Rowdies shocked Marsh. He was openly criticised by some of his former teammates, whom he describes as 'backstabbers' in his autobiography, *Priceless*. As he prepared to board the plane to America, Marsh took his famous parting shot at the game he was leaving behind, claiming that English football was 'a grey game, played on grey days by grey people'.

The Rowdies team that won the Soccer Bowl in 1975 had been a side without stars, without egos. The acquisition of Marsh, for a reported transfer fee of $80,000, gave them both, a fact that was underlined when the new signing was presented to the Tampa media. Having been introduced as the white version of Pelé, Marsh jokingly corrected the statement, by saying, 'Actually, Pelé is the black Rodney Marsh.' Such a comment was typical of the man and was intended to be light-hearted, but some reporters immediately marked him down as an arrogant Brit. The relationship was not to benefit by Marsh's reluctance to talk to the media and his habit of giving evasive and misleading answers on the rare occasions when journalists did corner him.

Meanwhile, there was concern in the Rowdies locker room that Marsh would upset the delicate equilibrium of team spirit. When Rogers appointed him team captain, it was against coach Eddie Firmani's wishes. 'Eddie didn't want him,' says midfielder Mark Lindsay. 'We hadn't had one player who was picked out as being a great player. The guys liked the idea that we were all considered reputable players. We all got time in the press and radio and everyone was happy. All of a sudden, Rodney comes in with all his history. The Clown Prince, good looking, blond hair. He leapt above everyone else.'

Tampa Bay striker Derek Smethurst remembers whispers about Marsh's salary. 'Rodney was flamboyant and when he came over he wasn't liked. There was a lot of animosity because he had been signed on a big contract.'

Defender Stewart Jump adds, 'I do remember a few times when there were conflicts in practice or in team meetings. In discussion, some things were brought up that gave you the impression there was not the harmony there had been a year before. But he was enjoyable to play with and fun to watch. Our style certainly changed a bit with Rodney in the team.'

Smethurst encouraged his teammates to look at Marsh's arrival as an opportunity. 'I thought, "It's none of my business what he earns." But I knew what he had done was to open the door to negotiate. I went up to him after about three weeks and said, "Thanks for coming." He looked at me as if to say, "What does this guy want?" He knew what the feeling was among some of the players and he said, "What do you mean?" I said, "You have given me the chance to negotiate a new contract. I can go in and take my salary up. What you get is your business." Of the other players, maybe Farrukh Quarishi was the only one who really understood it, but he had come up through the college ranks.'

Unrest in the camp aside, Marsh's impact on the Rowdies was immediate. In the final home game of the regular season of 1975, their championship year, just over 12,000 had seen Tampa Bay play Chicago, but for Marsh's home debut against the same opposition more than 32,000 watched their new hero score one goal and set up another in a 2–1 victory. 'He was like the Pied Piper in Tampa,' says Gordon Jago, Marsh's former manager at QPR and later to become his boss at the Rowdies. 'He was a showman, he played the crowd and he has to take a great deal of credit for the way the sport developed in that city.'

Says Adam, 'Rodney saw it for what it was and gave his all to the club and league in general. He as much as anyone, apart from Pelé, was responsible for promoting the league.'

Lindsay comments, 'I think Rodney was one of the reasons I stayed in America. The direct result was noticeable in the stands; we were going up by a couple of thousand every game. He was not only producing on the field but he was charismatic off it. Jasper Carrot came over to film a programme about us and everybody was talking about the Rowdies. I am still good friends with Rodney and it's fair to say he definitely sees himself as a focal point. He needs to be the focus of attention and a lot of people who thought they were that focal point found out they weren't. The average Joe Blow wouldn't gravitate to them, but to Rodney.'

Liverpool defender Tommy Smith, another new arrival at the Rowdies in Marsh's first season, recalls in his book, *I Did It The Hard Way*, 'You could never really get on his wavelength, never talk his language, which always seemed to be halfway between Freud and Donald Duck. He would do things purely and solely to surprise you. We'd go on a trip to New York for a couple of days and he would bring along a big bag that could hold a suit and all that business – and inside he had nothing except a toothbrush and a tube of toothpaste.'

Goalkeeper Paul Hammond adds, 'Rodney was a bit of a comedian. Some people thought he was a bit flashy, but I thought he did very well for us. He would do things like sitting on the ball and the Americans lapped it up.'

No one enjoyed Marsh's presence in the team more than Smethurst. During the 1976 season, the former Chelsea man scored 20 goals in 24 games, while Marsh notched up 11 goals and set up almost as many. Smethurst recalls, 'The press loved him and controversy followed him. But we were on the field one second and I knew it would be great playing alongside him. Any time he didn't look at me, I knew I would get the ball. If he looked at me, I knew I wouldn't get it and he wanted me to move.'

Lindsay adds, 'I was excited about a player of that quality coming in and he was a dream come true for a player like me. Every time you tackled and came up with the ball you would just stand up and he would be there, so you would just shovel it to him. The 35-yard offside rule stretched the game and was made for Rodney. He could find space, attract people to him, wind them up a bit and get a couple of fouls. Then he would go in the box for a bit and draw penalties. If he was playing against a young American kid he would pull a couple of free-kicks on the halfway line and then he would go forward and get a couple of penalties.'

Marsh was at his flamboyant best early in his first season when the Rowdies dismantled the Cosmos 5–1 at Tampa Stadium, with Smethurst scoring a hat-trick. Turning on the trickery for a crowd of more than 42,000 and a live television audience, Marsh terrorised New York's Northern Ireland international midfielder Dave Clements throughout the game and clearly felt his opponent had got away with one foul too many by the time the second half came around. As Clements challenged from behind, Marsh swung an elbow into his opponent's face, adding insult to injury by kneeling over the ball with his arms outstretched matador-style. Pelé was the player who reacted most angrily, grabbing Marsh by the head in a clash that made all the next day's newspapers.

Such performances by Marsh were all the more remarkable given that he admits his first couple of seasons in the NASL were set against a backdrop of marital problems, difficulty in coming to terms with the rejection he felt he had suffered at City, self-doubt over his decision to go to America and an increasing reliance on alcohol to escape from that cocktail of problems. Marsh confesses that he was often drinking a bottle of vodka a day at the depths of his dissatisfaction with life. In an interview given to the NASL's *Kick* magazine in 1979, he admitted, 'I had a nervous breakdown in 1975. It was a culmination of emotional, domestic and professional problems. When they come at the same time there's no way around it. You collapse. Your brain can't take it.'

Marsh's ability to make a consistent contribution on the field, even though 'psychologically, I had lost it', would have Tampa Bay challenging for honours regularly over the four years in which he wore their white, green and yellow uniform. And his career in America would produce its share of controversial headlines along the way.

Tabloid tales had been constant companions for the man who would become Marsh's great friend. Unlike the relatively unfulfilled Marsh, George Best arrived in America having won the biggest prizes available in club football, the European Cup and the First Division Championship. But while Marsh would win two division championships and achieve qualification for two Soccer Bowls in four NASL seasons, Best was embarking on a three-team, six-year American career that would feature only a pair of semi-final appearances and not a single division title.

Still just a skinny kid from Belfast, Best was in only his second season in the United team when he won the first of his two League Championship medals in 1965, a few weeks before his 19th birthday. It was when he destroyed Benfica in Lisbon in the quarter-final of the following season's European Cup that the George Best phenomenon really began. From the moment he stepped back on English soil after scoring two goals and inspiring United to a 5–1 victory, his life would never be the same, and would never be his own. Another First Division title, a great goal in United's 4–1 defeat of Benfica as they completed their fabled quest to conquer Europe, English and European Footballer of the Year awards, the dark good looks, the pop-star lifestyle, the Miss World girlfriends – it all added up to a frenzy of attention that had never before been lavished upon a British footballer.

Best rarely failed to match the hype with his performances on the field, yet by the end of the '60s, a decade for which he had become such a striking symbol, the signs of self-destruction were becoming evident. The '70s brought suspensions, dismissals, skipped training sessions, late arrivals at disciplinary sessions, missed trains to away games and eventually the first of his walkabouts and announcements that he was quitting the game. Best, who revealed in later years the part that an ongoing battle against alcoholism was playing in his life, twice announced his retirement in 1972, the second of which prompted the first interest from the New York Cosmos.

Back in the fold for the 1973–74 season, Best finally walked out on Old Trafford for good after Tommy Docherty's decision not to play him in an FA Cup game against Plymouth. A handful of games for Southern League Dunstable followed, a few more for Stockport County and, in an attempt to prepare for his first NASL season, three games in the League of Ireland for Cork Celtic, who then sacked him for 'lack of enthusiasm'.

The latest opportunity to play in America came via Los Angeles General Manager John Chaffetz, who, while persuading Best to head to California, asked if he knew of any other British players worth signing. Best put forward the name of one of his gambling buddies, Bobby McAlinden, highlighting his brief career at Manchester City rather than his subsequent moves to Port Vale, Stockport and Glentoran.

McAlinden, whose debut for City was the only League appearance of his career, recalls, 'George and I were pals. I knew him from when I was an apprentice at City. We were socialising together in Manchester and used to play five-a-sides together at the YMCA in Stalybridge. I had not played at all for four years, not even semi-professional, and George suddenly said, "Do you want to go and play in Los Angeles?" What did I have to lose? I was already in pretty good shape. I was not much of a night owl. George asked me in November and told me to get fit and ready to go out in February. I felt it was a second bite at the cherry for me and I was confident that if I did my best, it would be good enough.'

McAlinden would hold his own against some of the biggest names in world football and establish himself as a pivotal member of the Aztecs' midfield for the next three years. Having gone over as an unknown quantity on his pal's recommendation, he was quickly offered a year-round contract to stay and help with development work in the winter. Ken Adam remarks, 'Of all the people who came over here, the best example of someone who made a second career for themselves is Bobby McAlinden. He played his heart out.'

Sharing a house with McAlinden on Hermosa Beach and making the most of the exciting social life on offer in southern California, Best teamed up with former Wales centre-forward Ron Davies and ex-Chelsea and Scotland winger Charlie Cooke in the Aztecs' forward line. The powerfully built, fair-haired Davies, one of the most feared headers of the ball in the game, boasted more than 150 competitive goals for Southampton and 29 appearances for his country. Meanwhile, Cooke's 16-cap Scotland career and dazzling wing play in Chelsea's FA Cup and Cup-Winners' Cup triumphs early in the decade had brought inevitable comparisons with the trickery of Best himself.

Married to an American girl, Cooke had always planned to settle across the Atlantic one day and happily accepted the chance to join Best in his wife's home town of Los Angeles. He says, 'It was kind of strange playing alongside George. The truth was that soccer stars were not recognised here so you would go places thinking George would draw a crowd but there were only a few thousand.'

Those who did see the Aztecs in 1976 were lucky enough to witness Best's brilliance. Says Cooke, 'He still showed spurts of quickness and could spin on a dime. He could do things without exaggerated body movements. He was subtle and elegant and a little shimmy could get him two yards of space, where other players would have to work really hard to create that.'

McAlinden says, 'In that first year, George carried us. We wouldn't have been any good without him. He was enjoying himself. Five of us eventually bought into a bar called the Hard Times Tavern, which then became Bestie's – although it ended up with just me owning it. George was still well known but not to the extent that he was in England, so at first it was great for him. On the field, we had a good mix and even though our coach, Terry Fisher, was American, he knew the game. Most important, he knew how to handle George, which is to let him do his thing. George was very good that year and never caused any confrontations. He showed up, did his training and performed on the field. He never caused one second of worry.'

Needing to win and score three goals in the final game of the season to make the play-offs, Best scored the second in a 4–1 home win against Dallas, bringing his total for the season to 15 in 23 games. There were to be no more, however, as the Aztecs lost 2–0 to the same opposition in the first round of the post-season. Best wrote, 'It wasn't Manchester United, but I was playing well and enjoying my football again.'

San Jose Earthquakes defender Laurie Calloway remembers, 'George could do stuff that Pelé couldn't. I was playing left-back against the Aztecs and he would go one way and I would go the other. I have a couple of pictures of me holding his shirt, but I never got the better of him one on one. I traded jerseys with him and it's the biggest trophy I have.'

The winter of 1976–77 saw the now-famous partnership of Best and Marsh at Fulham. The venture was captured at its peak by the ITV cameras as the duo produced the full array of party tricks to beat Hereford 4–1 in a game that was more like the

Harlem Globetrotters than a scrap for a couple of Division Two points.

Best, in an echo of Marsh's story, admits that his 1977 NASL season was set against increased drinking, gambling and relationship problems, although he still managed 11 goals and a record-tying 18 assists for a team that went to the Soccer Bowl semi-finals with a swashbuckling style of attacking play. But by 1978, Best was falling into his old United pattern. He missed training and was suspended by the club. Liverpool defender Tommy Smith, one of Best's great adversaries, was the head coach in mid-season when Best and the Aztecs parted company. 'He more or less sold himself because he wasn't trying a leg,' Smith wrote. 'He never bothered his behind, he was that disillusioned.'

Best was traded to the Fort Lauderdale Strikers in June and his debut was against the New York Cosmos. He scored with virtually his first touch, added a second later in the game and helped his new team to a 5–3 win. But there were not to be too many happy days during Best's stay in Florida, where he ran headlong into a personality clash with Englishman Ron Newman, the former Dallas coach who had taken over at the Strikers in 1977. 'Ron was a great recruiter of players,' says one player, 'but George would have had no respect for someone he thought was limited in his knowledge of the game.'

Best recounts in his book, *Blessed*, that he was taken off during overtime in a 1978 semi-final play-off game against Marsh's Rowdies, claiming that Newman then expected him to participate in the shoot-out. Best says he had to remind Newman that only players on the field at the end of the game could take part in the sudden-death decider. 'I was fuming that the coach apparently hadn't fully understood the American rules of soccer,' he says.

Newman, who by that time was in his 12th American summer, counters, 'It was not George writing his book – it was Hans Christian Andersen. We had won the first play-off game at home and we lost the next game at Tampa, which meant we now had to play a mini-game followed by the shoot-out if we were still tied. I do remember pulling George off because he had become a nonentity and I did not want to play the mini-game with only ten men. It did go through my mind that it would have been useful to have George now that we had reached the shoot-out stage, but decided that the 35-yard run-up would be about 20 yards too much for him. If we had lost in the mini-game because I had left George on for the shoot-out, I would never have forgiven myself.'

Few of Newman's memories of Best are complimentary. He says, 'I realised what he was like – he could be a selfish son of a bitch. The promotion surrounding him was so huge that you had to say things you didn't believe. There was a radio guy who did a lot for us who wanted an interview with George, but went to the office instead of the stadium by mistake. He called and said, "Is George still there?" I said that he was and went to get George and asked him if he could wait. George said OK. The guy was there in a moment and when I asked if he had seen George he said, "No. I can't find him." Someone said he had got in someone's car and taken off. I thought, "You bastard, George Best. This is the kind of guy you are dealing with. He won't help the team or the game."

'He was good in practice but not in games. I thought we were carrying him most of the time because he was good PR and the press needed him. One of our players, Tony Whelan, had been at United when George was there and I asked him, "How good was George when he was really good?" I was a big fan of Ray Hudson in our midfield and Wheels said, "He was probably about ten times better than Ray."'

Strikers forward David Irving sticks up for Best, though. 'I thought Bestie was wonderful. He was our leader. George was a character and it was wonderful to play on the same field as him. But he and Ron didn't see eye to eye. As players you are aware of that situation but with the type of good professionals we had in that team we didn't let it affect the rest of us.'

The problems continued the following season, the start of which was delayed for Best by a dispute with Fulham. The London club had persuaded FIFA to ban Best after he played for the Detroit Express on their European tour, contravening Fulham's rights to Best anywhere outside the US. By the time the ban had been lifted, the 1979 NASL season had begun and Fort Lauderdale had signed legendary West German striker Gerd Müller and the Peruvian Teofilio Cubillas, who had almost single-handedly done for Scotland in the World Cup in Argentina.

David Chadwick, the former Dallas midfielder who was assistant coach under Newman at the Strikers, remembers Best being at his best when he joined up with his new teammates. 'When George was out and we couldn't play him, I was responsible for taking him for one-on-one training. We had to do extra work until we got the green light for him to play. Then Ron said he wanted to stage a full-scale practice match with George in the reserves to see if he was ready to play. At one point, the ball gets to George in midfield and he looks like he is going to hit it in the corner for Al Nijie, the winger. He must have seen the goalkeeper, Arnie Mausser, ten yards off his line. He just hit it and it went straight into the net from halfway. Then he got the ball on the left side a few minutes later. George never ran at you straight, always on an angle, and he goes past Ken Fogarty like he's not there and then bananas it in from the edge of the box. Cubillas is standing there clapping and Ron says, "OK. Put him in the team."'

Best's return to the team lasted only 70 minutes. With the Strikers leading 1–0 against the New England Tea Men, Best was substituted, his replacement Nico Bodonczy adding a second goal. 'He was tired because he had not played a full match,' says Chadwick. 'Ron says, "Chaddy, it's 1–0, we'll bring George out."'

Newman adds, 'When the second half started he was going red in the face. He was starting to kick young guys to stop them getting the ball off him. He gets a yellow card and I thought, "If he gets another he is out for several weeks. But he won't be bothered. He can sit on the bench and have some more drinks." Taking him out was the logical thing to do. He starts walking to the dressing room and then comes back towards the bench and starts pulling his shirt off. I am watching in my peripheral vision and he rolls it in a ball and throws it at me.'

Chadwick continues, 'We used to do a lap of honour and at the end of the game Ron says, "You take the guys round the pitch and I will get George." He grabs George by the arm and they run off together. Of course the press are all over it later, asking Ron if he is going to suspend George.'

Newman attempted to defuse the situation. 'I told them, "Everyone wants a George Best shirt and now I have got one. I will take it home and hang it above the mantelpiece. And if he does it again he will be hanging there with it."'

Newman's dissatisfaction over Best's attitude was matched by the player's concerns about his coach's tactical appreciation. Best remains fiercely critical of Newman for throwing away a 2–0 lead against the New York Cosmos a few weeks later when he took off experienced English players Hudson and Irving with 20 minutes to play and saw the Cosmos storm back to win 3–2. And there was to be another major run-in before the end of a disjointed season in which Best, suffering from a chronic knee injury, started only eleven games, appeared in eight more as a substitute and scored only two goals.

Newman claims, 'We helped to keep him teetotal for a year and eventually he broke down and missed training. The press were all over it and when he turned up the next day we just told them

George had not been well and we had given him the day off. The press called him and he said, "I am not sick, there is nothing wrong with me." We made him an alibi and he didn't use it. The next day his breath smelt awful of drink. He was already in the party to go to the game in Minnesota, although I was thinking, "Is this a one-shot deal or is he back on the drink?" We were sat around the table having the pre-game dinner and I decided he couldn't do what he had done and expect to play. I pulled him out and said, "George, it's not fair to the players if I play you." He said, "That's OK," and afterwards I thought, "You bugger! He wants to be sat down because he thinks we are going to get beat, so we will get stories saying that we can't win without Best." I played Clive Walker instead and he had a great game and we won 4–1.'

Not surprisingly, Best was not back in Fort Lauderdale in 1980, returning to California to play for the San Jose Earthquakes. With the condition of his right knee getting steadily worse, Best scored eight goals and assisted on eleven for an unsuccessful team.

In former Everton and Southampton rival Jimmy Gabriel, who joined Best at the club in 1981, he was about to find a coach who has nothing but good things to say about him. 'George was great, a super guy. He played some great soccer, but we didn't have enough good guys around him.'

Best's second season at San Jose was to be his final year in the NASL. With a new son – Calum Milan, the second name after Earthquakes owner Milan Mandaric, who had become a close and supportive friend – 35-year-old Best was attempting to beat the drink and prove he could still play the game that had brought him so much, both good and bad. Former West Brom defender Alan Merrick, a San Jose teammate, remembers, 'George was in the best of health with regard to his drinking habits. He was as sober as he could be and he was brilliant. I played against players like Cruyff and Beckenbauer but I regard George as the finest player I ever saw. I saw him do things on the training field you wouldn't believe, and then I saw him do them in matches. Wow! I was fortunate to see all of his good characteristics. The fact he had a bad knee that had to be drained before every game made his performance that year even more impressive.'

Irving, who played alongside Best once again in San Jose, adds, 'How he played at all that year was a miracle. His leg was like a question mark – he just couldn't straighten it.'

San Jose's American goalkeeper, Tim Hanley, recalls one of Best's tricks during training. 'Derek Evans, an American defender, made a little wager with George. Derek had been injured and had not had the chance to train with Bestie and felt George was a bit pampered. Derek claims he can strip George of the ball within a few seconds. George tells him he'll have a minute for $100 and sections off a 12-by-12-ft area. To this day I can remember the smirk on Derek's face. With Bestie holding the $100 bill in his hand, he proceeds to dribble the lights out. Derek pushed, kicked, grabbed and chased to no avail, and with ten seconds remaining – we were all counting down – George kicks Derek the ball, throws him the money and says, "There you go, son."'

San Jose may have been rooted to the foot of the division table again, but Best led the team with 13 goals and 10 assists, including what he considers the best goal of his career, scored, in the best theatrical tradition, against his former Fort Lauderdale team. Best began the move in the centre circle and received a return ball 25 yards out. With an impossible series of twists, turns and drag-backs, he made his way to within eight yards of goal, sending bewildered defenders this way and that – some of them making two or three attempts to halt his progress – before he lashed the ball left-footed past the goalkeeper.

Gabriel recalls, 'It was a fantastic goal and an amazing situation. George had lost his temper at the referee and Fort Lauderdale had just gone 2–0 up after what George considered was a foul for us. As he was arguing they took the free-kick and scored. After we kicked off, the ball was knocked to George and he stood back like he was going to whack it at the ref and I stood up and shouted, "George! No!" He could have been sent off if he had hit it at the ref, but he didn't. Instead, he ended up beating five men and stuck it away. The other team must have thought, "Oh no. We've ignited him and now we are going to see the best of him." He scored another and in overtime he beat three men and hit the foot of the post and one of our guys knocked in the rebound to win.'

Best's form was even rewarded with a brief recall to Billy Bingham's Northern Ireland squad, although he was taken out a week later because the Irish manager felt he lacked the necessary fitness. Best played his last NASL game in the Earthquakes' season finale against Vancouver, a low-key defeat. It was to be the end of Best's serious football career, although Bournemouth and a couple of Australian teams would benefit from his services for a few games.

San Jose's goal in Best's final game was scored by English midfielder Mark Lindsay, who played alongside both Marsh and

Best during his NASL career. 'George was completely different to Rodney,' he says. 'Rodney would go out looking for the newspaper article and the TV camera. George came here to play football and at the end of the day he would say, "See you tomorrow," and go home. Jimmy Gabriel's attitude was just, "Get out there and play" and for anything to do with tactics, free-kicks and corners, it was, "Ask George." That suited George. He'd say, "Throw it to me and let me take all the free-kicks." And he could still go by people even with a bum knee. I used to go out and play darts with Bestie. He was a very soft-spoken, nice guy. He was always smiling and I think he always looks at life in a positive way. And he threw great darts!'

10. ☆ Playing for Kicks

The NASL's 1976 season kicked off with 58,128 fans attending the opening game at Seattle's new indoor stadium, the Kingdome, where Pelé and the New York Cosmos were the visitors. Six years after lining up against him in the heat of World Cup battle in Guadalajara, England striker Geoff Hurst found himself renewing rivalry with the great Brazilian.

Hurst's journey from West Ham, where he had scored 180 Football League goals and earned 49 England caps, had gone via Stoke City, where he spent three seasons, and a handful of games for West Brom. Now pulling on the white and blue of Seattle, Hurst gave Sounders coach John Best immediate evidence that he had made a wise choice of player, even though he would record only a modest return of eight goals during the season. 'Geoff did reasonably well in terms of scoring goals, but the reason I specifically went after him was for his brains. Because of the World Cup hat-trick a lot of people tend to think only of his goal-scoring skills, but I was more interested in the wonderful timing of his runs and the positions he took on the field. Martin Peters used to score a bunch of goals because Geoff created space and opportunities for him to fill in. I felt in Seattle that we could get players to time their runs off Geoff.

'For that first game in the Kingdome, we'd only had the team in town for a week or so, whereas the Cosmos were coming off a world tour. There was no way we were as prepared as we would have liked and the players had not had long to get used to playing with Geoff in the team. I decided to put Jimmy Gabriel in to play alongside Geoff up front and within five minutes Geoff had made a near-post run and Jimmy had timed his run to fill in behind. Geoff had taken the defence with him and Jim got on the end of

99

the cross to score. That helped me show the other people what the opportunities were. Geoff was a great professional. He worked hard to improve his fitness and be very competitive.'

Meanwhile, Bobby Moore, Hurst's former Hammers and England captain, was donning the flashy, patriotic red, white and blue uniform of the San Antonio Thunder, where former Arsenal and England left-back Bob McNab, ex-Coventry and Nottingham Forest centre-forward Neil Martin, Aberdeen midfielder Eddie Thomson and Harry Hood, the former Celtic forward, were among his teammates.

Also in San Antonio was Aberdeen goalkeeper Bobby Clark, back for his second American summer after his club's 1967 journey to represent the Washington Whips. Clark recalls, 'Bobby Moore was obviously getting old and slow, but he was never fast anyway. He had such an accurate long pass. Sometimes he would tell me to just put it down at a goal-kick and he would knock a 40- or 50-yard pass right on to somebody's shoe. The other thing that struck me was that I thought he would do well as a coach because he took a lot of the coaching for Don Batie. Don had been a college coach and now he was handling all the pros and he gave Bobby a lot of responsibility. Bobby had a nice way and a nice manner and was very calm. I thought he would have done well as a coach. Those are my lasting images of Bobby.'

Since 1967, Clark had made his Scotland debut against Wales the following year and won the last of his 13 caps in 1973, although he was a member of Scotland's 1974 World Cup squad in Germany and would travel to the finals in Argentina in 1978. 'I'd just had knee surgery and I thought it would be the ideal way to get fit,' he remembers. 'Aberdeen had got themselves into relegation trouble. I remember going into the last game and, even if we had drawn, we could have gone down. I had come back into the team after my operation and they wouldn't let me go out to the US until they were clear, so I didn't get out until after the first few games and missed playing against Pelé. I remember finishing that last game against Hibernian, which we won, and getting on a train to Glasgow to get a flight with my family to New York.'

San Antonio's record of 12 wins and 12 losses would only be good enough for fourth place in the Southern Division of the NASL's Pacific Conference, Hood top scoring with 10 goals. McNab, who arrived in San Antonio after an injury-hit spell at Wolverhampton, struggled to accept Batie's coaching methods. A student of Don Howe, mastermind of Arsenal's Double-winning team of 1971, McNab admits, 'It is not one of my greatest abilities to bite my tongue if I don't agree with something. Bobby Moore didn't mind so much. He told me to forget it and just enjoy myself.

'I remember coming back after one road trip and I asked if the players who had not played were going to train. The players who hadn't played had not trained hard for six days. He said, "I don't know about you, I'm going home to my wife." I went and trained. At Vancouver in later years we started having a half-hour workout after every game, which became standard practice throughout the league. You would wait for the crowd to leave the stadium and the players who hadn't played a full game would have a hard workout. At San Antonio I saw players coming into the team or being given a chance from the subs' bench and they could not last 15 minutes because they were not fit.'

Finishing on top of the Southern Division were the San Jose Earthquakes, where Paul Child rediscovered his scoring touch by netting 13 times in 23 games. At the Dallas Tornado, former Atoms coach Al Miller led the team to second place in the division. Top scorer for Dallas was Derby County striker Jeff Bourne, who began five successful NASL seasons with a fifteen-goal haul. Former West Brom and Scotland midfielder Bobby Hope and Luton winger Jimmy Ryan joined him in the squad.

Former Philadelphia skipper Derek Trevis became player-coach of the new San Diego Jaws, the franchise having moved from Baltimore and changed its name. The squad included combative Welsh midfielder Trevor Hockey, who had played nine games for Wales and changed teams as often as he changed his facial hair during an eight-club Football League career that included more than 200 games for Birmingham. Peter Silvester moved with the team from Baltimore and his tally of a mere four goals was only one off the club lead.

The Western Division of the Pacific Conference saw the Portland Timbers entering the season among the favourites once again. The team had sold 12,000 season tickets, even though many of the successful squad of 1975 were not returning, among them centre-forward Peter Withe and captain Brian Godfrey. The Aston Villa connection was strengthened, however, with the acquisition of three old boys, midfielder Pat McMahon, installed as the new skipper, and defenders Neil Rioch and Brian Tiler. In addition, current Villa goalkeeper Jim Cumbes opted for a season in the United States, putting on hold his regular summer cricket career as a seam bowler for Worcestershire. Portland once again opened their season in pouring rain, but still attracted a crowd of 22,000 for a victory against great rivals Vancouver. But after winning four of their first six games the Timbers lost five straight and never recovered, finishing fourth in the division.

At Seattle, who finished second in the division, Hurst's British teammates included Southampton winger Tom Jenkins, the bald former Everton full-back John McLaughlin, Scottish striker Gordon Wallace who top-scored with 12 goals, former West Ham winger Harry Redknapp and the Stoke duo of defender Eric Skeels and Jimmy Robertson, a Scottish international winger who made his name at Tottenham, scoring for them in the 1967 FA Cup final, before moves to Arsenal, Ipswich and the Victoria Ground.

In Vancouver, Tommy Ord arrived from New York early in the season to finish as second-leading scorer with five goals, while the dark-haired Wolves goalkeeper Phil Parkes recorded six clean sheets in twenty games. When the two rivals from the north-west clashed in the first round of the play-offs, it was Hurst who had the decisive say with the only goal.

The NASL's new success story of 1976, following the grand entrances made by Portland and Tampa Bay a year earlier, was in Minnesota, where the Kicks – born out of the relocation of the Denver Dynamo – were clear winners of the Western Division.

The man at the helm was 42-year-old Freddie Goodwin, whose career as a wing-half had begun during the 'Busby Babes' era at Manchester United and continued at Leeds. As a manager he began at Scunthorpe but enjoyed little success at the New York Generals in 1967 and 1968 before returning to England to spend two seasons at Brighton and Hove Albion. In the summer of 1970, just as a 16-year-old prodigy called Trevor Francis was poised to break into the Birmingham City first team with a barrage of goals, Goodwin began a successful five-year stint at St Andrews, achieving promotion to the First Division in 1971–72 and an appearance in the semi-finals of the FA Cup in the same season. Goodwin and Birmingham parted company in the early weeks of the 1975–76 season, by which time the club had failed to win any of their first seven Division One games, and he returned to the US to take charge of the Kicks.

Like so many of the NASL's most successful start-up operations, the team constructed by Goodwin was built largely around British professionals. In goal, Geoff Barnett had been the non-playing back-up to Bob Wilson in Arsenal's Double-winning squad of 1971 before getting his chance, via Wilson's knee injury, to play in the 1972 FA Cup final loss to Leeds. By the time Goodwin called him away from the pub he had just bought in England, Barnett could already have been a New York Cosmos player. 'Arsenal wanted to sell me to the Cosmos and I met their people at Heathrow Airport with Ken Friar, our club secretary,' he recalls. 'But I always remembered something my father, who was ex-military, had taught me: if you have clean shoes and a clean white shirt you are halfway to making a good impression. I met their coach, Gordon Bradley, and he had a tatty shirt and dirty shoes. Admittedly, he had been on a transatlantic flight, but I turned the deal down, even though I had gone with my bags packed expecting to join them on tour.'

Of those recruited by the Kicks to protect Barnett, Frank Spraggon had helped anchor Middlesbrough's return to the First Division and Ron Webster had been a League Championship winner at Derby, while Steve Litt had played only 15 games for Luton. Peter Short, who had been at Denver the previous season, was adding an eighth NASL team to his résumé. To help anchor the defence, Goodwin signed West Brom's Alan Merrick, whose move came about after he turned down a move to a Southampton team on their way to winning the FA Cup. Merrick recalls, 'Albion had already spent the £75,000 they were expecting to get for me. Much to my chagrin, I also found out Freddie had been in to buy me four or five times for Birmingham, but Albion wouldn't sell to the team across town.'

The midfield included Alan West, an England Under-23 international who had been at Burnley before helping Luton to promotion to the First Division in 1974, and Middlesbrough's Peter Brine. Up front, Alan Willey, another fringe player at Ayresome Park, and Luton's Ron Futcher formed a partnership that would become one of the most prolific in NASL history.

The Kicks started steadily, winning their first four home games but losing five of their first six on the road. Nine wins in the final ten games captured the division title and underscored the growing enthusiasm for the team at its Metropolitan Stadium home in Bloomington. The final home game, a 6–2 win against Los Angeles, was watched by 42,065. 'The club had done a deal with McDonald's where anyone going to that game could go in and get a free Big Mac,' recalls Barnett. 'It was the biggest redemption of its kind that McDonald's had ever had.' The Kicks' average attendance of almost 24,000 was part of a general trend that saw NASL attendance rise by 38 per cent, although that still meant fewer than 11,000 as an overall average.

Merrick recalls, 'The marketing of the Kicks was exceptional. They had great knowledge of how to disseminate information to the public. The media relations guy was second to none in the area. He knew everybody. The public just jumped at it.'

West, who led the team with eight assists, adds, 'It was a unique situation that just built very quickly. We got to 20,000 in no time and when we played big teams it was 40,000. There was a great team spirit and the fact that we did very well in that first season meant it just took off. The great thing about America is that usually there are only home fans because of the distances involved in travelling. The whole atmosphere was very refreshing compared to the way things were in England at that time.'

The Kicks achieved the maximum three bonus points for goals scored in nine games, with Willey contributing 16 goals and Futcher 14. Even Ade Coker, signed from the Boston Minutemen late in the season, chipped in with four goals in the last three games. Willey explains, 'Ron would get stuck in and I would clean up the mess. He knocked defenders down and made them make mistakes. From day one we blended together. We read each other pretty well and with guys like Alan West around us we had good service.'

Merrick praises Goodwin's contribution to the Kicks' winning formula. 'Freddie was a smart coach and ahead of his time in some areas. He was innovative in his tactics and in the way he dealt with the players, although at times I didn't get on with him. He created some stability there over the years. He had his central part of the team – keeper, centre-backs, centre midfield and target players – that stayed pretty much the same, so all he had to do was put in some of the limbs.'

Over in the Atlantic Conference, Marsh's arrival at the Rowdies made them the team to beat in the Eastern Division, a task that no one was up to. Even the Cosmos, who were in the process of rebuilding their team around Pelé, trailed Tampa Bay by six points. As well as Marsh, the Rowdies added the former Charlton and Leicester left-winger Len Glover and Liverpool's pock-marked destroyer Tommy Smith. The owner of a single England cap, earned five years earlier, Smith had just won his third League Championship medal, Liverpool's battle to overhaul a stylish and surprising Queens Park Rangers keeping him in England until seven games of the NASL season had been played.

Midfielder Mark Lindsay recalls, 'When Tommy came over he was just as energetic and enthusiastic as if he was playing in the European Cup final. He would come up to me in a game and say, "I will kick your arse if you don't go and pick that guy up." The humidity and the temperature and the fact that the fields were stretched a lot more made it more difficult for defenders in general and he was exposed a bit at times.'

However, it was the Rowdies forward-line, with Smethurst scoring 20 goals, Marsh 11 and Clyde Best and Stewart Scullion 10 apiece, that gained most attention. In back-to-back games early in the season, Smethurst scored hat-tricks as Tampa Bay stuck five past Hartford and New York. Then, in a six-game stretch later in the season, the Rowdies scored twenty-five goals, including four tallies of four and a 7–0 crushing of poor old Hartford, Smethurst getting four this time. In the first of those games, Best scored a hat-trick in a dramatic 5–4 loss in New York, for whom Pelé scored twice. Lindsay recalls, 'We were 3–0 up at half-time and it was in the bag. All we had to do was keep possession.' The Rowdies' revenge over the Cosmos came in the play-offs, when Smethurst, Scullion and Marsh scored in a 3–1 home victory.

Washington's third place in the division behind Tampa and New York owed much to the form of Paul Cannell, the Newcastle striker, who scored 13 goals. Meanwhile, the Philadelphia Atoms had an unhappy season. Owner Tom McCloskey's interest had been waning since he was awarded the rights to the new NFL franchise in Tampa Bay (although he later declined the ownership) and he eventually sold the Atoms to a group called the United Club of Jalisco, an amalgamation of four Mexican First Division clubs. Club president Jose Cardenas released all the players before the 1976 season and started from scratch with players drawn from Mexico and the USA. Finishing below the Diplomats and Atoms in the division were the Miami Toros, whose new additions included the former Liverpool and England right-back Chris Lawler and the ex-Manchester United centre-half Jim Holton. 'Six foot two, eyes of blue, big Jim Holton's after you,' was the song the Stretford End came up with for the man who went on to win 15 Scotland caps. But the Toros often had barely 2,000 people inside Tamiami Stadium to strike up a chorus. Miami were not alone in their struggles at the gate and for every Minnesota, Portland and New York there was a San Antonio, Hartford and Philadelphia.

As the season began it had appeared that the big challenge to the Rowdies and the Cosmos in the Atlantic Conference would come from the Boston Minutemen, who were rivalling New York's spending in a bid to win the Northern Division. German coach Hubert Vogelsinger put together what had the potential to be one of the strongest teams the NASL had seen. Among the stars on the Minutemen roster were Portuguese legend Antonio Simoes, ex-Bayern Munich midfielder Wolfgang Sunholz, striker Ade Coker, goalkeeper Shep Messing and former Ipswich and Wolverhampton centre-half Derek Jefferson. But after six wins from ten games, owner John Sterge announced his money was running out and decided to offload his players, including Coker's trade to Minnesota and Jefferson's move to Washington. Boston, who began the season in front of crowds of around 7,000 ended up playing in front of fewer than 1,000, losing their final 12 games and using a total of 31 players.

Boston's self-destruction allowed Bill Foulkes's Chicago Sting to top their division, although they were beaten in their first play-off game by Toronto Metros-Croatia, who had signed Eusebio away from Boston before the season started. In mid-division, the Rochester Lancers were joined by the Hartford Bi-Centennials, for whom former Newcastle and Middlesbrough winger Alan Foggon joined a squad that included Chelsea and later Watford goalkeeper Steve Sherwood, West Ham midfielder Geoff Pike, former Hartlepool forward John Coyne and defender Bobby Thomson, who had played for Wolves in the USA back in 1967.

Having disposed of Rochester and Chicago in the early rounds of the play-offs, Toronto were expected to meet their match against the Rowdies in Tampa Bay in the Atlantic Conference final. Surprisingly, however, the free-scoring Rowdies were shut out for the first time in 16 games and Eusebio put the Metros-Croatia on the way to a 2–0 victory.

The final, in Seattle's Kingdome, saw Toronto as underdogs once again against the Kicks, who followed their division title with overwhelming home wins in the play-offs. With top scorer Willey sidelined by a bout of tonsillitis, Coker had continued his late-season surge by scoring twice in the 3–0 defeat of Seattle and he and West had each been on target in the 3–1 victory against San Jose, a game that attracted a crowd of 49,572. Earthquakes striker Paul Child claims, 'It was a fantastic game and it was incredible to see that many people but we got ripped off big time by the ref. We were ahead and scored what would have been a second, but he disallowed it.'

Toronto, the club who had defied the NASL by keeping the ethnic part of their nickname (commentator Jon Miller was forbidden by league officials from saying 'Metros-Croatia' on the air) were to cause another upset. They went ahead late in the first half when Eusebio's powerfully struck free-kick was deflected into the Kicks' goal. Merrick, the unlucky defender, says, 'I keep on seeing that ball going in. Eusebio grazed my right shoulder and it just ballooned over Geoff Barnett's head. At the end of the season Toronto had suddenly brought in about five top-notch players that no one had seen. They came out of nowhere. They were quality players and they gave them that boost.'

Barnett adds, 'We got a bit of a shock. By the time we met them in the final, they were a different team to the one we had played in a bruising battle earlier in the year. We probably didn't go in with the right attitude. The way we beat Seattle and the way we were playing, we thought we were better than we were. We were a good skilful team and Astroturf suited us because we were a good passing team. But we didn't play well.'

Toronto added two more goals in the second half and Willey, back in the team but forced to play wide on the right because of the form of Coker, admits, 'We were over-confident and they beat us pretty handily. It was a tough finish to the year for me. I had missed practice and lost some weight because of my illness and was stuck out on the right. I didn't play in the middle in the final until the last ten minutes.'

West adds, 'It was disappointing to lose 3–0, but I don't think it was such a big blow because we were a brand-new team and it was a fairy-tale just to get there. We were so thrilled at the season that the disappointment evaporated and we just savoured what we had achieved.'

English sporting eyes had turned towards America early in the summer of 1976, diverted from the West Indies' impending domination of the cricket season by the staging of an international tournament to celebrate the 200th anniversary of the country's independence. With no European Championship finals to look forward to after finishing behind eventual winners Czechoslovakia in their qualifying group, Don Revie's England were invited to join Italy and Brazil in the Bicentennial Cup.

The fourth contender for the trophy was Team America, a hybrid of the best American players and the NASL's leading international stars, under the guidance of New York Cosmos head coach Ken Furphy, the former Watford and Sheffield United boss. So it was that Pelé and Bobby Moore came to be lining up together on the international stage.

A newcomer to the NASL, Furphy consulted Tampa Bay coach Eddie Firmani before selecting a training squad that also included George Best, Rodney Marsh, New York's Northern Ireland international Dave Clements, Welsh defender Mike England, ex-England defenders Bob McNab and Tommy Smith and Tampa Bay forward Stewart Scullion.

Newspaper reports claimed that Marsh and Best pulled out when Furphy refused to guarantee them a place in the starting line-up, but Furphy supports Marsh's denial of that story. 'I picked George and Rodney to come to our training camp and

George didn't turn up. Rodney took part but always seemed a bit of an unwilling participant. He had no real desire about him and I decided I could not have players who would wander about, so I didn't pick them in the squad. I rang up Phil Woosnam and told him that George didn't turn up and Rodney didn't want to play. Woosnam said we have got to bring them even if they don't play, because of their publicity value. I said, "I want players available to play, not guys who won't play." But Phil said we had to pick them. We sent out notification to them and neither of them turned up. I phoned Rodney and he said he felt only Americans should be picked. I never got an explanation why George never turned up.'

McNab recalls the uniquely American circumstances that kept him out of the tournament. 'We were playing in temperatures of 120 degrees in San Antonio. At half-time, we would come into an air-conditioned dressing room with a good sweat on and the temperature would drop to 70 degrees. I was cooling down too much and then not stretching and I pulled a calf muscle five minutes into the second half of one game. I did it about three times before I realised what was causing the problem.'

Furphy's team kicked off the tournament in Washington DC against Italy. 'I told our guys, "Stay together and play together. Let's keep everybody tight in a 4-4-2. Don't rush forward and leave holes because, Smithy and Clements, you'll never get back." For 25 minutes it worked well, but then we lost the ball and they had a one-on-one against the keeper, Bob Rigby. He had been taught to come out with his feet first, not sideways to make himself big.' The goal was scored and Team America went on to lose 4–0. In the next game, America halved the deficit against Brazil, with Furphy claiming, 'We nearly beat them because they weren't used to Astroturf.'

Meanwhile, England had begun their programme by losing to a last-minute goal by Brazilian substitute Roberto in Los Angeles before taking on Italy in New York. Playing what would prove to be his only 45 minutes of international football, Arsenal goalkeeper Jimmy Rimmer saw two goals flash past him in the opening 20 minutes before making way for Manchester City's Joe Corrigan in a pre-planned half-time switch. Corrigan watched from the other end as England scored three goals in seven minutes, with stand-in captain Mick Channon scoring either side of a header by Liverpool defender Phil Thompson.

England did not award caps for the game against America in Philadelphia, where Scullion scored the host team's only goal of the tournament. By that time, however, Kevin Keegan had scored two goals and captain Gerry Francis had added a third. Brazil's 4–1 win against Italy in a game that saw three players sent off made them the winners of a tournament that attracted average crowds of 45,000 and further raised the profile of the soccer scene in the United States.

11. ☆ Furphy's Law

If Pelé's arrival in New York in 1975 had proved anything other than the man's pulling power at the gate, it was that one player, not even the game's greatest, could win a championship on his own. By the time Toronto were being crowned as surprise winners of the 1976 Soccer Bowl, the Cosmos were halfway through a two-year project to build a team worthy of Pelé's stature and their own rocketing ambitions. Yet it was clear that there was still a long way to go if the task was to be completed in time for him to sign off the following year by winning the NASL title.

The rebuilding programme had begun in the build-up to the 1976 season, which saw the Cosmos back in their original home of Yankee Stadium. Another part of the plan had been to move Gordon Bradley, the Englishman who had coached the team since 1971, into the role of vice-president of player personnel and development. 'There was a tremendous amount of work to be done,' recalls Bradley, who had discussed the new role with the Cosmos' general manager, another Englishman, Clive Toye. 'We felt I could do a better job on the organisational side, taking charge of the players,' says Bradley. 'It meant that we needed a new coach.'

The man chosen was 44-year-old Ken Furphy, who had recently been sacked as manager of Sheffield United. Born in Stockton-on-Tees, Furphy carved out a career as a wing-half, playing more than 300 league games for Darlington before moving on to Workington and Watford, filling the role of player-manager at both clubs. His most famous achievement at Vicarage Road was taking Watford to the semi-finals of the 1970 FA Cup, where they went down to eventual winners Chelsea after beating Liverpool in the quarter-finals. After Watford came spells in charge at Blackburn and Sheffield United.

Furphy was available for the Cosmos after his tenure at Sheffield United came to a surprise end early in the 1975–76 season. 'When I went to Sheffield in November of 1973 they were third from bottom of the First Division and we managed to get clear, even without Tony Currie, who'd had a knee operation,' he explains. 'The next year, with little money to spend, we finished joint fifth and missed out on Europe on goal difference and I was asked to manage the England Under-23 team that summer. So I certainly didn't think I was ready for the sack.

'We had been asked to go out to Tunisia in pre-season and we would get £10,000. I said it was no good going there; the grounds were too hard and the team would not be ready. I wanted to go to Europe as usual. But we went after only seven days' training and, sure enough, our three key players, Keith Eddy, Alan Woodward and Tony Currie, got injured. The season started and we drew against Derby, the champions, and lost to Arsenal, Manchester United and Everton. But there was no panic and I told the press I was not worried about relegation. I said, "I am not paid to worry about it, I am paid to make sure it doesn't happen." The club obviously didn't like that and I was told my services were not required.'

The phone was soon ringing with an offer to visit the Cosmos. 'I went out there and was interviewed upstairs at Warner by Steve Ross, the chairman. He didn't know anything about football either and he said he wanted me to go away and come back with a list of 12 things they had to do to make the club one of the biggest in the world.'

Furphy's plan included signing more world-class players at the end of their careers, setting up a reserve team of local players, and buying a small club in Ireland to use as a youth team to develop more American talent. The Cosmos liked what they heard and, announcing Furphy's appointment, Toye told the New York media that the club had found 'the kind of aggressive, progressive coach to take us on to the next stage of our build-up to becoming a powerhouse, not only in the NASL but in the world.'

The squad that was put together for the 1976 season was a mix of the exotic and the experienced. Falling into the first category were two Santos midfield players, the Peruvian Ramon Mifflin and Brazilian Nelsi Morais, who broke his leg on tour in Sweden and spent the winter and the first half of the new season at home regaining fitness. Signalling their intent to buy the best available players, whatever their nationality, the Cosmos spent $100,000 to acquire the NASL's leading Americans from the collapsing Philadelphia Atoms, goalkeeper Bob Rigby and defender Bob Smith.

Many of the other new signings spoke of Furphy's grounding in the no-nonsense business of the Football League – like full-back Charlie Aitken, who had played more than 600 games in a 15-year career at Aston Villa. To supplement the South American flair in midfield came Dave Clements, winner of 48 Northern Ireland caps during a long career at Coventry, Sheffield Wednesday and Everton, and Terry Garbett, who followed Furphy from Watford to Blackburn and Bramall Lane. Tony Field was signed by Furphy for the third time in his career, having scored goals for him at Blackburn and at Sheffield United, while winger Brian Tinnion, a Wrexham player for eight years, had begun as a youth-teamer under Furphy at Workington.

Joining his former coach in New York had been a long way from Tinnion's mind when he confronted Wrexham manager John Neal after being substituted in a vital end-of-season promotion battle. Neal explained that the Cosmos had made an offer for him and Tinnion went to meet Furphy in Sheffield. Tinnion explains, 'I went back to John and said, "I don't want to go and my wife doesn't want to go. Do you want me to go?" He said, "Yes, I do. For the £22,000 they have offered I can get three players who are better than you." So he signed Dai Davies from Everton's reserves to play in goal, got Dixie McNeil from Hereford, who scored loads of goals, and signed Bobby Shinton from Cambridge. They got £100,000 for him from Manchester City a few years later, so it was a brilliant deal.'

Garbett, meanwhile, considered himself 'washed up' as a player after three knee operations and considerable disillusionment during his two years at Sheffield United. 'I didn't like my time at United,' he confesses. 'The prevailing attitude in the team was that it didn't really matter. Everyone was just cruising. When Ken called, I had never even heard of the Cosmos and, to be honest, I went to see America, not to prolong my career. But Ken believed I could battle back and do something useful for him.'

To captain the side, Furphy turned to another faithful servant in Keith Eddy, who played more than 250 games for Watford before a four-year spell at Sheffield United. Furphy explains, 'When I asked Sheffield about Garbett, the manager, Jimmy Sirrell, said, "Do you want your mate, Keith Eddy?" I couldn't believe it. He was the rock the team was built around. He was very arrogant at times but that made him an even better player.'

Eddy remembers, 'Ken was fired and the next thing I knew I was sat there talking to the Cosmos people. My first reaction was, "Why the hell would I want to go?" I was 31 and captain of Sheffield United. But then I realised that my next move was probably to

Crewe. The money was attractive and a big selling point was that they had Pelé, so I went home and told my wife, "It looks like we are moving again." She said, "Where now?" and when I told her it was New York she just looked at me with her mouth wide open. The intention was to go for a short while, make the mighty dollar and get the hell out if it.

'New York were one of the first teams to come in and buy players outright and Dave Clements and I were the first two to be bought by them. My first impression was of the size of everything. I remember walking round Manhattan looking at the buildings, and even the people seemed big to me. It was the land of the giants.'

After the first game of the season, a 1–0 win at Miami, Eddy, to his surprise, discovered that he was to inherit the role of penalty-taker from Pelé. 'We were winning 1–0 and we got a penalty with ten minutes to go,' says Eddy. 'Pelé picked up the ball and rolled it straight at the keeper. I said to him, "Obviously you don't like penalties." He said, "No. People expect me to do something special with them because of who I am." From then on I took them. We had nine more that season and I scored eight of them. Ninety per cent were for fouls on Pelé.'

Pelé had posed some interesting pre-season problems for his new coach, including showing up a week late for pre-season training. 'He was out in Africa and got caught up in a civil war,' says Furphy. 'It shows you the power of the Cosmos that Steve Ross got Henry Kissinger to fly a private jet out there and they managed to hustle him to the airport and get him out. When he arrived he hugged me. Where I came from you didn't hug each other. It wasn't a manly thing to do!'

Before leaving chilly New York for a pre-season tour in some of the country's warmer states, Furphy was taken to one side by Toye. 'He told me that the discipline in the team, particularly among the South Americans, was dreadful. One of the players brought his wife with him without permission.

'On the first day of training I told the boys to be downstairs at 10 o'clock for the bus and if they were not there by 10.15 we would go without them. By 10.15, Pelé was not there and I decided I had to go without him. I thought that if I didn't treat him the same as everybody else we would have trouble. He eventually turned up in a taxi with his mate, Professor Mazzei. I told the Professor, "You warm him up and we will fit him back into the training session." The next day he was late again, so we went without him again. This time I said he was not training with us and told the Professor to train him on his own. I asked, "Why is he late?" The Professor said, "When he comes out of his room, there is a queue of people asking for an autograph – bartenders, waiters, guests. It takes him half an hour to get through the hotel." I said, "Well, get him up half an hour earlier." He was never late again. I got on well with him and he used to invite me along when he got asked out to dinner by millionaires.'

After the Miami victory, the Cosmos made a stuttering start to their home programme, losing two out of three games at Yankee Stadium. It was time for a new injection of talent – a player who had started his professional career by suffering rejection at Swansea and who would become the greatest goalscorer in NASL history.

☆

Giorgio Chinaglia was eight when his parents left Italy for Britain in search of greater employment opportunities, eventually settling in Wales. It was at Vetch Field that Chinaglia served his football apprenticeship, only to be released after starting four League games because he was considered lazy and difficult to work with. Returning to Italy, he rebuilt his career in the lower leagues and in 1969, three years after being kicked out of Swansea, signed for Lazio of Rome for £140,000. In 1974, Chinaglia cemented his place in the hearts of the local fans by leading Lazio to their first Serie A championship. He also earned selection for Italy's World Cup squad, but marked the end of his international career by making an obscene gesture – the Italian version of 'fuck off' – to coach Ferruccio Valcareggi after being substituted against Haiti.

In the fallout of his self-destruction in West Germany, life in Italy became intolerable and Chinaglia decided that America was where his future lay. Buying a mansion for his family in Englewood, New Jersey, in the spring of 1975, Chinaglia was forced to become a transatlantic commuter in order to play out the 1975–76 season for Lazio while he searched for an NASL team prepared to match his idea of his worth.

Aware of the opportunities Chinaglia presented to tap into New York's huge Italian population, the Cosmos pounced. Bradley, who travelled to Italy to see Chinaglia score a Serie A hat-trick, says, 'He already owned a mansion house in New Jersey, not far from Giants Stadium. When word got around that he wanted to play over here I persuaded him to come to New York after spending time with him in Italy. I persuaded Warner we needed a goalscorer to go alongside Pelé, although Pelé wasn't particularly thrilled about it.'

The Cosmos gave Lazio $750,000 and Chinaglia began his sometimes turbulent, mostly triumphant, career in New York. 'We did not have that good a team,' recalls Eddy. 'But when they signed Chinaglia things started to look a little more rosy.'

According to Bradley, it took time for the new Cosmos line-up to gel. 'It was difficult to get the players together. For example, Chinaglia was everything for Lazio but when he came here he was not the number-one man. He didn't set the world on fire to start with like Pelé did. Chinaglia felt a little bit out of it.'

Bradley explains that steps were taken to ensure that players signed for New York would fit in. 'We spent some time with these players before they came over. Some of those we tried to get might not want to come over at first but then they realised that the team was owned by one of the biggest businesses in the world. Once you have signed a player, maybe some teams don't do as much for him as he thought they would. But that was not the case at the Cosmos. They were recognised as top players and treated like it. But there were times when we struggled with Chinaglia. There were times when we had it out with him because we thought he could play better. True to his nature, he said once that he had a bad back before a game and that he couldn't play. We knew he was fit.'

Things could not have gone better on the Italian's debut, a 6–0 victory over George Best's Los Angeles Aztecs. Both Pelé and Chinaglia scored twice but it is the Brazilian's contribution that is remembered by Eddy, who grabbed two goals himself. 'Pelé was sensational. Playing against Best brought out the best in him. There was another game around that time when he ran onto a through ball on Astroturf and he beat the goalkeeper and two defenders without even touching it. There were a few body fakes this way and that way and he got credit for the goal, even though he didn't touch it.'

The combination of the Brazilian and the Italian looked as though it could not miss. Tinnion says, 'It was great. There was Tony Field on the left and me on the right and sometimes we were glorified spectators. Those two would play give-and-goes up the middle and when we did get the ball wide and crossed it, they got on the end of it.'

But, according to Furphy, Pelé took time to get used to the role that Chinaglia's arrival forced upon him. 'Playing in South America, I don't think Pelé had caught up with some of the changes that were going on in the game. Coaches would assign a player to sit on him and mark him and it took a bit of getting away from. I asked him to drop back into the hole so he would pull players away from Chinaglia and I don't think he was familiar with the role.'

The Cosmos management had to contend with a less than brotherly relationship between the two superstars. The fact that it was Pelé who was known everywhere the team travelled did not sit well with Chinaglia, who, says Eddy, 'had the biggest ego in the world'. Eddy adds, 'I liked the guy, but he would talk in the third person. "Chinaglia thinks this. Chinaglia thinks that." I said to him, "Use 'I' for heaven's sake."'

Furphy recalls, 'I had a message one day from the kit man saying Chinaglia wanted to throw his shirt to the crowd at the end of games. We'd ordered 100 shirts for Pelé so he could do that, but not for Chinaglia. Giorgio also didn't like the fact that everywhere Pelé went he got a suite. Chinaglia wanted the same treatment.'

Garbett's abiding memory of Chinaglia, apart from being 'the best scorer I have ever seen', was that 'I saw him hit more people than Muhammad Ali.' His victims included English teammate Steve Hunt, who was to join the club in 1977, and a team of stadium workers. 'There were a group of them cleaning the seats during one practice and they started jeering. Giorgio went up there and started beating on them. He was racing along the aisles after them. About ten of their guys went to join in and our guys went up there to pull Giorgio out. Ninety-five per cent of the time he was great, the other five per cent it was like he was on pills! I went into a nightclub in Rome with him and we had been in there one minute and he was fighting.'

Chinaglia's moods were something that those around him would learn to live with. More serious for New York's chances of success over the next two years was a recurring divide in the camp between the British contingent and other factions in the team. Off the field, Garbett recalls going to parties at Ramon Mifflin's house and says, 'Generally we all got on well.'

But Eddy says, 'On the field we did have a situation of South Americans against the English. The South American guys would only pass to Pelé. In midfield we had Mifflin, who had been captain of Peru, where he played as sweeper. He couldn't tackle a dinner. Brilliant on the ball, but couldn't do any defending. There was a real contrast in the philosophy of the game. I tried to be a peacemaker. If you win games it is not a problem at all, but we had had good games and bad games and there were still some holes in the team.'

One of those bad games was at Tampa, where goalkeeper Rigby pulled out of the game shortly before kick-off and inexperienced replacement Kurt Kuykendall, an American, was beaten five times. 'We'd been looking for another keeper but Gordon Bradley couldn't find one,' recalls Furphy, whose visit to Florida had got off on the wrong note after a grilling from local reporters about the Rowdies keeper Arnie Mausser.

'When I was picking the players for the American side in the Bicentennial tournament, Eddie Firmani, the Rowdies coach, told me not to pick his goalkeeper. He said he was not ready. So the first question I get when I show up for the pre-game press conference before we played Tampa Bay was, "Why didn't I pick their goalkeeper?" There had been a little hullabaloo about not picking him and the media had whipped it up. I didn't want to say that Eddie said not to pick him, but Eddie didn't stand up and say anything to help me.'

Back in New York on the back of a heavy defeat, the coach received a call at his Long Island home to attend an evening meeting in the Warner offices in Manhattan. 'Clive and Bradley and I went up in the elevator together and we didn't know who was going to be there. It was Steve Ross and the Ertegun brothers, Mifflin, Pelé and Professor Mazzei, and Chinaglia and his agent. I said, "What are these people doing here?" Steve said, "I want them here." He put on the tape of the game and stopped it whenever a goal was scored. Steve said, "Whose fault was it?" I said, "Ask Pelé and Chinaglia. They were playing." The answer was "the goalkeeper" every time they scored. The meeting finished with Steve saying, "Thanks, Ken. You're doing a great job." I said to him, "You have put me on the spot here. No way will I discuss a player with you when there are other players here. They have no real right to be in this meeting. I will not come to another meeting with players there."'

Furphy led the Cosmos on a road trip to Minnesota and Portland, but rumours were growing that the powerful Chinaglia wanted Furphy removed. 'But when he scored against Minnesota he made a point of running over to the sideline and he gave me a hug and lifted me off ground,' says Furphy. Yet the next time the Cosmos went away from New York, events did not work out so well. After a 4–1 loss at Chicago, the team travelled to Washington, where they discovered they were to play the Diplomats in the tiny Woodson Stadium instead of switching the game to a larger venue.

Furphy explains, 'Their coach, Dennis Viollet, pulled a fast one by changing the game to a small stadium. Ross offered them $50,000 to change to a big stadium because he wanted the share of the additional gate, but Washington wanted to get us on a university ground. There was four and a half inches of grass on the field and you wouldn't have played a junior game on it. Our players found it very difficult and their forward, Paul Cannell, collided with Rigby, who swallowed his tongue. Our young keeper had to go in again. Late in the game, they got the ball to the outside right position and he came rushing out like mad about 45 yards from goal. There was no need to do it and Cannell chipped it in and they won 3–2. Steve Ross called another meeting. I said, "I will come but not if players are there." He was a multi-millionaire and what he said went so I said, "Right, pay me up. I want out of here." If you lose control it soon gets back to the players and you are dead.'

Tinnion says, 'Furph was never going to be a "yes" man,' while Eddy ventures, 'Ken ruffled a few feathers and that came back to haunt him. When you have got a player like Pelé at the end of his career you have got to let him do what he wants to do. Ken was a little bit structured in his approach. If he wants to play a formation he wants everyone to play within the confines of that. You had to look at it as if we had ten men and then Pelé. Let him do what he wants.'

Bradley was asked to step back into the hot seat. 'I was comfortable doing what I was doing,' he says. 'But Steve said, "I want you to do it." I am looking at the boss of the biggest corporation in America, so I can hardly say no. And Steve was so enthusiastic about the team. When we moved to Giants Stadium, they had to put a seat belt on him to stop him falling out of the top tier.'

In the first game after Furphy's departure, Tinnion, who had started the previous eleven games and scored in the last four, was dropped to make way for the arrival of the Brazilian Morais and would start only one more game throughout the rest of the season. 'That's football,' says Tinnion. 'They say you are only as good as your last game but sometimes even that doesn't apply. It was Pelé's sidekick who came in and he was not even ready to come back after his injury.'

The Cosmos embarked on a run of six wins, and a total of eight victories in ten games under Bradley put them into the play-offs. They closed out the regular season with an 8–2 rout against Miami, Chinaglia scoring five goals, before Pelé and Garbett scored in a home defeat of Washington in the play-offs to set up a return to Tampa Bay. By that time, however, team captain Eddy was struggling with a serious groin injury, which had kept him out of the game against the Diplomats.

'Towards the end of the season I took a goal-kick for our keeper, Shep Messing, because he couldn't get the ball out of the damn area,' he recalls. 'I slipped and fell and my groin niggled at me for a while. The surgeon who had done Joe Namath's knee said I had a major problem. I was under a lot of pressure to play against Tampa because we thought that whoever won that game would win the championship. I said, "I can't play. I can't run. I can't finish the game." Pelé came to see me and said, "Keith, I really want to win the championship. Please play." They flew the doctor in and I had a Novocain shot before the game and another at half-time. At the end of the game I couldn't get on the bus. Whatever was wrong, I did it no good at all. I tore the tendon away from the groin. I had an operation but there was a 50 per cent chance I'd end up a cripple. I regret playing with those shots, but it was my own fault. It was my decision.'

New York, even with Eddy playing through the pain and Pelé getting on the scoresheet, were beaten 3–1. 'Our team was not very impassioned from what I could see and we didn't have the quality of players to dominate,' Garbett admits. 'We could have won most of our games, but sometimes we were like a non-league team.' The Cosmos clearly still had much work to do if Pelé's deadline was to be met.

12. ☆ Farewell to the King

The final Sunday in August 1977 may have marked the start of the last week of America's summer – before Labor Day brought it abruptly to a halt – but in Portland it seemed as though autumn had arrived early. Dark, dreary skies left the threat of rain hanging ominously over the Rose City, although not even the prospect of a good drenching could deter the 35,000 people who had squeezed themselves into Civic Stadium.

Americans viewing the scene on their television screens were greeted by commentator Jon Miller informing them earnestly that they were about to witness 'the most dramatic, emotion-filled Championship game in the history of the NASL, Pelé's last competitive game'. Announcements had been scarcely less solemn 12 days earlier when newscasters had imparted news of the death, at age 42, of Elvis Presley.

In contrast to the serious tones in the commentary booth, the chatter of anticipation going round the ground indicated the large number of youngsters in the crowd and gave the event the feeling of a summer fair, a very different atmosphere to the intimidating, tribal pre-game chanting to which British players were accustomed.

Soccer Bowl '77 was destined to be part-sport, part-melodrama, with 21 players on the field merely supporting actors to Pelé, the man attempting to win the one championship that still eluded him. Both teams were already lined up on the field when the star attraction jogged onto the worn-looking plastic surface, his sturdily built figure showing little sign of footballing middle age as he trotted around the centre circle waving to the crowd. Observing from the sideline was Seattle Sounders head coach Jimmy Gabriel, whose tough-tackling career at Everton and Southampton had contained little room for sentiment such as this day would yield.

His pre-game interviews had spoken of a belief in his team's ability to beat the Cosmos, but as he now looks back over more than a quarter of a century to the finale of the NASL's season, he is forced to admit, 'There is no way God was going to let Pelé go out a loser.'

Over the winter of 1976–77, while English fans followed Liverpool's journey toward European domination, the Cosmos had been adding the finishing touches to a team capable of ruling North America. There was no doubt they had the clout to match their ambition as they announced a move into Giants Stadium, the new 76,000-capacity venue in East Rutherford, New Jersey. But the soap-opera atmosphere that had pervaded the previous season continued, a predictable result of the club's volatile mix of personalities, politics and power.

Coach Gordon Bradley remembers it as being a world away from Carlisle's Brunton Park, where his career had begun. 'It was exciting every day,' he says. 'I remember the Cosmos offices were in one of the nicest parts of New York City, on 52nd Street. To think I could park my car ten yards away from Warner, where otherwise it would cost $60 a day, showed the power of these people. All these nice things came to us because of their power.'

Such influence meant that more stars to match Pelé's stature were on their way to New York. After nine games of the season, the Cosmos would welcome Franz Beckenbauer, whose elegant, visionary defensive play and inspirational leadership had helped West Germany to win the World Cup in their own country three years earlier. But as the 1977 season approached, Pelé himself, nearing his 37th birthday, seemed less bothered about whether or not he won the championship in the final year of his contract than the media, who were making it the season's storyline. Unhappy that a winning team had not yet been built around him, he skipped the entire pre-season and reported to the club overweight only a week before the real action began. He and Giorgio Chinaglia immediately resumed their feud, while the Brazilian's business interests seemed to be of greater importance to him than events on the field.

Apart from the impending arrival of Beckenbauer, the New York squad's most significant signing of the off-season was another English player, Steve Hunt, a 20-year-old left-winger from Birmingham who had started only four games for Aston Villa before being sold for £30,000. Another English import was not exactly what was needed to end the inter-nation feud that was still eating away at the club's harmony. While the South Americans continued to ignore opportunities to pass to the Europeans, the three leading Americans on the team, goalkeeper Shep Messing, defender Bobby Smith and Yugoslav-born Werner Roth, complained about the British influence on the club. Smith was even suspended by Bradley after throwing a tantrum when he was told he was to be left out of the line-up.

English midfielder Terry Garbett says, 'The Americans didn't want the British influence and there were a few comments. Smith and Roth used to moan about it. When Smithy was told he had been dropped from the side he went crazy, bashing the blackboard and screaming at Gordon. He thought he had a promise that he was playing but Gordon was a straight guy and would have hedged his bets. I thought we were going to have a big fight. The Brits all thought Smith should never have entered the building again. Now I have seen how Americans treat their players and they can get away with anything. I thought it was bad for discipline and team respect. In America, the players were allowed to talk back, but you would not have got away with it in England at that time.'

Messing was also benched briefly in favour of Turkish keeper Erol Yasin – a move inevitably linked to the influence of Nesuhi and Ahmet Ertegun – and Clive Toye, the long-time general manager of the Cosmos, decided he'd had enough interference. 'Before Pelé signed, the Cosmos staff was me and Gordon Bradley, plus a marketing and PR guy and one secretary,' he recalls. 'We were a pissy little club getting three or four thousand to our games if we were lucky. The next day we were a world-famous club with more media than we'd sometimes had people in the stand. We had to hire more people, but the people at Warner were still hands-off and I got everything I wanted.

'That lasted until after we had signed Beckenbauer and moved to Giants Stadium – over the strenuous objection of Warner. Then we drew 52,000 and suddenly everybody wanted to pick the fucking team. One day I got a phone call saying that everyone was going over to the stadium: Steve Ross, the Erteguns, several others. We all charged outside into a stretch limo to be driven to the heliport and flown across the river, where there were more limos waiting for us – just so we could argue about whether Shep Messing or Yasin should play in goal on Saturday.

'We would play a game and next day I would be told to go to the 32nd floor, where Steve Ross would be looking at the tape again. From some angle he'd see what he thought was a mistake by the referee and would be saying we had to protest. The year before, we'd been three goals down at half-time against Tampa Bay at Yankee Stadium and had correctly had two goals disallowed. I was told that Steve was going to tell the team not to go out for the second half in protest. I found him pacing outside the locker room and I had to plead with him, to point out the stupidity of not playing the second half. I told him it would ruin the game and the league – particularly when the referee was right. He agreed, but said, "You have to announce over the PA that the Cosmos are going to play the rest of the season under protest." So I had to go on the microphone and make this asinine comment. Then Pelé scored a wonderful goal and we ended up winning.'

The final straw for Toye was when Nesuhi Ertegun asked to see Toye's list of potential player targets. 'There were 11 players on the list. Nesuhi looked at the list and ticked off four names and said, "We'll sign them." Three of them were left-backs! I finally wrote a memo and said they either let me run the club the way I wanted, or else. They chose "or else".'

Toye would resurface as general manager of the Chicago Sting and, after two years, move on to take charge of the Toronto Blizzard. Bradley recalls, 'It was a difficult time. The Ertegun brothers didn't see eye to eye with Warner and Clive and I didn't see eye to eye with them. One of them thought he could play soccer just because he was from Turkey. They loved the team, but they were acting like they wanted to pick the team, move the stadium, everything. Clive left and took the position in Chicago. Who put the pressure on him? Chinaglia might have had a part to play. The Ertegun brothers loved Giorgio.'

Against such an unstable background, the Cosmos started the season slowly. But 10 wins in a stretch of 12 games, coinciding with Beckenbauer's introduction to the team, meant they were always play-off bound, even if the division title was beyond their reach. Former skipper Keith Eddy was not to be part of the season beyond the opening few games. 'The start of the year was very exciting with the move to Giants Stadium. Crowds doubled overnight. Yankee Stadium was a shit hole. I wouldn't let my wife go to the games there, but Giants Stadium was a great facility. But it was looking more and more like I was on the way out. I was injured and Beckenbauer was on his way.'

The captaincy passed to Roth and, before long, Bradley was gone from the touchline, meaning the club's English trio of general manager, head coach and team captain had vacated those positions in quick succession. Bradley had taken a huge risk by leaving out Chinaglia for the home game against Los Angeles, which was won 5–2 thanks to a Pelé hat-trick. Eddy recalls, 'Giorgio was having a bad time. He was not getting the service and he was making excuses and I said to him, "It's just not working for you at the moment. You have to work hard." If I had been the coach I would have left him out. Before the game, Steve Ross came into the locker room and said to him, "Why aren't you dressed?" Giorgio said, "Because I am not playing." Steve said, "Yes, you are," and told him to get changed, but to be fair to Giorgio, he didn't.'

Chinaglia returned and after a couple more games Bradley was moved back to his role behind the scenes, to the delight of those fans who had taken to bringing 'Bradley Must Go' banners to the games. The coaching position passed, amid considerable bitterness, to Eddie Firmani, who had suddenly resigned a few weeks earlier from arch-rivals Tampa Bay Rowdies. Keith Eddy tells a story that shows the influence Chinaglia wielded. 'Giorgio was so into the ownership that after my injury I had a call from him, asking, "Would you like to coach the team?" I said, "One, I don't want to and, two, you are not in position to ask me." He said, "Oh yes, I am. And if you don't do it I will get Firmani." A few days later, Eddie was in the job. Whatever Giorgio wanted, he got.'

Firmani had reportedly been seen dining with Chinaglia the night before he resigned from the Rowdies and Bradley recalls, 'Firmani and Chinaglia were best friends.'

The Rowdies players were far from surprised when Firmani, who walked out after the team won seven of their first ten games, accepted the Cosmos job. Goalkeeper Paul Hammond says, 'There were rumours that he had been talking to New York a month before the season. One day out of the blue, he just left. They were weird circumstances. It upset our chemistry a bit.'

One man, however, was pleased to see Firmani move on. Rodney Marsh had never seen eye to eye with a coach who always seemed to be urging a player renowned for his artistry to become more of an artisan. 'We disliked each other as a player and coach,' said Marsh, 'although I liked him as a man.'

Firmani's first act in New York was to reinstate Smith to the Cosmos defence, but that won him few points with the English players and the perception grew that Chinaglia was pulling the strings. Garbett argues, 'To be honest, what the hell do the Cosmos need a coach for anyway? How are you going to coach those players? Give them the ball and let them knock it around for an hour – that was generally how it was. There were no supreme tactics. Where Eddie was good was that he was a great picker of a team. He knew where to put people, knew different players could do different things. If we needed someone to come in he would find the right player.'

The Cosmos made their final personnel move with less than a month remaining of the regular season, when former Brazilian skipper Carlos Alberto arrived to take over the role of sweeper, meaning that New York now included the last two captains to lift the World Cup. Eddy states, 'Carlos Alberto was the most outstanding player I ever saw play in America. He never lost the ball. I thought I was composed, but this guy made me look like a raving idiot. And he couldn't even get a team in Brazil to sign him at that time.'

Garbett recalls a 'very nice guy' who could be 'an absolute bloody animal', explaining, 'He had wonderful skill, but he was a maniac. A controlled maniac, which I loved. He was lethal. No wonder Brazil won the World Cup with players like that in the side. He had a mean streak and you couldn't screw around with him. World soccer never gave him the credit he deserved. He and Beckenbauer used to knock the ball about in the dressing-room. They would stand either side of a bench and keep the ball up for ever. We used to watch them open-mouthed. One day we came in and Franz was stood there with the ball and Carlos was injured so me and Bobby Iarusci dived into the showers real quick because we weren't going to try to kick it around with Beckenbauer.'

By the end of the regular season, Chinaglia and Pelé led the team with 15 and 13 goals respectively, while Englishmen Hunt and Tony Field topped the assists with ten and nine. Hunt, fair-haired with a splay-footed style of running that belied his athleticism, felt he had proved a point, admitting, 'The fact that Villa were ready to let me go after I had helped them win promotion from the Second Division really hurt. I felt they had not given me the chance to prove myself. I had a choice between joining the Cosmos or dropping down into the Second or Third Division. I chose the Cosmos and never regretted it for a moment. Going to the States was the making of me. Playing alongside the giants of the game like Pelé and Beckenbauer gave me new confidence and a better understanding of the game.'

The Cosmos' play-off journey began with a home game against Tampa, the team who had ended their title hopes the previous season. The Rowdies had not been the force of the two previous years, finishing only third in the Eastern Division amid the upheaval of Firmani's departure and the ex-Chelsea man John Boyle's appointment as interim head coach. The Rowdies won only seven of their sixteen games after Firmani quit. With Stewart Scullion and Clyde Best having moved on and Marsh scoring only eight goals, it was Derek Smethurst who carried the weight of the forward line, scoring nineteen goals in twenty-one games – many set up by South African Steve Wegerle, the older brother of future Rowdies, Luton, Queens Park Rangers and Blackburn striker Roy.

Davie Robb, the former Aberdeen forward who had won five Scotland caps in 1971, added eight goals, while Australian forward Adrian Alston arrived from Cardiff to score seven.

It was at the goalkeeper's position that controversy reared its head at the start of the season. Arnie Mausser, one of the top American goalkeepers in the NASL, had been signed by the Rowdies from Hartford in 1976 and was rewarded for an outstanding year by selection for the league's all-star team. While the American soccer community had to accept the relatively slow development of home-grown players, the goalkeeper's position was the one where many of the locals could compete on equal terms with the imports. It was with some surprise, then, that news was received of Firmani's decision to release Mausser for the 1977 season, opting to give the position back to Hammond, who was returning from Crystal Palace. Justifying the decision, Firmani said he had gone for Hammond's additional experience, which now included helping Palace to an FA Cup semi-final in 1976.

'Because of the Cup run, Malcolm Allison didn't want me to go until the end of the season so I ended up missing the 1976 season in America,' says Hammond. 'Then in February of '77, Eddie asked me if I wanted to come out full-time. I knew Arnie very well. He was a good keeper and he had a very good year in '76. But when I got there I managed to keep the number one job and he got traded. I didn't feel like it was anything to do with me. Things like that happen whenever you get a newcomer.'

In front of 57,828 fans at Giants Stadium, the Rowdies were no match for the home team, Pelé scoring twice in a 3–0 win to set up a two-game series against the Fort Lauderdale Strikers, winners of the Eastern Division but two-time losers to the Cosmos during the regular season.

The Fort Lauderdale Strikers had been born out of the Miami Toros' decision to relocate further up the south Florida coast. After a season in California in the American Soccer League, Ron Newman was brought back to the NASL to take the position of head coach and, as he had at Dallas in previous years, set about building a team around English players. In defence were Bobby Bell, a former Crystal Palace and Ipswich man, Ray Lugg, on loan from Crewe, and Tony Whelan, a former Manchester United apprentice who arrived from Rochdale. In midfield, Dave Chadwick, a player under Newman at Dallas, was joined by Ray

Hudson, who had been fighting unsuccessfully to win a regular first team spot at Newcastle, and former Plymouth and Portsmouth wide man Norman Piper. The forwards included Gordon Fearnley, ex-Bristol Rovers, and David Irving, an England youth international who had struggled to make his mark at Everton after leaving Workington.

The most familiar name signed by Newman also represented his biggest gamble. Gordon Banks, England's goalkeeper in the 1966 and 1970 World Cups and undisputed in his status of number one keeper in the world, had not played a competitive game of football since 21 October 1972. The next day, while driving home for Sunday lunch, he had been involved in a head-on collision with a van. Surgeons fought unsuccessfully to save the sight in his right eye, and a career that spanned 73 international appearances and had seen him named Footballer of the Year only months earlier was over. Or so it seemed. As the years went by, Banks found that his basic goalkeeping instincts had remained intact. 'I had mentally accepted the fact that I would never again be able to play as a top-line goalkeeper,' he wrote in his book, *Banks of England*. 'But while taking part in kick-about training matches and friendly fixtures it slowly dawned on me that even with one eye I could still do a useful job at the back of a defence.'

Banks's progress had not gone unnoticed and Newman made his move, convincing the proud former England man that he would not be treated as some kind of freak in the promotion-driven world of American soccer. Newman admits, 'It was a huge risk. But we needed someone of Gordon's calibre to attract other good players. I had seen he was beginning to play again, so I went to England and thought, if I could get him, I would have a name and reputation to sell to the other players. And I could afford him – it cost only $20,000 for the whole year. That was our top money. We could only sign players to seasonal contracts and we were up against the Cosmos, who were spending millions.'

Aware that the American media might not be familiar with the ability of Banks, and would be dubious about the signing of a one-eyed goalkeeper, Newman used their knowledge of Pelé to introduce his new signing. 'I found this brilliant story in the centrefold of a magazine about the save he made against Pelé in the Mexico World Cup. I made about a hundred copies and covered them in plastic and used them as place mats at the lunch we held for the media so they could read about him before I presented him. It worked.

'Banksy was terrific. I tried to cut our training short and everyone would be leathering the ball at him. I'd walk away and Banksy was still there stopping the ball. I'd have to say, "Banksy, I'm trying to save you."'

Chadwick, the team's assistant coach, adds, 'Gordon was unbelievable. He never talked about his injury and I was real worried when Ron signed him. He showed good authority and he adjusted. He still had the ability to read the game and the ability to throw the ball out and start an attack. His overall positional sense was just incredible. We played in Las Vegas and it was 104 degrees on the Astroturf at eight in the evening. You could feel your feet burning. He was unbelievable. He got to balls and flung himself from God knows where. I was training him and I said, "You tell me what you want." He said, "I want one good session a week. I can't take a beating every day like I could. Give me one good session and the rest of the time I would like to play with the guys and run." That's what we did.'

Based further north in Florida, Rowdies keeper Hammond remembers having many opportunities to watch Banks in action. 'It was amazing what he could do with one eye, tremendous the way he could work his angles. I tried it once, playing with my hand over one eye, and all the angles were wrong. He was always a positional goalkeeper and great at communication.'

Banks would end up being named as the NASL's leading goalkeeper for 1977, admitting, 'That gave me a lot of pleasure and satisfaction. I knew I was only 75 per cent of the player who had won a World Cup medal with England in 1966, but this accolade was a tremendous boost to my confidence.'

Accepting that he could not afford the great individual talent that the Cosmos had acquired, Newman made sure his team could match anyone in the physical side of the game. 'I realised that with the level of quality on my team, our biggest advantage was coping with the heat in the second half of games. I ran the players on the sand and between the piers in Fort Lauderdale. They could have run up Mount Everest.'

The results bore out Newman's methods, opening the season with four wins and clinching first place in the Eastern Division by winning twelve of their final fourteen games for a league-record nineteen victories in all. The goals were shared around, with former Oldham left-back Maurice Whittle top scoring with six. Although a defender, scoring goals was nothing new to the team captain and penalty-taker, who had notched more than 40 in his career at Boundary Park and had gone six years without missing from the spot. Standing only 5 ft 8 in., and weighing less than 11

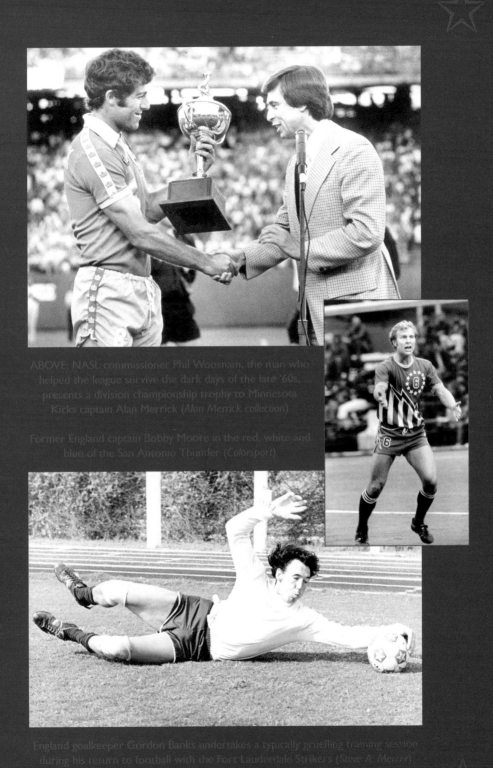

ABOVE: NASL commissioner Phil Woosnam, the man who helped the league survive the dark days of the late '60s, presents a division championship trophy to Minnesota Kicks captain Alan Merrick (*Alan Merrick collection*)

Former England captain Bobby Moore in the red, white and blue of the San Antonio Thunder (*Colorsport*)

England goalkeeper Gordon Banks undertakes a typically gruelling training session during his return to football with the Fort Lauderdale Strikers (*Steve A. Mercer*)

Putting the 'England' into the 1978 New England Tea Men. Back row (left to right): Kevin Keelan, Colin Powell, Peter Simpson, Kevin Welsh, David Eyre, Chris Lloyd, Dennis Wit, Roger Gibbins, Mazzy Mazur, Mike Flanagan, Keith Beardon. Front row: Joe Bourdon (trainer), Peter Carr, Ringo Cantillo, David D'Errico, Laurie Abrahams, Noel Cantwell (head coach), Keith Weller, Dennis Violler (assistant coach), Gerry Daly, Tim Hunter, Benny Brewster, Brian Alderson, Dick Hobbs (equipment manager) (Tom Cross)

Tampa Bay Rowdies and former West Ham midfielder Graham Paddon prepares to cross to Rodney Marsh. Fort Lauderdale's John Ridley (5), George Best (3), Gary Jones (13) and Maurice Whittle stand guard.
(Alan Merrick collection)

Tea Men on tour... Lauris Abrahams makes a name for himself, despite the misspelling. Mike Flanagan and Roger Gibbins stroll in the California sunshine, while Gerry Daly enjoys an off-duty dip. (Vince Casey)

Rodney Marsh is shadowed in the 1979 Soccer Bowl by Alan Ball, who had helped to talk his Vancouver teammates out of going on strike on the eve of the game. (Colorsport)

Rodney Marsh makes his displeasure known after being substituted in the 1979 Soccer Bowl, the final game of his career. (Colorsport)

Former England forward Keith Weller (left) on the
attack for the Fort Lauderdale Strikers (*Alan Schwartz*)

Former Arsenal defender
Peter Simpson 'felt a right
prat' when asked to display
his ball-juggling skills to
promote the Tea Men
(*Tony Crabb*)

Brian Kidd gets in a shot for Fort Lauderdale, despite the attention of San Jose Earthquakes defender Steve Litt (Kingsley R. Labrossi)

Two of English football's 'Mavericks' in action as Alan Hudson, linchpin of the Seattle Sounders midfield, takes on the Tampa Bay Rowdies' Frank Worthington (Joanie Komuro)

Brian Kidd aims a shot past New York Cosmos goalkeeper Hubert Birkenmeier *(Jim Singh)*

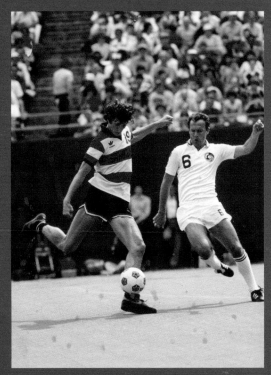

Roger Davies is challenged by Franz Beckenbauer during the former German captain's comeback season for the New York Cosmos *(Alan Merrick Collection)*

Former England centre-half Dave Watson battles with Fort Lauderdale Strikers and ex-Derby forward Roger Davies (Alan Merrick collection).

stones, Whittle packed enough power to have his shots timed at 70 mph and earn the nickname 'Thunderboot'.

Newman was named NASL Coach of the Year, one year after achieving the same honour in the American Soccer League, and by winning their division the Strikers avoided the opening round of the play-offs, which had been expanded to include 12 of the league's 18 teams. They eventually headed to New York for what proved to be one of the most memorable games in the league's history, although the Strikers were only too keen to erase the events of 14 August 1977 from their minds. On the day after Kenny Dalglish made his debut as Liverpool's new number seven in a goalless Charity Shield at a packed Wembley, a comparable crowd of 77,691 – an NASL record – saw the ball find the net 11 times in Giants Stadium. 'I'd always said I'd bare my rear end in Woolworth's if we filled that place,' says Garbett. 'It was downright amazing. I arrived two hours before the game and I remember thinking there must be a big event at the race track because all the parking lots were full. They had to delay the kick-off half an hour.'

With many fans exposed to the torrential rain that fell on the Meadowlands, what transpired in front of them left Ron Newman claiming that the Cosmos were beginning to wield too much power over the American soccer scene. 'After looking at the forecasts we expected rain, which was always difficult on Astroturf,' he explains. 'We were familiar with the type of shoe we needed. There were no special shoes made for Astroturf at that time, we just used to wear worn-down studs. We knew if it was wet we needed a newer cleat, a sharper image.

'I'd heard that Pony had come up with brand-new shoes that were brilliant for Astroturf in the rain. I asked if they could supply us if it rained at Giants Stadium. We trained on Astroturf, but the shoes they had sent us were terrible. They had small cleats with a lot of little edges and the players were coming through the shoes. When they stopped, the foot came right through it. The soles were all right but no one could wear them. There was no time to do anything about it, so we wore old shoes with old cleats. Banksy was slipping and sliding everywhere and Steve Hunt was cutting round us like an ice skater.'

The result was an astonishing 8–3 victory for the Cosmos, with Chinaglia scoring a hat-trick and the sure-footed Hunt adding two goals. Newman continues, 'After the game, I said to the Cosmos, "Can I see your shoes?" They were the Pony shoes we had tried. They had the same moulded cleat, but they had been made with kangaroo leather. I have no proof, but I believe pressure might have been put on them not to supply us with the most up-to-date shoes they had. I wouldn't put it past the Cosmos. They were big-time, they had to win at all costs.'

At least in the format of the play-offs, an 8–3 loss was no worse than defeat by one goal, so the Strikers were still in with a shout four days later at Lockhart Stadium. Even so, it was a daunting task for a such a collection of unremarkable players to take on the all-star squad of the Cosmos. Irving, who only went to America as a late replacement when Sunderland striker Vic Halom's wife became pregnant, recalls, 'We were so unknown that when Ron Newman came to meet me and Maurice Whittle at the airport he didn't know who was who. But we were all good players, good solid pros, and we felt like gunslingers because we weren't meant to be there. Playing on Astroturf was a big advantage for the Cosmos because you couldn't get close to them and they kept the ball away from you. But on grass you could get close and shut them down and they were not as effective.'

Following goals from New York's big guns Pelé and Chinaglia and Fort Lauderdale's lesser names Irving and Whittle, the game went into overtime. The teams could still not be separated, so it was on to the new shoot-out introduced by the NASL at the start of the season, where, instead of taking traditional penalties, attackers advanced one-on-one against the goalkeepers from the 35-yard line and had five seconds in which to attempt a shot. New York prevailed and Pelé's dream of a fairy-tale farewell was still alive.

'We all knew he was going to retire and we wanted to fight for him to win the championship,' says Garbett. 'He is the nicest guy you would ever want to meet in the whole world. If I had asked him he would have tied my shoelaces for me. I suppose that when you are driving a Ferrari you don't have to prove you can beat a Ford. He could be nice to everybody because he had nothing to prove to anyone.'

In the Eastern Conference final, another two-game series, Chinaglia and Hunt scored in a 2–1 victory at the Rochester Lancers before the Italian added two more – giving him eight in five play-off games – to help the Cosmos to a 4–1 win in front of a home crowd of 73,669.

It was the Seattle Sounders who battled through the Western Conference to confront the Cosmos in Soccer Bowl '77 at Portland's Civic Stadium. The team was now under the leadership of Jimmy Gabriel, promoted from player and assistant coach when John Best moved on to become general manager of the Vancouver Whitecaps. There was no Geoff Hurst in 1977 and his former West

Ham colleague Harry Redknapp played only the first month of the season, but Seattle brought in several other new British faces to help them to the play-offs, even though they finished only third in the Western Division. They included Mel Machin, a versatile Norwich and ex-Bournemouth player who made the all-league team at right-back, and Steve Buttle, a midfielder who arrived from Bournemouth. Another ex-Dean Court man, Mickey Cave, was the team's top scorer with 12 goals. An important late-season signing was the much-travelled Tommy Ord, who arrived from Vancouver after scoring only three goals all season and proceeded to hit five in his six regular season games for the Sounders.

Seattle began their play-off run with Machin and Ord scoring in a 2–0 win at the Whitecaps. Ord was on target in each game as the Minnesota Kicks were dispatched in two matches, meaning the Sounders had knocked off the two teams who had finished ahead of them in their division. The Los Angeles Aztecs were then beaten in two games, Scottish forward Jocky Scott getting the only goal in a Kingdome victory that clinched Seattle's place in the final.

Before the Sounders and Cosmos did battle, there were some formalities to go through when Pelé was honoured at a banquet at the Portland Hilton. Commissioner Phil Woosnam stood up and told the audience, 'He put his reputation on the line. Deep down inside this man is a missionary zeal that very few people have. Tonight we would like to pay tribute to Pelé, the man who gave us credibility.'

With such a build-up, the Sounders could have been excused for feeling like the team who toured the world with the job of losing every night to the Harlem Globetrotters. But Gabriel recalls that his team, watched by 12,000 travelling Sounders fans, were determined to do more than make up the numbers. 'We'd hit a rich vein of form and beaten some good teams on the way, so the players felt very confident we could do it. The game was on Astroturf, which suited us, and we played really well, as well as I could have hoped for. The plan was to get out there and get at them. I never coached a team that sat back. If they force us back that's one thing, but tactically I don't like sitting back and I wasn't going to do that.'

The Sounders lived up to their coach's promise, forcing the green shirts of the Cosmos back towards their own area with waves of high-tempo attacks. Cave headed wide from a good position and then had a goal disallowed when he was ruled offside following up a rebound, before Pelé made his first contribution by firing wide from a free-kick. The occasion seemed to be earning the Brazilian some sympathy from the referee, with Machin penalised for high kicking when Pelé had clearly bent down into the Englishman's boot and no foul being awarded when Pelé chopped down Jimmy Robertson on the edge of the box

Ord was close with a header, but, against the run of play, the Cosmos took the lead after 19 minutes, thanks to the quick thinking of Hunt. Canadian keeper Tony Chursky had taken the ball off the winger's feet, but made the mistake of rolling it in front of himself with his opponent still in the vicinity. Alert to the possibility, Hunt stole the ball and smuggled it into the net.

But minutes later, with the US viewers watching a commercial, Cave robbed Beckenbauer in the Cosmos half and some slick passing around the edge of the box set up Ord for a low drive past Messing's right hand to level the score. Then Robertson, causing concern as he switched from one flank to the other, almost gave Seattle the lead after cutting in from the left and firing over.

As the rain poured down during the interval, Firmani told Garbett he was being taken off and word was spread to the media that the midfield man had an injured groin. But the player reveals, 'I was not injured and I was very upset at being taken off. I was playing quite well compared to some of them, who were playing bloody useless. Seattle were a tough and uncompromising team and we couldn't get the game going. Thank goodness for Steve Hunt, who was absolutely dynamite. It was an astonishing exhibition and a great goal. He was powerful and strong and, boy, could he run.'

The tempo of the game in the second half dropped noticeably from the frantic pace of the first period, picking up again only in the final 20 minutes, with the Sounders again the catalysts. Scottish defender Dave Gillet hit a fierce first-time shot from 25 yards that Messing spectacularly pushed away and Scott forced another save moments later with a header. But with ten minutes left, Hunt, voted the game's Most Valuable Player, stretched beyond Machin on the left and delivered a cross that Chinaglia headed in from the edge of the six-yard box.

Pelé, whose finishing had not been equal to a couple of moments of sublime footwork around the penalty area, was too high with one last attempt to finish his career with a flourish, but as Seattle scampered to take a goal-kick the full-time whistle sounded. The sideline photographers rushed the field to capture the great man in his final moment of glory. The pictures they took showed Pelé bare to the waist, having tossed his shirt to Seattle's 20-year-old American full-back Jimmy McAlister as soon as the game ended.

The significance of the moment was not lost on Gabriel. 'It was like saying, "Hey, I am handing over to the young Americans. Go and run with it." Pelé was very thoughtful about these things. He could have handed it to anyone but he handed it to a young American kid. I was upset because we lost, but if we were going to get beaten by anyone it was great to go that way. There was nothing I could take back or say that we could have done better, although the goal we had disallowed for offside was kind of ridiculous. Overall, it was a wonderful day for American soccer.'

13. ☆ New Kids on the Block

If you had plotted the well-being of the NASL like a hospital patient's graph, the start of the 1978 season would mark its peak of health. Coming off a memorable and emotional climax to the previous season, the new campaign saw the realisation of Phil Woosnam's dream of reaching 24 teams. 'That was as far as we wanted to go with expansion,' he says. 'If other cities wanted to come in, they would protect us in case we were losing a city. We didn't need any more. It was a great satisfaction to me to achieve that number but credit goes to others as well.'

The final foundations for Woosnam's 24-team tower had been the successful 1977 season. Driven by the Cosmos and Pelé, NASL attendance had increased by 33 per cent to roughly 13,000 per game, with an average of more than 29,000 for the play-offs. Seven games were televised on the TVS syndicated network, the most soccer seen on US screens for almost a decade.

There had, as usual, been changes at the beginning of the 1977 season, with the Boston and Philadelphia franchises going into receivership and several other teams moving. As well as Miami's switch to Fort Lauderdale, San Diego went to Las Vegas, Hartford ventured to New Haven to become the Connecticut Bi-Centennials, and, most intriguingly, San Antonio became Team Hawaii under Austrian coach Hubert Vogelsinger. Among Hawaii's new acquisitions had been Brian Tinnion, who had been told he had no future by Cosmos coach Gordon Bradley when the club made plans to sign Yugoslav forward Jadranko Topic.

In Hawaii, Tinnion discovered a franchise doomed to failure. 'For our second game we were at home to New York and only drew a few thousand. Everyone else was getting 30,000 for games against the Cosmos. With all the travel we had to do as well, you could tell it wasn't going to last.' It was fun for a while, though. 'Some of the single lads thought they had gone to heaven,' Tinnion adds. 'There were plenty of pitfalls in places like Hawaii.'

The San Jose Earthquakes welcomed an English player who revelled in the showbiz atmosphere of the NASL. Alan Birchenall had carved out a decent career as a forward at Sheffield United, Chelsea, Crystal Palace and Leicester, the final three of whom had all paid six figures for his services. Birchenall's outlook on the game, and life, was that it should be approached wearing a smile. With his eye-catching shock of blond hair, 'The Birch' had been one of English football's most colourful characters in the past decade, although injury had robbed him of his one chance of real glory in Chelsea's 1970 FA Cup run and the missing ingredient of a Marsh or a Bowles had limited him to four England Under-23 caps.

Legendary for his one-liners and his penchant for belting out a tune in front of a band, Birchenall was the perfect showman for the US audience. 'He should have been a damn comedian,' says Earthquakes teammate Paul Child affectionately. 'He was a good player, but he was just so funny – a great guy to have on the team. He was a fantastic leader. I remember being on the road with him and if we won he would be leading the singing in the restaurant. He'd be singing "Alouette" and he would have the whole place joining in, even though they didn't know what they were singing. The guy could damn well play as well. I used to love playing with guys like him, not a selfish player.'

Birchenall explains his decision to go to America. 'I'd had a few problems at Leicester, a disagreement caused by personalities really. I was about 31 and in those days when you got to 30, no matter how fit you were, they considered you on your last legs. In those days it was a barrier. Jimmy Bloomfield said five clubs had asked about me and he had no objections. I didn't fancy Chicago, but I remembered "Do You Know the Way to San Jose?" and chose the Earthquakes.'

On arrival in San Jose, Birchenall was instantly presented with his company Cadillac. 'I got my car straight away at the airport so I knew that I was well thought of, but a lot of guys came and went without getting anything after playing a trial. There were a lot of names who came over and had apparently played for Yugoslavia in internationals or for Holland. Where they had caps from, I don't know. I think they must have embellished their careers a bit.'

Birchenall scored only three goals in seventeen games and did not always see eye to eye with Manadaric about the role he had been signed to play. 'I was having a bad game against Las Vegas and

Eusebio, who had dodgy knees by then, brought me down. A few of our fans started throwing cans at him. Tony Simoes, who was Eusebio's pal, came over and said, "Birchy, get up if you are not too bad or else we could have a riot on our hands." I got up. Because we were so near the crowd you could practically touch them, so, to take the heat out of the situation and take their attention from Eusebio, I picked up a couple of empty cans and pretended to drink, then staggered up the line. The crowd loved it, but the owner, Milan Mandaric, didn't see the funny side. He banned me from a road trip and fined me.

'I still carried on the way I had been all my career. I loved the game, but I liked to live life. They had an image of English people being dour and I was something different. I would be joking with fans during the game and I was such a one-off to them. The Yugoslav owner did not have a great sense of humour.'

Eusebio's transfer from Toronto to the Las Vegas Quicksilver made him a teammate of Englishmen Gerry Ingram, top scorer with seven goals following his transfer from Washington, and Chris Dangerfield, the former Wolves and Portland forward. 'I could have gone to Hawaii, but Vogelsinger had a reputation for curfews and other crazy things,' Dangerfield remembers. 'Eusebio could still do stuff on free-kicks, but with his bad knee he could not do as well as some of the other older players.'

Englishman Derek Trevis failed to last the season as Las Vegas head coach, being replaced by the former Southport and Philadelphia centre-forward Jim Fryatt as the Quicksilver slumped to the foot of their division. Bill Foulkes was another English coach replaced during the season, his coaching job in Chicago going to the American Willy Roy. The Sting team included the Scottish midfielder Jim McCalliog, who had won the FA Cup with Southampton a year earlier to round off a top-flight career that took in Sheffield Wednesday, Wolves and Manchester United. He, like Tranmere forward Ronnie Moore, who scored a team-high eight goals, was playing in his only NASL campaign. Meanwhile, Scotland international winger Willie Morgan, who had made a high-profile move from Burnley to Old Trafford shortly after Manchester United's European Cup triumph, was in the first of his four seasons in America, splitting his years between the NASL and Bolton Wanderers. West Ham forward Bill Jennings, part of the Hammers team that beat Fulham at Wembley, gave the team another recent FA Cup winner.

The Connecticut Bi-Centennials saw one English coach, Bobby Thomson, make way for another, Malcolm Musgrove, who, in his playing days, had been one of West Ham's famed academy of future coaches and had gone on to be assistant to Frank O'Farrell at Leicester and Manchester United.

Former Philadelphia coach Al Miller led Dallas Tornado to the Southern Division title, with English keeper Ken Cooper recording the league's lowest goals-conceded-per-game average. Former Scotland centre-forward John O'Hare, a Football League champion under Brian Clough at Derby and soon to win another title at Nottingham Forest, finished second in the team with ten goals, one behind the American Kyle Rote. Ten years earlier, O'Hare's final action for his first club, Sunderland, had been in Vancouver as part of the United Soccer Association.

The Los Angeles Aztecs looked to a pair of Football League veterans to shore up their defence, signing Phil Beal, veteran of 330 League games and various cup successes for Tottenham, and Terry Mancini, whose lack of finesse sometimes matched his lack of hair, but whose great humour and spirit had endeared him to fans at Watford, Orient, QPR and Arsenal. After play-off wins against San Jose and Dallas, the Aztecs' season was ended by Seattle in the Pacific Conference Championship.

Minnesota's English contingent repeated their previous year's division title success, Alan Willey top-scoring with 14 goals, but the Portland Timbers, meanwhile, won only 10 games under new head coach Brian Tiler, who had succeeded his former Aston Villa manager Vic Crowe. In Washington, Dennis Viollet failed to get the Diplomats into the play-offs with a squad that now included Southampton FA Cup heroes Bobby Stokes, scorer of the Wembley winner against Manchester United, and Jim Steele, the big Scottish defender, plus former Saints keeper Eric Martin. Top scorer with nine goals was Coventry City forward Alan Green.

John Sewell's St Louis Stars finally opened the door to more foreigners, with ex-Tottenham right-back Ray Evans and Crystal Palace's Peter Wall bolstering the defence sufficiently to help St Louis to a play-off berth. Wall recalls, 'St Louis was traditionally the country's soccer centre, but eventually they realised they needed to bring in other players to compete. If it caused problems with the American players, it was never shown. Deep down, I am sure some were disappointed that they were now on the subs' bench, but most were willing to recognise we had something to offer.'

☆

With overseas players having been accepted in the American heartland of St Louis and some brand-new teams on the scene, excitement surrounding the NASL had never been greater than at the start of the 1978 season. The Colorado Caribous, Detroit Express, Houston Hurricane, Memphis Rogues, New England Tea Men, Oakland Stompers and Philadelphia Fury were the brand-new kids on the block, while several other teams moved to new neighbourhoods and Connecticut evicted themselves from the league entirely. Hawaii became the Tulsa Roughnecks in Oklahoma, coached by Bill Foulkes, while Las Vegas and St Louis headed to California to become the San Diego Sockers and the California Surf, who played on Walt Disney's doorstep in Anaheim.

The league featured an American and National Conference, each with three divisions, and a 30-game schedule. A major television contract was still absent, with the NASL having to settle for a nine-game package with TVS Sports, for which ratings would be disappointing. Some games were not shown until late on Monday nights. For some observers, the rush to expand and the bank-breaking attempts of teams to keep pace with the Cosmos without the support of major television money would mark the start of the NASL's slippery slope. Critics of the spend-for-success philosophy felt it was more important to develop American talent and, in the meantime, to set on-field objectives that were in line with realistic team budgets.

Former Sheffield Wednesday defender Don Megson, the new coach of the Portland Timbers, says, 'I looked at it as though we would have success if we won our division. You could have a good year and win something without getting to the Soccer Bowl. I saw that as being a bit like the FA Cup, something extra, because it was a bit optimistic to think we could turn over the likes of the Cosmos and Tampa Bay. The way the league worked meant it was possible for everybody to achieve a little success.'

Megson had been an interesting acquisition for the Timbers, the first English manger to quit a Football League job to take a post in the NASL. During five seasons at Bristol Rovers he had led the team to promotion from Division Three and had taken his team to Portland for an end-of-season friendly. 'I liked it right away. Portland is a beautiful place and I saw that they had a good training facility.'

Jim Smith, on the move from Blackburn to Birmingham, had been the club's first target, but when they could not sign the man whose nickname of 'Bald Eagle' would have made him the perfect choice for an NASL job, they turned to Megson. 'I had a call from a guy called Keith Williams who said he was booked into the hotel at the side of my home and did I want to meet for breakfast? I think I had gone as far as I could with Rovers. It was very exciting when we won promotion and had the best team in the division, but in the Second Division our team was not quite good enough and everything was negative. It was really difficult to compete and we were hanging on week in and week out, trying to claw results. It can get you down after a little while. And the Timbers were offering me twice the money I was on at Rovers, so obviously that was a consideration.'

Another English manager on his way back to the NASL was Gordon Jago, whose acceptance of an offer to coach the Tampa Bay Rowdies had been precipitated by the BBC. After returning from his ill-fated stint as the Baltimore Bays head coach, Jago was appointed manager of Queens Park Rangers early in 1971, leading them back to the First Division before resigning in September of 1975. Less than a month later, he was installed as manager of Millwall.

Tampa had come calling after Eddie Firmani resigned in 1977, but their bid to secure Jago's services reached its turning point in December of that year, when Millwall's hooligan element was highlighted on BBC's *Panorama* programme, a show that took viewers inside the violent world of groups who revelled in names like F-Troop and Treatment. 'It was a disgraceful programme,' Jago recalls angrily. 'That killed it for me. We had worked so hard to try to change the image of Millwall, with identification cards, supporters' trains, open days for the fans to meet players, a Sunday morning market, going to clubs and schools. I was in the New Cross area virtually every night because it was all part of changing the image. *Panorama* asked if they could do a feature on what we were trying to do.

'It was my impression that they had produced a concocted programme. I even heard a rumour that they took people to a pub in Catford and got them drunk and interviewed them. That was F-Troop. We had one problem against Chelsea around that time but we were winning the battle. It was a carve-up job. I knew then that no one would come to Millwall to see their team play, which would hurt us. Instead of 15,000 with visiting fans, we would get 10,000. We needed the extra revenue to make the club run.

'We went to see the BBC. Ted Croker, the FA secretary, was there, so was the producer of the show, a head guy from the BBC and Denis Howell, the Minister of Sport. Between the BBC guy and the minister I have never heard two people insult each other so well with their use of the English language. The Millwall chairman, Herbert Burnidge, turned round at the end of the meeting and said, "Your programme has cost me my manager and if I could I would resign." The club let me out of a year and a half of my contract to go to Tampa.'

Jago's arrival led to several Rowdies stalwarts departing the club, including the old Palace trio of Paul Hammond, Stewart Jump and Mark Lindsay, who all found their way to Houston. Coventry's Mick McGuire and West Ham FA Cup-winner Graham Paddon were brought in to strengthen the Rowdies midfield. Lindsay, who still lives in Tampa, explains, 'Eddie Firmani asked me if I wanted to go to New York. Where would I play? I was happy in Tampa and I got married in '76 and we had built a house. But it was Jago's decision to bring in his own players and, being naive and immature, I said a couple of things I shouldn't have. I was negotiating a new contract but Gordon had no intention of me signing it. My beef was that they should have told me if they were not interested. "If you want Paddon and those guys, that's fine. It's part and parcel of football, but don't keep me coming into work and negotiating a contract." It was tough leaving Tampa. The Rowdies were a much tighter organisation than any I played for after that.'

Striker Derek Smethurst recalls, 'I went in to renegotiate in '78 and found out they were going to spend several hundred thousand dollars on an unproven player. It didn't happen in the end, but I knew I had hit a nerve and I doubled my salary.'

But Smethurst and his salary were soon on their way to San Diego in a trade for former Luton midfielder Peter Anderson. The striker's memories of the Sockers and coach Hubert Vogelsinger are not happy ones. 'Nobody knew who was fighting who at that team. And I ran into a coach who could not trap a bag of cement. He was like sandpaper to my whole character. The players knew he knew nothing as well but wanted to stay living in San Diego.'

Smethurst's transfer would not have happened at all if his alternative career move had worked out after the 1977 season, when he tried out as a kicker for the NFL's Tampa Bay Buccaneers. 'I was winning the job, but I tore a thigh muscle. I'd told them I needed a two-week rest because of a thigh injury but they made me carry on and I tore a quadricep muscle.'

Replacing Smethurst in the Rowdies' forward line was the Brazilian Mirandinha, who managed only one goal in 14 games. But the Rowdies, with Marsh recording 18 goals and 16 assists, comfortably made the 16-team play-off field by finishing second in their division behind the New England Tea Men, one of two expansion teams led to division titles by British coaches.

The Tea Men were guided by head coach Noel Cantwell, who had won 36 Republic of Ireland caps during a playing career at West Ham and Manchester United, where he skippered the team to their 1963 FA Cup triumph. Having been manager at Peterborough and Coventry, Cantwell was getting ready to retire from football and concentrate on running his pub when Phil Woosnam and then the Tea Men themselves contacted him. Cantwell admits, 'At first I said I wasn't interested because I had done enough in the game, then the Tea Men offered me this and that and I agreed.'

Without a team in place, Cantwell's first move was to appoint NASL veteran and former United teammate Dennis Viollet as his assistant, explaining, 'He was already established in America and I didn't want to go out there blindfolded.'

Deliberately setting out to build a team of British players, Cantwell's choice of goalkeeper was the Indian-born Kevin Keelan, whose long career at Norwich had earned him a reputation as one of the country's best uncapped players. Another who had fallen into that category was Arsenal's Peter Simpson, a Double winner, who anchored a defence that included Chris Turner, who had played for Cantwell at Peterborough, and former Carlisle full-back Peter Carr. In midfield, Irish international Gerry Daly had played a major part in Manchester United's renaissance after relegation to Division Two before a £175,000 transfer to Derby in the spring of 1977, while Keith Weller had jumped from Millwall to Chelsea to Leicester in quick succession before settling at Filbert Street and winning four England caps. Brian Alderson had joined him at Leicester from Coventry and Roger Gibbins was signed from Norwich, while winger Colin Powell had been one of non-League football's best-known figures at Barnet before moving to Charlton. The south London team also provided the thrust of the Tea Men's attack, with the inexperienced Laurie Abrahams teaming up with Mike Flanagan, approaching the peak of his career at 25 and soon to be pushing for England recognition.

Flanagan marked his intentions early in the season, scoring all the goals in the Tea Men's first three victories, a pair of 1–0 wins and a four-goal thrashing of Chicago, who were on their way to losing their first ten games, spelling the end for coach Malcolm Musgrove. By the time New England had played nine games, Flanagan had hit 12 goals and would end the regular season with 30 in 28 games, including all five in a victory against California.

Flanagan earned the league's MVP award and Weller recalls, 'Flano was a good player and could score goals if you gave him a chance around the box. He wasn't really like a target man, he had pace and a good left foot and could beat people. He surprised a lot of people when he kept banging in the goals. People thought it would dry up soon, but with the service he was getting he was always capable of scoring.'

Cantwell adds, 'His finishing was as good as anyone in England at that time. He was clinical and he was good in the air. He was never the fittest and best athlete in the team, but he conserved his energy for playing. In England, where they trained and worked hard every day, he had less energy for games, but it wasn't like that in America. You didn't take much out of them in training because they were in good condition anyway and it was enjoyable because you were always out in the sunshine. That helped Mike. Also, he was something of an unknown threat and he had more room in the American game.'

In Detroit, the Express were winning the Central Division of the American Conference under the leadership of Ken Furphy, back for another shot at NASL success after his unhappy stint in New York. The Express were owned by Jimmy Hill, the face of football on the BBC, who had introduced a lot of American-style razzmatazz and promotions as manager of Coventry in the '60s. The ex-Fulham midfielder and former head of the Professional Footballers Association was looking to invest the money earned by his company, World Sports Academy, from a lucrative contract to oversee soccer in Saudi Arabia.

After departing the Cosmos, Furphy had accepted an offer to coach the Fort Lauderdale Strikers for the 1977 season, but fell out with the ownership before the season started. 'I came back to England and I read in the papers they had accepted my resignation,' he says.

It almost marked the end of Furphy's career in football. 'I was not in the best of health and was ready to call it a day. I had been affected by years of working in pressure positions and went through a stage when I wanted to hide away from people. It was a nervous reaction. I was asked to help out with some part-time coaching at a school and I was fine when I was working, but in company I wouldn't say anything and went into a shell. The doctor said all I needed was a job, and then the letter came from Jimmy Hill wanting to discuss running the new team in Detroit. The wages were not as good as the Cosmos but I decided to go.'

The Express, based at the impressive indoor Pontiac Silverdome, pulled off one of the coups of the season with the signing of Trevor Francis from Birmingham. Francis had burst onto the scene as a 16 year old in the 1970-71 season by scoring 15 goals in only 21 games and was now approaching the peak of his powers and establishing himself as an England international. After missing the opening weeks of the season because of international duty, he arrived to score 22 goals in 19 games, including five in a 10–0 defeat of San Jose. Francis, reported to have earned £50,000 for his summer's work, would return to England to become the first million-pound player in British football when he was sold for £1,150,000 to Nottingham Forest, heading the winner three months later in the European Cup final win against Malmö.

Furphy recalls, 'Jimmy had been talking to Jim Smith at Birmingham and he asked me if I wanted Trevor Francis. When I met Trevor I said to him, "These are the drawbacks. The people know nothing about soccer, you are going to play on Astroturf and travel 4,000 miles for matches. But you'll have an apartment, a car and everything you need." He was going to go and play for Noel Cantwell in New England but he did the deal with us. Trevor has said to me since that his times in Detroit were the best he ever had in football. I kid him that we turned him into a million-pound player. He was superb. On Astroturf you had to play to feet and have great agility. He would play in the inside-left position, check back in on his right foot and – whack! – it would be in the net. Put a ball to him anywhere in front of goal and he could middle it because he could control his balance so quickly.'

Partnering Francis was Alan Brazil, a blond, 19-year-old Scot on loan from Ipswich, the new FA Cup holders following their 1–0 Wembley upset of Arsenal. Brazil was attempting to make an impact at Portman Road behind strikers Paul Mariner, Trevor Whymark and David Geddis, but Furphy recalls, 'I threatened to send him back after two days. His first game was at home and obviously he felt Astroturf was not his cup of tea. I took him off and he went around saying, "I didn't come over here to sit on the bench." I had him in my office and handed him a return ticket. I said, "We are paying terrific money and if you can't enjoy yourself and improve your game, you can go." He asked me to give him another chance and responded very well.'

Brazil went on to score nine goals in twenty-one games and admitted, 'Before I went to the States I lacked pace, but when I returned to England I was two yards quicker. It must have had a lot to do with playing on the Astroturf, plus the top-class company in which I played and the draining humidity. The trip gave me tremendous confidence.' Brazil would return to become a regular in the Ipswich team, going on to win 13 Scotland caps before injuries ended his career while still in his twenties.

Helping to supply the Francis–Brazil duo were the coach's son, Keith, who scored 11 goals himself, stalwart Queens Park Rangers midfielder Mick Leach, and ex-Blackburn and Sheffield United player David Bradford. At the back, lanky centre-half Eddie Colquhoun, who had won nine Scotland caps and spent a decade at Sheffield United, was joined by ex-Everton stopper Steve

Seargeant, Norwich full-back Ian Davies and ex-Blackburn and Newcastle player Graham Oates.

Meanwhile, Philadelphia's new franchise, the Fury, failed to enjoy the immediate on-field success of New England and Detroit. With an ownership group that included rock stars Rick Wakeman, Peter Frampton and Paul Simon, the club understood the need for a flamboyant front man and turned to former Chelsea centre-forward Peter Osgood. One of the most skilful number nines in English football over the previous ten years, Osgood, scorer of more than a hundred Chelsea goals and winner of four England caps, had won the FA Cup at Chelsea and Southampton, for whom he had been playing since March 1974. He was introduced to the Philadelphia public in a television advert that featured him juggling a ball across the Walt Whitman Bridge to the accompaniment of Mike Oldfield's 'Tubular Bells' while a group of worshipping children trailed in his wake. Osgood's skill and personality suggested that he was a natural for success in the slower-paced NASL, even in his 32nd year, but in 22 games he was to score only one goal. 'But he had a great time socially,' laughs former Burnley centre-half Colin Waldron, a mid-season Fury signing from Tulsa. 'But to be honest, the team never really clicked. We stuttered along.'

A large British contingent had joined Osgood, including a midfield axis of Johnny Giles and Alan Ball. 'It was great playing on Johnny's team for once,' says Ball, who spent more than a decade locked in fierce battles against the Leeds man for Everton and Arsenal. It seemed somehow appropriate that the two combatants should finally be brought together in the City of Brotherly Love. Former Manchester City keeper Keith MacRae was the Fury's last line of defence, with Irish international centre-half John Dempsey, Osgood's former Chelsea teammate, partnering Waldron.

Coaching the team was Richard Dinnis, sacked as Newcastle manager the previous autumn when his team reached the second week of November with only two wins to their credit. Things were not to go much better for Dinnis at the Fury and in June he was fired again, to be replaced by Ball. 'Richard was a former schoolteacher who had never played the game at a high level,' Waldron explains. 'To go anywhere and have Ball, Osgood and Giles on your books, you would have to have great character and balls to cope with that. I felt sorry for him because he was a nice man. Those were great players but big personalities and it was tough for anyone to handle them.'

Instead of asking anyone else to take on that task, the Fury looked inside the team for a new coach. Ball recalls, 'They asked

Johnny Giles and me if we wanted the job. Johnny didn't, but I said I would do it to help them out, rather than have them go and look for someone else. I didn't think of it as the start of a coaching career at the time. I thought I had four or five years left as a player.'

Waldron adds, 'Bally took over and he was a great pro. But he was a bit hard verbally on the younger players, especially the Americans. I think he used to forget what a great player he was and expected the others to live up to his standards.'

Decked out in yellow uniforms dreamed up by an award-winning fashion designer, the Fury finished last of the four teams in their division. Such was the generosity of the NASL play-off system, however, that they prolonged their season with a knock-out game against Detroit, decided for the Express by a goal from Francis.

The Memphis Rogues, under head coach Eddie McCreadie, included several familiar British faces for their first season, but the play-offs were always out of reach. Defenders Bobby Thomson and Phil Beal, midfielder Alan Birchenall and forward Tony Field, signed from champions New York, were among those with previous NASL experience. John Faulkner, the big centre-half whose FA Cup exploits for non-League Sutton United eight years earlier had earned a transfer to Leeds, former Tottenham schemer Phil Holder and winger Jimmy Husband, a vital member of Everton's 1970 League Championship team, were among the newcomers. Former Scotland and Chelsea left-back McCreadie, who inherited the Rogues job when first-choice coach Malcolm Allison was dismissed during pre-season, saw his team lose their first nine games.

In Denver, the extravagantly named Caribous of Colorado had appointed former Cosmos midfielder Dave Clements as head coach. His team included former New York teammate Brian Tinnion, but, just as one year earlier in Hawaii, Tinnion knew instantly that he had made a bad decision. 'I had verbally agreed to go to Colorado when Ken Furphy called me and offered me a job in Detroit. I wanted to go there but I had already said yes to Dave. First home game they were anticipating about 30,000 but it rained so hard they had to postpone it and only had a few thousand when they played it again in midweek.' Clements was another coach who failed to last the season, dismissed from a team that would win only eight games. Clements's departure did, however, allow Tinnion to escape to Detroit.

Further west, turmoil prevailed at the Los Angeles Aztecs, where Liverpool defender Tommy Smith had returned for his second NASL tour of duty and was installed as player-coach after Terry

Fisher was fired by the club's new ownership. The Aztecs' owners clearly did not know enough about Smith's reputation as a player to know that he was not a man to be messed with and when he discovered they had traded Charlie Cooke without telling him, his reaction was one of anger, even though he had earlier agreed to the sale of the disillusioned George Best. Furious that the local media were blaming him for the player departures, which soon included centre-forward Ron Davies, Smith grabbed a baseball bat and went looking for team boss Larry Friend. He never did find him. 'In the end he made his team the laughing stock of soccer in the States,' says Smith. 'It was a nightmare and I was truly glad to be out of it.'

The Aztecs won only nine games all season and English midfielder Bobby McAlinden says, 'It all went south. Tommy took over and was all for the lads but had not had any coaching experience. Once you get that losing mentality you are no longer competitive and there is no time to work with the players and change anything. It all fell apart and they got rid of everybody.'

A few miles away in Anaheim, George Graham, who had been to Manchester United, Portsmouth and Crystal Palace since helping Arsenal win the League and FA Cup in 1971, was wearing the number eight shirt for the Surf, who also fielded former Fulham left-winger Les Barrett. Graham's Palace teammate Peter Wall had helped persuade the elegant midfielder to accept an offer to go to the NASL, although the uneven surface at Anaheim's baseball stadium led to an ankle injury that ended his season prematurely.

Wall believes that the injury could have changed the course of football history, pushing Graham towards a management career that saw him win two League Championships and four other trophies at Highbury. 'That injury led to a big change in his life. If he had not gone home because of it, I am quite sure he would have stayed in America. He loved it there, thought the competition was good and thought there was a good future there.'

Meanwhile, Charlie George, the man whose Wembley strike had clinched the Gunners' Double, signed on loan from Derby for the Minnesota Kicks, who duly won their division once more. While Alan Willey was leading the team with twenty-one goals, George scored nine times and had eight assists in eighteen games for the Kicks. Former Aston Villa midfielder Ian 'Chico' Hamilton led the team with thirteen assists, while Willie Morgan added seven in the first of his three seasons with the club.

Elsewhere, former Liverpool and England left-back Alec Lindsay played in 28 games for the Oakland Stompers, who saw five men take turns in coaching the team, including former Tranmere defender Ken Bracewell, who had last been in charge of an NASL team in Denver four years earlier.

The Dallas Tornado's season was dominated by the goalscoring of Jeff Bourne. Back in Texas after a one-year absence, Bourne scored twenty-one goals, the highlight being a four-goal haul in less than five minutes in a 5–3 win against the mighty Cosmos in the final game. Bourne's record for the fastest four goals in NASL history followed up his achievement a week earlier, when he had grabbed two goals only forty-one seconds apart against Houston.

By the time New York were being beaten in Dallas, the Cosmos had long since clinched another division title, winning 24 games, tied for the best record in the 1978 season. They had clearly proved they could win without the physical and inspirational presence of Pelé, whose place had, in part, been taken by Manchester City and England forward Dennis Tueart.

Beginning his career at Sunderland, Tueart had been part of one of the great FA Cup upsets when helping the Second Division club beat Don Revie's Leeds at Wembley in 1973 before moving to City for £275,000 a year later. Having forced his way into the England team and scoring a spectacular winning goal for City in the 1976 League Cup final against Newcastle, Tueart's transfer to the Cosmos late in 1977 was the first time a current member of the England squad had chosen to make a permanent move to an NASL club, although he would not add to his six England caps following his transfer.

Manchester United had reportedly made a £300,000 bid for Tueart after he scored his third hat-trick of the season in a Boxing Day 1977 win against Newcastle, but his refusal to consider a cross-town move was thought to be evidence of his desire to move overseas. In mid-February, the Cosmos completed the signing, with newspapers quoting a £1,000-per-week salary on top of a £100,000 signing-on fee. Earlier in the season Manchester City chairman Peter Swales had addressed the exodus of English players to America after the Cosmos had bid £150,000 for midfielder Paul Power. 'This trend is certainly a challenge, but I think it's a healthy development,' he said. 'It will keep us on our toes. I firmly believe in competition and I am also convinced that the growing interest from America is going to lead to an even better deal for footballers in Britain.'

While Giorgio Chinaglia led the Cosmos attack with 34 goals, Tueart weighed in with 10 goals in his 20 games, while Steve Hunt added 12 with 12 assists from wide on the left. Before the season ended, Hunt agreed to return to England at the end of the summer in a £40,000 transfer to Coventry, a decision that amazed his teammate Terry Garbett. 'I was given the job to persuade Steve not to go back. I remember speaking to him in an elevator coming down Rockefeller Plaza. He said he was going back because he wanted an England cap. I said, "That is nice, but they have offered to give you your apartment beside the Hudson River and pay you in excess of $100,000 and I don't think you are going to get that deal in England. You are going to regret that decision." But when we are young we have these aspirations and he did it with his heart and not his head. He had this place wrapped up. They loved him and he was doing TV ads and all sorts.'

Hunt explained later, 'I needed to prove to myself that I could make it in the First Division. A lot of people thought I was mad leaving the Cosmos when I had it made, but money is not everything. The Cosmos offered me a fantastic contract to stay on for another couple of years but I had this burning desire to return to England and show I could hold my own.'

The Cosmos opened their play-off campaign against the Seattle Sounders, the team they had beaten in the previous year's Soccer Bowl. Bobby Moore had returned to the NASL to play in the final seven games of the season as Seattle edged their way into the post-season field, but his presence did little to deter the Cosmos, whose 5–2 victory featured a pair of goals by Yugoslav Vladislav Bogicevic, an instant hit with the New York fans after scoring 10 goals and 17 assists during the season.

The second round paired the Cosmos with Minnesota, who hosted the first game of the two-match series. Astonishingly, the Kicks tore the Cosmos apart 9–2, with Willey scoring five times. 'It started off as a so-so game,' he recalls. 'Then Charlie George crossed the ball and the keeper collided with one of his own players and it went in. Then I got a second and another one just before half-time for 3–0. I scored another early on after half-time and they just kept coming and coming. Unfortunately, the newspapers were on strike in New York, so no one back there knew much about it.'

The Cosmos exacted emphatic revenge, Chinaglia and Tueart sharing the goals in a 4–0 win, but the mini-game decider ended scoreless. 'I almost got a winner,' says Willey. 'Ron Futcher headed back a ball from Charlie and I had a header from the penalty spot and the keeper made his only save in two games.' New York prevailed in the shoot-out and then had an easier time of it against Portland, winning 1–0 and 5–0 to advance to the Soccer Bowl, to be played on their own turf.

The one-game format of the first round of the play-offs had lent itself to surprise results and, sure enough, the New England Tea Men, one of the tournament favourites, fell at the opening hurdle when they went down 3–1 at home to the Fort Lauderdale Strikers. Tea Men coach Cantwell says, 'We thought we had a very good chance of going all the way. The team was playing well together, we had a fair deal of experience and Flano was scoring a lot of goals.'

Keith Weller claims, 'We could have won the whole thing. We had beaten the Cosmos twice. Against Fort Lauderdale we were winning 1–0 and had a penalty just before half-time. I usually took them, but Noel let Mike Flanagan take it and he missed. Instead of 2–0 it was 1–0, and then Roger Gibbins sliced one into his own goal from a corner and we ended up losing.'

The Strikers team was largely unchanged from the previous year, with the notable addition of Liverpool midfielder Ian Callaghan, who had just completed an 18-year Liverpool career that took in more than 800 first-team games. Remarkably, Callaghan, selected for one of the group games in the 1966 World Cup finals, his second cap, had not added to his collection until recalled to the side for two games early in his final season at Liverpool. Callaghan was joined later in the summer by George Best, who began his stormy Strikers career with two goals in a 5–3 defeat of the Cosmos.

Having beaten New England, the Strikers came up against another division champion, Detroit, winning the home leg in a shoot-out after a 3–3 draw. Ken Furphy still questions the way the game was officiated. 'The refereeing standard was dreadful. Why we didn't get one of the imported referees for that game I will never know. If you got one of the American referees you were in trouble. We were winning and the referee gave them a penalty. He never looked me in the eye when I asked about the decision. You never knew what was going on over there and some people involved in the game had tremendous power.'

Furphy also recalls with obvious pain his team's defeat in the shoot-out. 'Trevor just had to hit his one in to win and I thought, "We have got this all wrapped up." The Fort Lauderdale players were shouting at him and telling him he was going to miss. He turned round towards them and the ref blew his whistle before he even got to the ball. He wasted a couple of seconds and had to run and hurry his shot and missed.' Alan Brazil squared the series with a winner back in Detroit, but the Strikers forced a one-goal win in the mini-game.

At home to the Rowdies in the first game of the American Conference championship series, the Strikers won 3–2, with goals by Whittle, David Irving and Best, but the Rowdies were comfortable 3–1 winners when the action returned to rain-soaked Tampa. In the mini-game, Strikers coach Ron Newman made his infamous decision to substitute Best before the contest reached its goalless conclusion.

Yet another shoot-out ensued, but Newman remembers the difficulties faced by the players in the wake of the evening's deluge. 'There were puddles all over the field. I sent out Tony Whelan, our first shoot-out taker, to check the location of the puddles, fearful that he might get the ball stuck in one. Sure enough, on the run-up from 35 yards, Wheels pushed his ball into a puddle and it stopped, forcing him to try to drag the ball with him. The Tampa goalkeeper, Winston Dubose, smothered the ball before Wheels could get a shot off.

'The league's Director of Officials, Eddie Pearson, came into the dressing-room later and asked me why I didn't protest about Whelan's kick. He explained that Dubose had slid right out of the area and came up with the ball in his hands in making the save. The referee should have awarded us a penalty. But it was impossible to see the field markings from the bench because the floodlights caused a sheen on the wet field.'

Rowdies coach Jago recalls, 'We had an unbelievable year and I was very confident when we got to the semi-final. I called home and invited my father and mother and some friends to come over if we got through. It was gone midnight when Rodney Marsh popped in the last goal in the shoot-out and I was calling people at two in the morning to say, "You are on the way." I knew in my heart of hearts there was not much chance of beating New York, but we would have a great time.'

The best hope of a Rowdies upset obviously lay at the feet of Marsh, a player who seemed to reserve his best for when the stakes were highest. His habit of pacing himself during games, taking breathers and conserving energy for the vital moments, could sometimes seem like he was loafing, but he explained, 'That's my style of play. That is the reason I will win games in the last few minutes when the others are flagging. What I do in the first minute I will do in the last.'

But on the morning of 27 August, Marsh met with the Rowdies medical staff and informed them that he would not be facing the Cosmos. A gash he had suffered in his left shin had become infected and, although the doctors said later they would have allowed Marsh to play, he withdrew himself from the Tampa Bay line-up.

Jago still finds it hard to comprehend the decision. 'It was a downer on the whole team. There will always be a question about whether he could have played, but I always left it to the players. Maybe Rodney felt it was sufficient to stop him playing well and all the European press were there. I knew that even *with* him playing it would be difficult.'

Inevitably, the Rowdies attack lacked penetration without Marsh and the Cosmos went in at half-time two goals ahead, Tueart and Chinaglia having scored. Jago introduced Mirandinha as a second-half substitute and, with the Rowdies raising the tempo, the Cosmos were on the back foot for a while. The Brazilian reduced the New York lead with 17 minutes to play but the goal stung the Cosmos back to life and Tueart added a second, decisive, goal to round off a successful debut season in America.

14. ☆ Death of a Salesman

The Fort Lauderdale Strikers may never have won a Soccer Bowl, but they certainly knew how to make an entrance. Head coach Ron Newman, a man who had once dressed up as George Washington for a holiday promotion – 'complete with wooden teeth' – recalls, 'We had this PR guy called Ken Small who was a great promoter and we had this track that went round the field. He said, "Let's come out in different ways every week." It was a real gimmick and we kept it a secret. We would come out standing on the running boards of mafia-type limos or on horseback.'

As former England international Keith Weller, who spent four seasons at the Strikers, explains, 'I don't think I ever entered the stadium the same way twice. I remember sitting on the back of a fire truck one time to go in and other times it was different kinds of cars or Harley Davidson bikes.'

Strikers player and assistant coach David Chadwick recalls, 'Ron loved the game and went along with some of the wacky stuff and stupid things we did to sell it. The marketing department put us on different vehicles every week and you can imagine some of the ribbing Gordon Banks and those guys got. I remember it was a London bus one time. But the funniest one was something I didn't even know about and I was as close to Ron as anyone.'

One particular stunt has gone down in NASL lore. The Strikers, division champions in 1977, had lost their first three games of the new season and were due to play host to the Los Angles Aztecs. Newman recalls, 'The papers had run headlines saying, "Are the Strikers dead?"' Chadwick adds, 'There was build-up in the press all week. We came out in hearses, with the death march playing as we entered the stadium. We all got out and the front hearse had a coffin.'

Newman corrects Chadwick's memory by saying, 'I don't want to break the myth, but there was never an actual coffin – the players would have nailed it shut. I was lying on this roller thing with a sheet over the top. I thought it was better that I did it rather than one of the players. The plan was that they would pull out the dead body. I threw back the sheet and grabbed the microphone and shouted, "We are not dead yet!" Actually, the microphone was not on!'

Despite the audio problems, the crowd responded wildly. 'We couldn't believe it,' says Chadwick. 'And we went out and won the game. It was typical of the crazy things we did to get the game in front of people.'

Every team in the NASL took part in some kind of marketing activity. Some went down the route of staging stunts in the manner of the Strikers, others focused their efforts on organising clinics for children, building at the grassroots level.

As well as the appearances at local schools and coaching clinics, there was another important cog in the public relations machine: the need to speak frankly, and frequently, to the press. At a time when most Football League players were becoming more remote from the journalists who wrote about them, contact often restricted to brief encounters in stadium car parks after games, they now entered a culture that insisted on them being available to reporters on a daily basis, including in the changing room after the game.

Vince Casey, whose role as public relations director of the New England Tea Men meant introducing this notion to his English players, recalls, 'I think they actually looked forward to it. Talking to the media about the game at length was something they had never done before. It was fresh and new to them. There was none of the suspicion that they had in their relationship with the British press. To them, it was just one more example of those crazy Americans.'

Casey recalls his fear at how head coach Noel Cantwell, brought up as a player in the old school of Upton Park and Old Trafford, would react to female reporter Lesley Visser, now one of America's leading NFL broadcasters, being around the locker room. 'Lesley was a young reporter for the *Boston Globe*. I'd had a bunch of things to talk to Noel about as we put the team together, explaining how we did things in America, but one thing I didn't talk to him about was women in the locker room. First game, we are up in the press box and Lesley comes up to me and I am just ecstatic that the *Globe* is covering us. She asks, "Will I have any trouble getting into the locker room after the game?" My worst fears are coming true. We are being covered by a woman reporter and this can only lead to something negative. I thought, "Damn it, I never asked Noel." I don't have time to go down to the locker room so I have to call him from the press box. An hour before our first game I have got to call him over what, in his experience, is totally inconsequential but for us is a big deal. I was very nervous about his reaction. I explained we had a woman reporter who would like to come into the locker room after the game. He said, "Well, will she mind?" I said, "No." So he says, "Well, then we won't either." That was symbolic of the whole team's approach. It was as though they were being allowed to talk to the press for the first time and now they couldn't stop talking.'

For each team, the aim was the same: to sell the sport of soccer. Just about every player who went from Britain to take part in the NASL has memories of being such a salesman. 'I remember going to places where the kick-off was delayed by 20 minutes,' says former New York Cosmos captain Keith Eddy. 'I am getting uptight about the game and a guy comes out dressed in a gorilla outfit. I am thinking, "Jesus Christ, get me back to England." But one thing the Americans do well is marketing. Someone thought all these gimmicks were a good idea.'

Minnesota Kicks goalkeeper Geoff Barnett adds, 'Our first game was at San Jose. Being from England we were used to running out five minutes before the game, warming up and kicking off. They had us lining up in our positions while the mascot, Crazy George, was going in and out of us on a three-wheel bike and then he was climbing up the stanchion of the goal banging his drum. It was something of a culture shock.'

Steve Earle has similar memories of pre-game antics in Tulsa. 'At one game we had someone called Captain Dynamite blowing himself up at half-time. We often had people parachuting in before the game and one time they missed the stadium and landed in the bleachers and broke some woman's legs.'

Combating the locals' lack of knowledge of the sport was a vital part of the sales process. Fort Lauderdale forward David Irving explains, 'When we first went over, people thought we were a rock band with our long hair and our accents. Once we did a clinic in a Catholic school run by nuns. We had shown a lot of tricks with the ball and afterwards the Sister came up to me and said that the kids had really enjoyed it. "One question," she said. "How do you stand on those skates and kick a ball?"'

For outgoing personalities like Alan Birchenall, the PR work was a welcome diversion. 'All the personal appearances didn't bother me. I was up at six o'clock the first morning in San Jose and they drove me into San Francisco to do a breakfast show. There was no breakfast TV in Britain at that time so I thought, "Who the hell is going to be watching this?" But it was like peak-time viewing over there. The interview was a joke, though. The guy was just interested about the difference between posts in football and American football.

'I wasn't the best player San Jose had, but the fans liked me for my after-game performances. They would have a big tailgate party in the Californian hills with live bands and I would get up and sing. I was even asked to sing the American national anthem in front of 18,000 fans before a game. Some of the notes were a bit hard, but when you have a load of armed marines as guard of honour you make sure you get it right.'

Birchenall's teammate, Laurie Calloway, had a similar outlook. 'I bought into the whole public relations thing very early. A lot of Brits come over and criticise anything Americans do. After a couple of years of seeing what they were trying to do, I felt they should do more of it back home. I did some wacky stuff, like taking part in fairs and rallies and sitting in a dunk tank while people fired baseballs at you to knock you in the tank. Some thought it was bullshit and didn't have the personalities for it. But when I ran on to that field I felt like I had 20,000 relatives in the stand. They did a survey at one game in 1978 and 90 per cent of the people there had either met or been in the company of an Earthquakes player. The fans looked at you like buddies and friends. You never had to battle to get over a loss of confidence because they always supported you.'

Tampa Bay striker Derek Smethurst adds, 'The only thing I didn't like at first was when we had to go to all the schools. It was tough. I knew why we had to do it and we shared the load. A year after we got there suddenly soccer balls were being seen and not just baseballs. Most of the players hated all the promotional stuff and I didn't like it initially. You would train and then have to go back in the afternoon and go to a school. We were messing about with a basketball one day and I headed it through the hoop and they all went bananas. I wouldn't do it again, though. It hurt.

'I had decided after three or four months that I was staying and I had got used to the selling and the publicity. And I realised that I was getting out and meeting people who would be good for my future after I finished playing.'

New England defender Peter Simpson, brought up in the traditional football environment of Highbury, recalls, 'We did a lot of coaching with the kids and I remember going into one of the stores and doing a routine. Four or five of us were playing "keepy-uppy" and I think I was given a gold chain for doing that. I felt like a right prat. It was not the sort of thing I would ever have anticipated doing when I was at Arsenal.'

David Chadwick, formerly of Dallas and Fort Lauderdale, says, 'A lot of guys on my teams were English and some had never really played at a high level, maybe only non-League. They were great guys and worked so hard for the game. We were asked to do two clinics or speeches a week and the young Americans showed such great energy that I enjoyed it. But I think some players came out and took the money and ran. Some of the guys didn't give a shit about the promotion of the game and didn't give a shit about the sport. Fort Lauderdale is one of the nicest places in the country, with its beaches and restaurants. There were guys who came over and trained and then went on the beach and hit the nightclubs. But there were some who did want to promote.'

Defender Mick Hoban coordinated much of that promotional work at Atlanta and Portland. 'It was not just a question of going out to the occasional hospital to visit, it was a planned campaign every day, utilising the players so that when we got to games we had got to know everyone. In other sports, the players were so well compensated they didn't worry about anything else. Basketball players either weren't motivated or capable of talking through a business presentation. I was well educated and had been a head boy, so I was used to having to stand up and make speeches and it served me well.

'You had to browbeat some of the guys. Some of the old guys from Britain wanted the easy life. You had to coerce and threaten them and I was given the responsibility of doing that. It was a good ploy because a team is cliquey and when you employ someone from outside it can be difficult. You have to be a player to converse with the players and they were a lot more helpful for me than for someone from outside.

'You weren't talking to guys who were thinking about their post-football careers, but I told them, "This is the best way to meet people if you want to stay here and work – plus you can meet people who can give you deals on holidays and cars." We had to train the guys, show them what to do if we went to a school assembly in a gymnasium. After two or three times they got it. We had pre-packed speeches for Rotary Clubs, ladies' clubs, something for every group.'

Portland defender Neil Rioch recalls, 'I had interacted with the fans a bit at Villa. At that time if you were not married you lived in lodgings and, of course, you were with an elderly couple, so in the evenings you found yourself wondering what to do. I was in digs with Pat McMahon and Chico Hamilton and the three of us used to go down to the supporters' club and sit with them and play cards or dominoes. So I was used to mixing with fans when I got to Portland. After every game it was compulsory to go to the hotel and meet the supporters and I developed friendships I still have to this day. And the appearances we did held me in good stead for later on in business. I learned the importance of promotion and marketing.'

Peter Wall, who played and coached in St Louis and California, explains, 'You had to do as much as you could in the community to get people to come to the games. Part of the contract was to do it. You had no choice. The soccer camps were a big money-maker for the clubs. They lasted eight to ten weeks during the summer holidays and you would usually have half a dozen players there each week. Actually, they were fun. You were working with kids and the weather was nice.'

Alan Merrick, one of the senior players in Minnesota, had a background that helped him tackle his PR duties for the Kicks. 'I had done some public speaking and some teaching at a private school so it was relatively easy for me to integrate into the PR stuff. Some players shied away from it, but the club gave coaching and instruction, protocols to abide by, a dress code, media training. They told them the pitfalls if they were not prepared.

'To the public who don't know soccer, the game is from Mars and we are the Martians. You have to tell the public what your skills are and how the people can enjoy it. Then it makes sense. Eight of us stayed on for the first winter and I went to every high school in Minnesota. Some days it was three schools in a day, presenting in front of the whole school. We showed highlights of the previous year; what we had done and who we were. Then we would have a skills session and we would pull out five of the teachers, who were either the nerds or the good sports, and we'd have fun and play a game, keeping the ball away from them. The kids just loved it.'

Peter McParland, whose Atlanta club was one of the first to launch grassroots initiatives in the '60s, says, 'When we demonstrated soccer drills at high schools, the American football coaches would often want to get their guys playing as well. They saw that soccer could get their players moving around on their toes and develop a nimbleness of feet that they could bring into American football.'

It is ironic that Ron Newman, who helped to launch many of the league's grassroots programmes in Atlanta and Dallas, ended up as a master of the pantomime-style gimmickry that, in many places, took over from youth development as the main form of promoting the sport. Although Newman regrets the trend, he understands the difficult line that clubs had to tread. 'When, in the later years of the league, teams started getting crowds without having worked to get kids playing soccer, I got a little pissed off. Nobody had done the work I had done. Soccer had become a promotional thing. But just because proper promotion will bring the crowds in, it doesn't mean you should not do the thing with kids. But simply believing that if we had kids playing we would get them to the stadium was wrong as well. They trained twice a week and played on the same day as we did. In the end, Mum and Dad were soccered out.'

15. ☆ The Price of Success

'The locals were calling us the English mafia. Vancouver is very multi-cultural and many people didn't like having players from one place. But ònce we had a winning streak we became their team.' That is how former England international goalkeeper Tony Waiters remembers the reaction to the Vancouver Whitecaps' transformation from a nondescript, unambitious club into the team that would loosen the New York Cosmos' stranglehold on the NASL in the late '70s.

Vancouver had first played host to Sunderland in the United Soccer Association days of 1967 and had been back in the NASL for three seasons when John Best arrived from the Seattle Sounders to take up the position of general manager. He found a club ill-equipped to take on the best in the NASL. 'All the players were part-time,' he says. 'They were mainly a Canadian team and had only a few imported players. I didn't feel the club was fully determined to take a professional approach. You couldn't have players who were part-time and play in a premier league.'

The makeover began with the removal of German head coach Eckhard Krautzen, whom Best felt was distracted by being in charge of the Canadian national team. Tony Waiters, who had spent almost five seasons as manager of Plymouth, was chosen to take over. Born in Southport, Waiters won five caps in England's goal during nine years at Blackpool and came back from a three-year retirement to finish his playing career with Burnley in the 1970–71 season. After coaching the England youth team, Waiters arrived at Home Park and led Argyle to promotion to the Second Division in 1974–75.

Having been fired by Plymouth, Waiters packed his bags as soon as the call came from America. 'Phil Woosman had approached me a couple of years earlier and I was not interested. But being fired is a great motivation for you. The NASL seemed like a good opportunity.'

The Whitecaps won only three of their first nine games in 1977, but recovered to take second place in the Western Division before losing to eventual Soccer Bowl finalists Seattle in the first round of the play-offs. Waiters had strengthened the squad by bringing in former Birmingham and Bolton winger Gordon Taylor from Blackburn Rovers and Derek Possee, whose 107 Football League goals included 79 in a 6-year stint at Millwall. Possee, out of contract at Orient, was an instant success with 11 goals in 16 games.

Major rebuilding work followed in the winter as Best and Waiters made a policy decision to recruit only English players to play alongside the Canadians. In front of Wolves goalkeeper Phil Parkes, who returned to Canada after missing the previous season through injury, a rebuilt defence included former Blackpool, Crystal Palace and Coventry man John Craven, Blackpool full-back Steve Harrison, a future England coach under Graham Taylor, and long-time Derby utility man Peter Daniel. In the hub of the midfield, former Arsenal stalwart Jon Sammels arrived from Leicester to team up with Filbert Street colleague Steve Kember, whose name had been made at Crystal Palace and Chelsea. In front of them was Kevin Hector, scorer of 147 League goals in 426 games for Derby following a transfer from Bradford Park Avenue, where his scoring rate had been 113 in only 176 games. Hector's two England caps included an ill-fated appearance as substitute in the 1973 game against Poland at Wembley, where he nearly rescued England's World Cup qualification hopes with a late header.

Hector had a familiar figure feeding him from the left wing, former Derby teammate Alan Hinton. Waiters recalls, 'A big turning point was when Alan joined as player and assistant coach in 1978. He was approaching 36, a good stone overweight, but we got him fit. He didn't do a lot of running but his crosses were fantastic.'

Hinton had spent the previous NASL season in Dallas after concluding a First Division career that had begun at Wolves, continued at Nottingham Forest and achieved its greatest success at the Baseball Ground, where his consistency was an integral part of two League Championship-winning teams. The winner of three England caps, Hinton was one of a talented group whose international ambitions were left on the shelf after Alf Ramsey achieved World Cup success without employing recognised wingers. His arrival in Vancouver not only marked the beginning of a successful second career as a coach but also saw him sign off as a player with a record-breaking 30 assists, setting up almost half of the Whitecaps' total of 68 goals.

Waiters continues, 'We brought over players who would not be seen as outstanding international players, but were good professionals. Everyone was trying to be a mini New York Cosmos at that time and overstretching themselves. A lot of the players that teams signed didn't mean a lot in America anyway, so we went for guys who were good for the team. If you were on our budget and needed journeymen, you went with what you knew, which for us meant players from England.'

Sammels adds, 'When Vancouver set about buying players, they didn't want the Jack the lad types who would go out for the ride. They brought players into the side who would integrate and not be aloof. We had good team spirit and good young Canadians, who were better than the Americans. Then Tony and Alan Hinton instilled the ethos that we wanted to go out and play.'

Vancouver lost two of their first four games in 1978 before making their intentions clear by winning five straight. And when they thumped Tulsa 5–1 it signalled the start of 13 consecutive wins to the end of the regular season. They finished by scoring six goals twice in the last three games to win their division with a won–lost record of 24–6, matching the Cosmos for the best record in the league. Hector was the top scorer with 21 goals, while Bob Campbell, a future Northern Ireland international, arrived late in the season from Sheffield United to score 9 goals in 13 appearances. Canadian midfielder Bobby Lenarduzzi, who had played 63 Football League games as a teenager at Reading, contributed 10 goals and 17 assists.

Campbell added two more goals in a 4–0 victory against Toronto in the first round of the play-offs to set up a contest with Portland, who had finished as division runners-up behind Vancouver. Portland had failed to score in two defeats to the Whitecaps in the regular season, but a Clyde Best goal was enough to earn them the first game in Portland. Best scored again in the return at Vancouver's Empire Stadium, along with winger Willie Anderson, to bring a premature end to the Whitecaps' season. 'We screwed up,' says Possee. 'We treated the second game like a European game where goal difference counted, even though it didn't matter because of the mini-game system. We looked at it as though we needed to win by two goals and pushed forward too early and they caught us. We played wrong tactically and we learned a lot that helped us the next year.'

☆

It was more than the team's shirts that changed – from red and white to royal blue – over the winter of 1978–79. Waiters' first task was to replace his right-hand man, Alan Hinton, who accepted the head coach's position at Tulsa. Bob McNab, who had played in the NASL for San Antonio three years earlier, answered the call after his wife, Barbara, spotted a newspaper advertisement for the position.

'She had lived in Vancouver and after my season in San Antonio I had driven up there and spent a few weeks on vacation,' McNab recalls. 'I went down to Plymouth and Tony must have felt I was something like the person he needed. Alan Hinton had been player-coach and had a great season as a player, but I think Tony was looking for someone to do more of the coaching. Tony felt he wanted someone with my background, from a top-class club.'

Waiters made changes along the spine of the Whitecaps team. At the back, former Everton centre-half Roger Kenyon, veteran of 12 seasons at Goodison Park, added height and strength, while Chelsea's Ray Lewington brought young legs and hard graft to the centre of midfield. Up front, a partner for Hector was found in the shape of Trevor Whymark, scorer of 74 League goals in almost 250 games for Ipswich. The slightly built forward, effective in the air, had earned one England cap in a World Cup qualifier in Luxembourg, but had missed out on one of the biggest days in Ipswich's history later in the same season when injury robbed him of a place in the 1978 FA Cup final victory over Arsenal.

'I'd had a knee ligament injury and Bobby Robson said he was willing to let me go,' says Whymark. 'I spoke to Lawrie McMenemy at Southampton but in the back of my mind was that I was not as fit as I wanted to be. I didn't think I could do myself justice in the First Division so I went to Vancouver and thought I would finish my career there.'

To provide service from the flanks, the Whitecaps flew Scotland winger Willie Johnston across the Atlantic in the hope that his trip would be happier than his World Cup journey to Argentina. Johnston, a skilful player with a belligerent streak that resulted in more than 20 dismissals during his career at Rangers and West Bromwich Albion, had played 22 times for Scotland, including their 3–1 defeat to Peru in the opening game of the 1978 World Cup finals. While the Scots were trying to rebuild their shattered confidence, Johnston was revealed to have failed a drugs test and was sent home. To operate on the opposite flank to the veteran, the Whitecaps signed Carl Valentine, a 20-year-old, express-speed winger from Manchester who had made his Oldham debut three years earlier.

Vancouver won three of their first five games, but McNab, who played a couple of early-season games while Lenarduzzi was preparing to switch from midfield to left-back, says, 'We were just scraping wins, although we were a much better side. We played both our wide men as wide out as possible so that we had four up front. What we weren't doing was winning second balls from dead balls and goal kicks, because teams had twice as many men in the midfield area. I mentioned it to Tony but he said, "I don't want any of that Arsenal defensive stuff."'

By the time Hector grabbed a hat-trick to beat Edmonton, the Whitecaps had won eight out of ten games. But their previous game, a 2–0 win against the Philadelphia Fury, had presented an opportunity to further strengthen the side. McNab recalls, 'We lacked a bit of craft and confidence in midfield. Barbara and I took Alan Ball out for dinner before we played against Philadelphia in Vancouver. He said, "Get me out of Philadelphia." They had excellent players but they were all stars and not enough workers. Ballie was magnificent in the first half of our game and I said to Tony, "I have seen the man who is going to help us: Alan Ball." Tony didn't agree with me but I asked him to take a look at the tape of the game. Ballie was not even fully fit, but he was unbelievable in the first half until his lack of fitness showed. I knew Ballie, warts and all, from England and Arsenal and I knew he could do it for us.'

Ball remembers things a little differently, claiming, 'I was quite happy in Philadelphia and didn't go looking for a move. But with Vancouver being primarily an English team, they came in and traded for me. It was a mutual thing.'

In the few weeks it took for Ball's trade to be arranged, Vancouver lost three out of four games before getting their season back on track with a 4–1 thrashing of the Cosmos. 'I think I was the icing on the cake for them,' says Ball. 'They wanted a bit of experience on the pitch and someone to provide some leadership.'

In 15 games following his arrival in Canada, Ball scored 8 goals, provided 10 assists, and proved to be an inspiration. 'He absolutely had a new lease of life,' says Best. 'There was space for him to use his skills and he played in a small radius instead of trying to pick out players from 30 or 40 yards.'

Possee describes Ball's character and confidence as 'the missing piece of the puzzle', while McNab adds, 'Ballie was the difference, with his class and his ability to get more out of his teammates. He was, and still is, the best one-touch footballer I have ever seen.'

Whymark says, 'When Alan joined it made you realise how good a player you had to be to play with guys like that in their prime and made you realise how far off top-notch you really were. He had lost his legs a bit but not upstairs. He was a great influence on the players around him.'

Vancouver retained their division title, with Hector and Whymark scoring 12 and 10 goals respectively and Johnston leading the team with 12 assists. Says Best, 'Apart from his goals, Kevin Hector was such a composed player in the area. Put him on the edge of the area or the corner of the box and play to his feet, and he was always able to wriggle round people and put you in dangerous positions. And Whymark was a classy, skilful, goalscoring striker.'

Waiters, however, admits, 'We had a more spectacular team in '78 and played better football. But the '79 team did their job better. They were used to the Astroturf field, which required a possession game, playing to feet.'

Dallas were beaten in two games in the first round of the play-offs, Craven netting both goals past former Manchester United and England keeper Alex Stepney in the home win. Next up were the Los Angeles Aztecs, who were coached by former Holland World Cup coach Rinus Michels and had been steered towards the play-offs by 13 goals from Dutch superstar Johan Cruyff, lured out of retirement by a reported $700,000-per-season deal. Playing alongside the 32-year-old former Ajax and Barcelona genius, the league's MVP was English forward Chris Dangerfield, making his sixth NASL stop in five seasons. After scoring nine times in the regular season, Dangerfield's three goals helped ease the Aztecs past the Washington Diplomats in their first play-off series.

Dangerfield recalls the thrill of playing in the Aztecs environment. 'The best coach I ever played for was Rinus Michels. He and Cruyff were like father and son. They were on the same wavelength and were able to adjust to things on the park. All I used to do was make runs and it was like Joe Montana finding Jerry Rice for the San Francisco 49ers. As a team player, Cruyff added a little more than, say, George Best. Johan could play several positions and make coaching decisions. And what was not recognised was that he was so relaxed in America. He spent time with the young players after training and would share his experiences. He became one of the lads.'

The first game of the National Conference semi-final series

seemed to be going smoothly for the Whitecaps in Pasadena's Rose Bowl after Valentine scored twice. But Waiters recalls, 'With about 15 or 20 minutes to go, Valentine played a little square ball that was intercepted and they scored. Then Lewington repeated the same thing. It was a case of young players doing naive things.' Those goals, including one by former Southport defender Bobby Sibbald, took the game into extra-time and the Aztecs went on to win after a shoot-out. 'From being in control of our destiny we were facing a game where, even if we won, we would only be at 1–1 in the series and facing a mini-game.'

Three days later, the Empire Stadium heaved to accommodate more than 32,000 fans. 'The stadium was completely full but it was eerie because people knew we had to win two games to go through,' says Waiters. 'They were hardly cheering because they were as nervous as we were.'

McNab, a veteran of Arsenal's triumph in the 1970 European Fairs Cup, urged Waiters to be patient. 'Tony had no experience in Europe and playing in the play-offs was very similar to European games. I said, "Let's play tight and outwork them. You can't let them score." Tony wanted to bring on Carl Shearer, a big defender, and put him up front after about 15 minutes. I said, "If we win in 89 minutes that's OK. You have got to approach the game properly, be cautious and sensible until the last few minutes."'

The Whitecaps prevailed 1–0 and McNab could sense that the 30-minute mini-game was there for the taking. 'We were fitter and LA were dead by the end of the game. Cruyff could not walk in the mini-game.'

Hector's decisive goal brought the Whitecaps up against the reigning champions from New York. Once again, the Cosmos had not stood idle following their victory in Soccer Bowl '78, adding Holland's World Cup midfielder Johan Neeskens, Dutch defender Wim Rijsbergen and the striking blond Brazilian left-back Francisco Marinho. Giorgio Chinaglia was in no mood to be pushed into the shadows, however, scoring 26 of New York's league-high tally of 84, while Dennis Tueart netted 16 times and added the same number of assists.

The only bump in the smooth road to another division title was when coach Eddie Firmani was fired and replaced by Lithuanian-born American Ray Klivecka. It was a shock decision, given that the Cosmos had won 10 out of 12 games at the time, but the coach had upset the Ertegun brothers by preferring Canadian Jack Brand in goal over their fellow-countryman Erol Yasin and leaving out Marinho. A year earlier, Firmani might have survived, but he had lost the support of his great ally, Chinaglia, during the 1978 season when he substituted the Italian late in a game at the Memphis Rogues.

Without the powerful Chinaglia in his corner, Firmani was exposed to the whims of the management and Klivecka stepped up from his position as assistant coach to help the Cosmos cruise to the play-offs. After disposing of Toronto, New York suffered a shock 3–0 defeat at Hinton's Tulsa Roughnecks, for whom ex-Derby centre-forward Roger Davies scored twice. Normal service was resumed at Giants Stadium, where another 76,000-plus crowd saw the Cosmos reverse that scoreline and advance to face Vancouver after Chinaglia bagged two goals in the mini-game.

The Whitecaps approached the Conference Championship series as underdogs, despite having scored four goals in each of their regular season victories against the Cosmos. McNab recalls, 'I loved taking on New York. They had wonderful quality players, like Beckenbauer and Carlos Alberto and Chinaglia, but all of those lads were past their best and only wanted to play when they had the ball. When you get older you don't want to do the grunt work, so we needed to outwork and outfight them. They also played with a sweeper and man-for-man marked. I had played against that system many times in Europe and always thought it a poor way of using your players.'

Possee adds, 'The Cosmos used to hate playing against us because we didn't give them any respect. Some other teams would think, "Oh, my God. We can't beat the Cosmos." We said, "Screw it. We can sort them out."'

Whymark recalls an explosive regular season game between the teams. 'Willie Johnston was up against Eskandarian, the Iranian, who was not the most popular player to be playing in America at that time. They got in a brawl and Chinaglia got involved and kicked Willie and as he turned to get away from the referee Craven put him down with a crunching right-hander. I think all four of them were sent off and it was chaos for a few minutes. Pelé, who was watching the game, came on in a white suit to calm everything down.'

Whymark and Johnston were on target as the Whitecaps continued their dominance over the Cosmos with a 2–0 home victory in the first game of the play-off series. 'We fought and pressurised them everywhere, even in their own half of the field,' says McNab. 'We were dropping off and encouraging the goalkeeper to throw the ball out to their back men then flying into them. Ballie was being man-marked, which teams had been doing to him without success since 1966, and he bossed the midfield.'

Three days later came another of those dramatic occasions that only the NASL's play-off format could produce. 'It was incredible,' says Ball. 'We kicked off at eight o'clock and didn't finish until half past eleven.' By the end of the night, the Whitecaps were through to the Soccer Bowl.

It began with the teams battling to a 2–2 draw, Chinaglia scoring twice for the home team, Craven and Johnston for Vancouver. The Cosmos kept alive their hopes of a third straight NASL title when the Whitecaps could only score once in the shoot-out. For the decisive mini-game, the Whitecaps left out Lewington in favour of Sammels, whose hamstring injury had made him an absentee from the play-offs until his appearance as substitute earlier in the evening, and played Possee from the start in place of Hector. Having already played 120 minutes in 88-degree heat, the teams, like heavyweight boxers rising from their stools for the 15th round, squared up for another half-hour of battle. Valentine recalls, 'There was so much on the line. No one wanted to make any mistakes and you were just going on adrenalin.'

Tempers became frayed and both teams had goal attempts ruled out before the decisive match ended scoreless. For the second time in an hour, the outcome depended on sudden-death attempts on goal. It looked bad for the Whitecaps when Canadian defender Bob Bolitho missed their second attempt, but Beckenbauer followed suit. After Possee scored and New York's Ricky Davis missed later in the shoot-out, Ball wasted the opportunity to clinch a Vancouver victory. That left Brazilian Nelsi Morais with the chance to beat Parkes and extend the competition to a sixth round of kicks, but he failed to get his shot away in time and New York's reign was over.

That it was Possee whose shoot-out goal proved decisive brought some deserved glory for a man who, McNab recalls, 'worked his socks off. He was magnificent'. Possee says, 'I had come in for Trevor Whymark for a while that season and did very well, but they wanted Trevor back in the team. I was in my thirties and had the experience to understand about the team and that it takes a lot of people working together to win. You get your glory where you can and the semi-final was my game.'

With only the Tampa Bay Rowdies standing between them and their first NASL championship, it should have been a time of celebration and anticipation for the Whitecaps. Instead, it became one of bitterness and animosity. 'The players felt they should have got a bigger bonus and they might have in other soccer environments,' says Waiters. 'The attitude in the club was, "That is your contract. You signed and that's what you get." The bonus was about $5,000 or less and they wanted it doubled. I recommended to the board they found a way of doing it. In the end we tried to build in a bonus the next season but it was messy.'

At the root of the players' problem was the NASL's policy that all bonus money for play-off success was paid by the league. Best recalled, 'A number of the owners could have paid huge bonuses if they had wanted to, whereas a club like ours could not compete. That's why the league decided the best way was for them to control the bonuses.'

Whymark continued, 'We knew a lot of the players from Tampa Bay and, as always happened, money came into the conversation somewhere. I think they had offered their players and wives a holiday in Hawaii just for getting to the final. We formed a little committee, led by Ballie and John Craven, and they went to the management. But they were told the club would not break the rules and regulations. Ballie and John told them they didn't know how the players would react.'

Best told me, 'A couple of the players came to me and said they wanted extra money under the table as a bonus for reaching the final. I had anticipated something like it. I met with the players and told them we could not do that. One of the players who came to me said, "You are going to have worse problems than you can imagine," and was threatening me. What made a mess of things was that a couple of players got hold of a couple of our directors at a social function. The directors said they would throw in some money for the players. When the chairman heard about it he went crazy. From the players' perspective it just seemed like the management was being tough about it.'

Possee claims, 'They screwed us, basically. All we asked the Whitecaps was if they would match the league bonuses. They wouldn't even think about it, but said they would reward us on our next contract. Then they got rid of a load of us, so we never got anything.'

Feelings were running so high that the Whitecaps players even talked about boycotting the Soccer Bowl, although Possee admits now, 'It was all bravado really. We wanted to play.' The fact, however, that the Cosmos had been beaten in the semi-finals and that the final was now being played in Giants Stadium only accentuated the Whitecaps players' feelings of being poor relations. Says McNab, 'Our guys were on 36,000 Canadian dollars and the New York players were on about 360,000. The Cosmos spent more on programme sellers than we did on players.

'I remember Tony having a meeting in the dressing room the day before the game. It was not nice. After Tony had finished speaking,

I said to the players, "You get very few chances in your life to win things. You have worked your socks off to get where you are now. Whatever is going on, arguments or disagreements, you can't jeopardise this one chance of making a little history or you will never forgive yourselves."

'During our warm-up that evening, the grumbling and complaining was still going on so I decided to give them quite a hard session. The players were soon swearing at me and saying, "How can we be doing this when we have got a game tomorrow?" It turned their anger towards me and it seemed to change their focus for a while. We finished the practice with a small-sided game, which turned out to be extremely physical. I think most of the players were trying to kick me.'

The bonus issue was still on the players' minds as the game approached, until Ball decided to speak up. 'The money side of it was a nuisance,' the former England captain admits, 'and being a senior member of the team I decided to speak to them, away from Tony and Bob. I said, "This is a fantastic thing you have achieved. Don't let the monetary side of things get in the way." I think the fact that it came from me made a difference. It was different to one of the management team trying to get through to them.'

Waiters says that 'Ballie helped save the day, even though he was one of the ones stirring it up,' while Whymark remembers, 'Ballie was absolutely superb. He spoke about how the cup finals he had played in had gone so fast and that he was going to enjoy every single minute of this one. He instilled that feeling in everybody and kept everybody calm.'

But there had been more unhappiness in the Whitecaps ranks when the team to face the Rowdies was announced. Sammels, who had at one time been the team captain, did not even make it on to the three-man substitutes' bench. For the 34-year-old midfielder it brought back haunting memories of 1971, when, out of favour with the North Bank fans, he had lost his place in Arsenal's first team and had missed out on the Double-clinching FA Cup-final victory against Liverpool.

McNab, who had seen the torment that Sammels had gone through at Highbury, recalls, 'I still remember the sick feeling in my stomach when Tony told me that Jon could not even be on the bench. Jon was very upset and I don't think he has ever forgiven me. He deserved to be playing and it left me feeling very uncomfortable, even though it was not my decision. But it was the only decision that Tony could possibly have made. Roger Kenyon had a calf-muscle injury, so we had to have Peter Daniel on the bench to cover for him. We had to cover the forwards with Derek

Possee and league rules stated that you were only allowed two foreign players on the bench.'

Meanwhile, the Rowdies team that arrived in New York in the hope of erasing memories of their previous year's Soccer Bowl defeat were not without their own problems. Rodney Marsh, the charismatic club captain, felt that the club's new general manager, Chas Seredneski, was forcing him into early retirement. Wanting to release the 34-year-old after the season, but fearful of the public reaction, Seredneski had offered Marsh the first testimonial game ever given to an NASL player if he would go quietly. Tempted by the prospect of a pay five times his annual salary, Marsh accepted, but felt he had been 'blackmailed' by the club.

Rowdies coach Gordon Jago believes that, one year after being denied Marsh's services in the Soccer Bowl through injury, he had been left with a distracted star player. 'Rodney was upset about not receiving a new contract and maybe felt I was partly responsible. I think he felt they weren't treating him right. He had been Mister Soccer in Tampa. It weighed on his mind and I don't think his concentration was fully there. There might not have been the determination to win there would normally have been.'

It had been a determined, slimline Marsh who reported to the Rowdies for pre-season training, weighing a stone and a half lighter than a year earlier. Marsh explained that the criticism of his no-show at Soccer Bowl '78 had been a spur for his programme of self-improvement. 'At the end of the season, with the bad publicity I got, I went into a bit of a depression. I was drinking a few beers, eating lots of stupid food, and I was really upset by what went down. So I decided to cut out beer and junk food. Later I went on a religious diet, eating pure health foods. I had no drink at all, apart from champagne and white wine.'

With a reunion with his wife, Jean, aiding his mental health, Marsh totalled 11 goals and 14 assists, many of them to set up his new strike partner Oscar Fabbiani, scorer of 25 goals. At the back, the Rowdies had added former Millwall stopper Barry Kitchener and ex-Tottenham full-back John Gorman and they won the American Conference's East Division with a defensive record bettered only by the Whitecaps. Detroit and Philadelphia were beaten in the first two rounds of the play-offs, before San Diego forced the Rowdies into a mini-game decider in the Conference Championship.

The stage should have been set for Marsh to emulate Pelé two years earlier and bring the curtain down on his career with a glorious finale. But in front of more than 50,000 in Giants Stadium, he was denied twice by Parkes and the Whitecaps took the lead through Whymark.

Having missed Ipswich's big day a year earlier, Whymark had feared the ankle injury he suffered against New York would keep him out of another big occasion, but he recovered in time to receive specific pre-game instructions from McNab. 'He told me that every time I got the chance I should get myself turned and take on Barry Kitchener because if I got him on the turn I would be through. After about a quarter of an hour I got the ball, turned Gorman on the halfway line and had about 20 yards to Kitchener. I ran at him full pace and checked out to the left. As I took it past him I hit it and it flew into the net. McNab was full of praise for himself!'

Despite Dutchman Jan Van der Veen's equaliser ten minutes later, the Whitecaps remained confident of victory, with Whymark having a further attempt disallowed and Hector hitting the post. 'We were constantly attacking,' says Whymark. 'We played very well throughout the team, and bossed it, apart from a ten-minute spell when they scored. In the second half they ran out of steam and we came more into it. Ballie laid the ball off to me and said, "Hit it!" I whacked it and it clipped someone's heels and flew inside the near post.'

The Rowdies had more than half an hour in which to salvage the game, but with only ten minutes remaining Jago decided to take drastic action. 'I could see it was not going to be Rodney's day,' he remembers. 'I thought, "Bugger it. I will make the change." I'd had a similar situation with him at QPR when he wanted to go to Manchester City and was affected by it. That may have been in the back of my mind.'

Marsh threw down his shirt in the dug-out, distraught at the way his career was being brought to an end. Jago explained he felt he needed more pace up front and Marsh, recalling his response in his book, *Priceless*, shot back, 'How long have you known me? Fifteen years? And with ten minutes of my career left you've realised I'm not fucking quick enough.'

The Whitecaps were on their way to victory and Waiters saw Marsh's withdrawal as a testament to his team's professional display. 'We knew we had to keep Marsh quiet and he didn't do much. It was a very workmanlike performance, an example of the team doing its job.'

Jago still claims his team should have had a penalty in the

opening minutes, while McNab believes that the loss of an early goal could have spelled the end of the road for Vancouver. 'I am convinced that if they had scored first we would have lost because of the frame of mind the players were in.'

But it was the Whitecaps' day. 'We played terrific football all the way through,' says Ball. 'We were in control of it, very comfortable and very professional. We were a good English side who were very well drilled.'

But, true to the build-up to the game, there was more unhappiness when the Vancouver players returned to their hotel to find their suitcases packed and their rooms – originally booked in anticipation of the Cosmos making the final – occupied by new guests. McNab explains, 'The league assumed the Cosmos would win the semi-final and would not need the rooms the night of the final. We had rewritten the script but no one changed the booking. What a mess. What should have been a great evening was a real let down.'

McNab recalls Sammels and Hector making plans to fly home direct from New York instead of joining the celebrations in Vancouver, where 200,000 would line the team's parade route, while John Best admits that the players' mood was not as it should have been among newly crowned champions. 'It was virtually impossible to overcome the money situation. People had taken their positions.'

The hotel issue would be brought up again at the NASL's winter meetings, but was put savagely into perspective when one team owner replied, 'That was terrible, but who really gives a fuck? This league lost $20 million this year.'

The Whitecaps' response to the players' simmering discontent was to offer a considerable wage increase. 'The players seemed to have a great resentment against the league and some of them accused the Vancouver club of cheating them,' says McNab. 'For the 1980 season, all the players were given a 30 per cent increase on their existing contracts, which I felt was generous since the owners had still lost more than $500,000 for the 1979 season – even though we had sold out nearly every game, won Soccer Bowl and had 16,000 season ticket holders. We could win it again and the owners might lose $2 million. I remember telling the players, "This is a great club and the only thing that will happen is that this team and the NASL will fold if you keep up with your demands."

'Phil Parkes got Dionne Warwick's agent, who wrote to the club asking for three-quarters of a million over three years. Phil left for Chicago before the 1980 season, but it was a terrible decision for both sides. The club lost a fan favourite and a good goalkeeper and Phil lost Tony Waiters, who spent much of his time and effort coaching him. I heard Phil received a $70,000 contract with Chicago.'

Into this atmosphere of unrest came a pair of new signings from England – Leeds and Scotland goalkeeper David Harvey and the former Burnley and Leeds striker Ray Hankin. 'I'd had four good years at Leeds and asked for a transfer,' says Hankin. 'There were a couple of inquiries to keep me in the First Division, but I thought a change of pace might suit me better and I knew Tony Waiters and I knew the city was a beautiful place to live so I decided to take the plunge.'

But what Hankin found in Vancouver was far from the idyllic picture he had imagined. 'There was a lot of bad feeling in the team because the players felt they had been promised this and that. It was very difficult to settle. The team was not doing well and the players were always talking about the bonuses. I wondered what the hell I was doing there. That first year was really difficult.'

This time, however, not even Alan Ball was in the mood to help resolve the situation. Before returning to Canada after playing the 1979–80 season for Southampton, Ball accepted an offer to become manager at Blackpool, the club with which he had started his career. He explains, 'My playing career was starting to come to an end. Vancouver knew what my thoughts were and I said I would play another season, but I would like to go home early. In hindsight I shouldn't have gone back at all. I was starting a brand-new career and my mind was in turmoil. But I felt obliged to the club and the fans wanted to see me and the other players back, so I decided to go.'

McNab says, 'I wanted to cancel his contract. There is no way anyone can give his best for any team and manage a professional club 5,000 miles away at the same time. He was spending all his time managing them by phone. He became mischievous. As good as he had been the previous year supporting Tony and me, he became a huge negative for the team and the management. I had witnessed both sides of Ballie at Arsenal and knew what a disruptive influence he could be on the other players if the situation was not to his benefit. I wanted to get rid of Alan and Willie Johnston before the season started. Willie had become almost impossibly disruptive as he felt his popularity with the fans gave him the leverage to demand more money. I hoped that releasing both Ballie and Willie would salvage the rest of the squad.'

Playing for Uncle Sam

The season began with five defeats in seven games, while McNab's own situation added to the uneasy atmosphere. 'Tony was totally organised and his administration skills were fantastic. But after 1979 I had a meeting with him. He was supposed to be taking over as general manager at the end of the 1980 season and he did not see me as his future head coach.'

Yet, after returning to England, McNab received a call from Waiters asking him to return as assistant coach. With no other job offers, McNab accepted. 'A few days later Tony called again and said, "I have been told to ask you if you will come back as the head coach." I could not believe my ears. Tony explained that John Best wanted to set up an English system of manager and coach. I accepted, knowing that Tony was not on board with the idea at all. From what I understood later, he thought I had tried to get the head coach's job from him. How he could think that has always been a mystery to me. Tony had been NASL Coach of the Year and was treated like a god in Vancouver. It would be like taking over from Arsène Wenger at Arsenal – a suicide mission.

'I accepted responsibility without authority. Essentially I had the same position as in 1979, but with a different title. Tony still picked the team but sat in the stands and left me getting booed down on the bench. The players were in revolt against everything at the club and the respect I had gained from them the previous season was lost.'

Waiters explains, 'We had a troubled ship and it was always going to be difficult to deal with that situation. There was confusion in the players' minds about who was making the major decisions. I should have made it clear I was running the team and sorted it out. In the end, I let Bob go and I have mended the fence since. He is a good friend.'

Best adds, 'It was impossible for Bob. It was a difficult situation for an experienced head coach and he was not an experienced head coach. I hired Bob again as a head coach at an indoor franchise and he had a great impact in terms of developing young players, but as head coach at Vancouver he was very different to what we were looking for.'

Ball's departure came at the end of June. Waiters admits, 'I had to let Ballie go, which was tough because I had known him since he was 14. He is dynamic, aggressive and an assertive leader, but not only was he unhappy with the financial situation at Vancouver, he had taken the Blackpool job. He was winding up Willie Johnston and we had other players who were being affected by the whole situation.'

174

Ball's final game in a Vancouver shirt was also Johnston's farewell appearance – for a couple of years, anyway – and, after the 1980 season, Johnny Giles arrived to succeed Waiters as head coach. The Whitecaps would enter a new, less dramatic, chapter in their history.

16. ☆ A Fistful of Dollars

Anyone arriving at Heathrow Airport in the summer months of the late '70s ran the risk of tripping over a Football League player with his bags packed and tagged for anywhere from California to Connecticut. When the pop anthem 'Go West' hit the charts in 1979, it could have been the theme tune for the British professional footballer. And, in many cases, the uniforms they ended up wearing weren't much less flamboyant than those of the Village People themselves.

There was certainly no shortage of volunteers ready to don the red and yellow hoops of the Fort Lauderdale Strikers, the orange and blue of the Detroit Express or the gold jersey of the New England Tea Men with its distinctive scarlet 'T' running across the shoulders and down the torso. And it was agents like Ken Adam who provided a vital link between the American clubs and players keen to take advantage of the opportunities, if not necessarily the fashion, on offer across the water.

'Once you have taken some of your own players over there, like Rodney Marsh, Tommy Smith and Alan Ball, you become the person everyone thinks of when they need players,' says Adam. 'The clubs looked to me to help them, but I was always a player agent first. I started getting calls from all kinds of players. I remember Bobby Lennox from Celtic, who I had never met, giving me a call to see if I could help him. I knew most of the owners because I went to league meetings.'

Although some American teams paid transfer fees to purchase the contracts of their British imports, the majority of Football League players heading across the water were still doing so as part of loan deals between the US and British clubs, with the player often caught in the middle of some unseemly haggling. The

American season began before the Football League programme wound down, while the NASL play-offs overlapped the start of the new season back home. It meant that delicate negotiations were required to ensure that the NASL teams had their players for the maximum number of games. 'The loan system was a major pain in the arse,' Adam recalls. 'It was not a very practical solution. At some point one of the sides was going to be pissed off.'

Former Bristol Rovers manager and Portland Timbers head coach Don Megson experienced the system from both sides and says, 'If the American team did well their season cut into ours in England. You wanted your own player back and the NASL team may have promised they would come back. But then the NASL started insisting that if you signed a player for the season he had to stay until you were out of the competition. It became a very difficult situation to manage.'

According to various sources, often the only way the American teams could ensure that they had their Football League imports for the maximum number of games was to give an off-the-books payment to the English club's manager. 'For sure it happened,' says Adam.

Former NASL commissioner Phil Woosnam explains, 'I went to a Football League board meeting and asked if we could make a loan agreement. I said they could set the standards but insisted that the players couldn't come back until they were out of our competition. That was where Vic Crowe got himself into trouble in that first year in Portland. They were in the semi-finals and Vic said Peter Withe had to leave. I said, "Vic, he ain't going back. You have got to find a way that he doesn't go back, otherwise you are going to get killed." And somehow he did it.'

Woosnam denies knowledge of how Crowe solved his problem, adding, 'No one ever came to me and told me about any backhanders.'

But Fort Lauderdale Strikers coach Ron Newman recounts, 'Payment to managers did happen. Otherwise, sometimes the player would be a week late arriving or he would have an injury they still had to repair.'

Newman also claims that there were opportunities for payments to go in the other direction, into the pocket of the NASL coach. But he insists, 'I never got involved in it, although I know it happened. A couple of agents said they would put something in there for me, but I couldn't do that.'

New England Tea Men coach Noel Cantwell explains, 'When you were trying to get players from England, good players like Archie Gemmill or Gerry Daly, clubs didn't want players to go for nothing.

The clubs had to think about what state they were going to be in when they came back. Some clubs, like Arsenal and Manchester United, wouldn't let players go at all unless they were young players who needed experience.'

Former New York Cosmos and Detroit Express head coach Ken Furphy adds, 'We were often asked for payments by English managers, but refused to pay it. My clubs never got involved in it, even though it probably cost us a few players.'

John Best, coach at Seattle and general manager at Vancouver, adopted a similar stance. 'There were a number of people who were reported to be making those kinds of payments to overseas clubs. But I felt that once you went though that door all was lost. It was going to be a monster that would grow and grow. It was a shame that the loan system operated, but something like that was needed at the time to upgrade the quality of the league.'

According to Adam, even a gradual erosion of the loan system did not prevent some English managers lining their pockets. 'There were many instances of players being given a free transfer, but someone getting money as a transfer fee. The Americans were very generous with some of their expenses.'

Such generosity meant that a stint in the NASL offered veteran British players a lucrative alternative to remaining at home. Former Fulham and Leicester forward Steve Earle says, 'My basic wages at Leicester would have been about £100 a week and I was on double that when I signed for Detroit. And the club provided us with everything so I was able to rent out my house in Leicester to Ray Illingworth. Some players were getting fees of $35,000 to sign on. My Leicester teammate, Alan Woollett, was offered a great deal by Detroit but wouldn't go because he didn't want to leave his dog! He went to Northampton and knew he'd made the wrong decision when they pulled up at a Wimpy and they were given a £1 voucher each to get a meal.'

Brian Tinnion recalls turning down an opportunity to earn some extra money during a game for Hawaii. 'We got a penalty and this little Portuguese guy, Diamantino Costa, came up and said, "I take penalty." I reminded him I was the penalty taker, but he said, "No, no. I take it. I give you money." I took it and missed the bloody thing. It turned out his contract had him on a thousand dollars a goal.'

Some players viewed a move to the NASL career as a great family opportunity. Alan Merrick, who swapped West Bromwich Albion for Minnesota, explains, 'I might have earned a little bit more in America, but that wasn't the reason I stayed. I sensed the kids would have a better opportunity. If I had gone back to England I would have had to send them to a private school for them to have the same opportunities.'

Others looked at their careers beyond football, with Neil Rioch saying, 'It was a fresh direction, to see how the Americans went about preparation and coaching. I thought it would be very educational.'

And for players like Laurie Calloway, whose Football League career had been played out in the lower divisions, it was a chance to taste the big time. 'We had sell-out crowds in San Jose and suddenly I was playing in front of 35,000 instead of being in the Third Division. I made the all-star team the first two years I was there and from an ego point of view it made you feel good. In the Third and Fourth Division I was making the same money as my bricklaying mates. In San Jose, I was somebody.'

Once in America, most British players found every need taken care of. Vince Casey, former public relations director of the New England Tea Men, remembers Helen Viollet, the wife of assistant coach Dennis, taking on the role of interior designer. 'She was the one who chose everything, from the knives and forks to the bed sheets and furniture. So while the team was at Charlton Athletic preparing for the season, she was in the US outfitting the apartments.'

Alan Merrick remembers, 'I was picked up at the airport by a guy called Don Byerly. No one in the world would know him apart from in Minnesota. He had a grocery store with carpets. It was like walking into your own house, but with food everywhere. He drove us to an apartment that was fully furnished and had a fully stocked refrigerator. The next day we were escorted to a car dealership to get our brand-new cars. They were taking the plastic off the seats as we were pulling away.'

Portland's Mick Hoban recalls, 'The Timbers set up sponsors so that when you got to town you were given a family. They told you everything from where you got buckets, to where the kids could go to school. Most players still have ties to those people.'

Casey recalls Charlton winger Colin Powell watching in amazement when Tea Men general manager Bob Keating changed the player's flat tyre in his business suit. 'The attitude was, "Let's just get it done." Colin was so impressed that executives in the organisation would change a flat tyre, but to us it was no big deal. It was just the way you put together a club. The British players seemed overwhelmed by that.'

For those players looking to extend their tenancy in America, some things were more important than car maintenance, soft furnishings and even money. Often additional dollars would be foregone for the promise of a green card, the prized document granting the right to remain and work in the United States. Tampa Bay Rowdies striker Derek Smethurst explains, 'After 1976 I decided I was going to try for $60,000 a year. But then I told them, "I will take $40,000 but I want a green card within six months." I knew it could be got and I negotiated it that way, otherwise the lawyers would have let it get delayed. It was hard to get a green card without the club behind you. I was officially the groundsman for two years.'

Former Portland and Los Angeles Aztecs forward Chris Dangerfield says, 'Peter Short was negotiating my contract at LA and he said he would give me this and that and added, "I will give you a green card." I thought, "Whatever," but that turned out to be the greatest thing I could have had. Life in America was that one day you were here and the next you were traded. I was one of those guys who had more clubs than Tiger Woods, but when I decided to stay in America, that green card gave me flexibility and security.'

Tinnion adds, 'The green card was the best Christmas present I ever got. I applied for one when I was in Hawaii and then in Colorado but both those teams folded. I applied again when I was in Detroit under Ken Furphy, but one day Ken said, "We are struggling for money. I am going to let you go." I asked him if he could do me a favour and keep me on just until I got my green card. That was some time in November and on 23 December it came though.'

British players took a little time to get used to a system where teams could trade them at a moment's notice, in the manner of children swapping soccer stickers in the playground. Former Burnley centre-half Colin Waldron says, 'When you are transferred you have no say in it. Tulsa came to me and said, "You are sold to Philadelphia." I said, "No, I am not. I am not going where I don't want to go." In the end they explained the financial side of things and I said I would go.'

Knowing the way the system worked was, according to Smethurst, a vital asset. That knowledge paid off when the Tampa Bay Rowdies attempted to send him to the San Diego Sockers in exchange for former Luton midfielder Peter Anderson. 'Most players thought that if you were traded you had to make the deal,' says Smethurst. 'But I knew they had to get your signature on a contract. They offered me what I was making at Tampa Bay and I said, "I am not making the deal." I knew it was not a trade until I signed and I knew San Diego did not want Peter Anderson back, so they came back an hour later and made a better offer. Most guys were in fear and would sign anything.'

Finding players willing to accept their offers of cash, cars and whatever else was not a problem for NASL teams. The art came in making those offers to players who would give their all in return. Ken Adam says, 'There were instances where the players saw it as a cross between a paid holiday and a chance to stay in shape. The players were offered reasonable money and apartments and cars, which added to the holiday atmosphere. The better-known players were coming over with nice big numbers. But the journeyman player could make pretty decent money as well.'

As an agent, Adam was cautious about recommending anyone he felt would see the NASL as a meal ticket and deckchair in the sun. 'From a business and reputation point of view, you can't send a player thinking he is going to take the money and run. You can't always tell, but most of the players I brought over did really well – guys like Ron Davies and Tommy Smith. Bobby Stokes and Jim Steele went to Washington from Southampton and made the best of it. I brought over Alan Ball and he could play in a Sunday League game and would give it his all.'

Former Cosmos captain Keith Eddy explains, 'The players in New York took it very seriously, although there were instances at some teams when players didn't do that. It wasn't like the Football League, where there were win bonuses or appearance money. You got paid whether you won or played or not, so it was party time for some guys.'

Scottish international Jimmy Gabriel, former head coach of the Seattle Sounders, recalls, 'By 1978 and '79 everyone was going for higher-class players instead of guys who just wanted to give it their all for a couple of years and then finish. We were looking at 27 and 28 year olds and it became a bit of a holiday for some. They were picking their games a bit. Also, instead of players from the lower divisions who were delighted to be playing against Pelé or Geoff Hurst, it was guys who had been playing First Division anyway. Something was left behind when they came over. These guys weren't as willing to sign autographs, or go to places where fans were having a drink. We started losing the connection with the fans. At times you had to look at the players and say, "Are you giving me everything?" Maybe I should have sent some of them home and in the end it cost me a bit as a head coach. It got out of hand.'

Alan Merrick adds, 'Some players didn't really look for opportunities to contribute. They just came over for a giggle and to get some spending money. They were detrimental to the game and we found them out pretty quickly. They were just mercenaries.'

Whitecaps coach Tony Waiters reveals, 'Players realised that public relations was part of the job and most of them accepted it. But one player who came from Ipswich in '78 didn't fit into the North American scene. He thought it was going to be a busman's holiday, so we sent him back.'

John Best helped to build successful teams in Seattle, as head coach, and at Vancouver, where the team he constructed as general manager was almost exclusively British. 'We took 10 per cent of the budget for the team and put it towards scouting and recruiting. We had local scouts and we also paid guys in England. Without the budget of the New York Cosmos, I felt we needed to do better than anyone else in scouting and assessment. What was the player's value to the team, his impact, and what would we accomplish with him? That was the basis of evaluating contracts. Obviously, the rest of the league also influenced us. Players would knock on your door saying, "If so-and-so in California is getting this, I should get this." You could not always control your own labour costs.'

When British players came face to face with the game in America, it was like being greeted by a relative who had settled across the water and picked up a mid-Atlantic accent and a new dress sense. The changes may have been small and cosmetic but they were the first thing you noticed and seemed to induce a complete personality change.

As well as the colourful kits – 'uniforms', as the Americans insisted on calling them – there were the artificial pitches. In the days before Queens Park Rangers, Luton and Oldham introduced synthetic playing surfaces to the Football League, few players had experienced such conditions outside of five-a-side games in training.

Former Aston Villa defender Neil Rioch, who played on plastic in Portland, recalls, 'Our stadium had Tartan Turf, which, instead of having blades like Astroturf had a knitted surface. I never got used to it because the ball would bounce too high and far. Our goalkeeper, Jim Cumbes, had a terrific kick and got nicknamed Big Foot. He would kick the ball and it would bounce on the edge of the opposition area and over the crossbar.'

Fellow Portland defender Mick Hoban adds, 'You had to wear under-shorts because the biggest problem was getting infections from what was on the turf – dirt, grime, even cigarette ends. It required better technique because if you hit a 30-yard pass it had to go within a certain margin. If you played the ball short it bounced up around your chest. It became a midfield game. You couldn't hit the ball inside a full-back because it ran out of bounds.'

Former Derby centre-forward Roger Davies, who thrived in Seattle's Kingdome, argues, 'If you could play a little bit it suited you, but if you were a defender who liked to dive in and kick people it didn't. The touch play suited me and if you had a bad first touch the ball went away. The only problem was that, with the field being laid on concrete, it was very hard and it took you longer to get fit again after injuries because of the pressure on your joints and ligaments.'

Ironically, former Ipswich striker Trevor Whymark found that the Vancouver Whitecaps' artificial surface eventually cured him of the after-effects of the knee ligament injury that had led him to quit English football. 'Everything in my knee had dried up and I could not get full traction in the knee joint. For the first half a dozen games in Vancouver I got strange sensations in my calf and back muscles and put it down to playing on Astroturf. Then we had a training session and it was wet and I slipped over. I fell back on my knee, sat on my ankles and felt terrific pain in my knee. I thought, "Christ, it has gone again." By the time I hobbled to the physio's room it had eased up. It seemed to have loosened everything up and from then on I had no more problems.'

Together with the large number of artificial surfaces on which games were played, it was the 35-yard offside rule that made NASL football different to the rest of the world. Former Arsenal and Leicester midfielder Jon Sammels, who spent two seasons in Vancouver, says, 'You had much more space and I like to think it showed who could play. Give a bad player a lot of space and he will look bad. If you were the sort of player who relied on physical power you could not do it over there. We played against teams who had well-known British players and some of our Canadian boys couldn't believe they were seeing so-and-so from a big English club because their game could not be adapted.'

Phil Woosnam had been pushing for a new offside law since telling reporters in England in 1969, 'From what I can see of football in Britain it is time for drastic changes to be made if the game is to stay alive.' He explains, 'The back lines were all squeezing up to the halfway line and taking all the space for the creative players. It was happening right through the First Division. Another reason for bringing in a new rule was because so many of our fields were very narrow. Good players can't play unless they have space and they were getting squeezed both ways.'

English football had briefly experimented in the 1971–72 Watney Cup, a short-lived pre-season competition contested by the two highest-scoring teams in each of the four divisions. No offside was given outside of an area marked by a line drawn across from the edge of the penalty area and Woosnam was keen for the NASL to be similarly ground-breaking. 'We had always told FIFA they could use us to experiment with the rules and they said this was the one they would like to start with, so they approved it in the first place. Then, in 1982, they said we had been trying it for several years and it was time to go back to how everyone else was doing it.'

Opinions are diverse over the success of the experiment. Keith Eddy says, 'I loved the offside rule. Now I only had to get to the 35-yard line and I found it a stroll. I could have played until 40. After every game at Sheffield United I was mentally and physically drained, but I could have played two games at a time in the NASL.'

Veteran Football League midfielder Terry Garbett felt he had taken up a brand-new sport when he joined the New York Cosmos. 'I was surprised at the lack of pace. I remember in one of our first games getting the ball and knocking it off. All of a sudden someone shouted to me that I had plenty of time. Next ball, I turned and looked and there was no one near me. After years of players pounding on top of you, to turn around and have seven or eight yards of space was a strange experience.'

Striker Derek Smethurst describes the NASL offside system as 'the greatest thing that ever happened'. He adds, 'Even people who were intimidators on the field had a hard time because it opened up the field so much. But I think some of them liked it because it gave them the chance to play. You would not bypass players, so even guys like Tommy Smith would get the ball a hundred times. I didn't hear a complaint about it.'

Smethurst clearly never spoke to Steve Earle, who argues, 'It was the biggest fallacy in the world that it would create more goalscoring chances. If you are a forward who relies on pace and likes to get behind defenders you couldn't because there was no space. If you played alongside a big man, all his flick-ons went straight to the keeper. I saw some guys come over and it ruined their game because they couldn't spin and get balls over the top.'

Former Chelsea winger Charlie Cooke adds, 'I used to get frustrated with the way they experimented with things without any qualms. I am old-fashioned. I didn't think the offside rule made any difference.' Ex-Derby and Nottingham Forest forward John O'Hare concurs, saying 'Because the league was full of people who played with the old rule all their lives, they didn't change their game that much. I didn't think it was that beneficial.'

Bob McNab, Arsenal and England full-back, contends, 'The 35-yard offside rule was like communism – a great idea but it did not work. You just ended up with three defenders versus two forwards on each 35-yard line. There was so much space and teams would just drop back behind the ball. It was extremely difficult to hit long through balls into space behind the last defenders because on Astroturf the ball just keeps rolling through to the goalkeeper. As a defender you are always conscious of the deep threat, but you could mark tighter because you were not worried about the ball over the head.'

Another identifying element of the NASL was the sudden-death shoot-outs that were introduced in 1974 to eliminate drawn games. At first it was a penalty kick competition after 90 minutes, changing the following year to allow 15 minutes of sudden-death extra-time before resorting to spot kicks. In 1977, the rule changed again to introduce the 35-yard against-the-clock competitions that became one of the NASL's trademarks.

Unlike the offside rule, the shoot-outs were enjoyed by most players. And Woosnam pointed out their success, noting that in the three seasons immediately before their introduction 33 per cent of games ended level after 90 minutes, but in the five years after the introduction of sudden death the figure had dropped to 18 per cent. Woosnam cited the elimination of the desire among coaches to play for a draw.

Don Megson says, 'To be sat on the line watching the shoot-out gave you a huge adrenalin rush. The first game I was involved in was against Seattle and the league had brought over a referee for his first season. He was disallowing goals because the ball had not gone over the line inside five seconds. He didn't know the rule was that you had to get your shot away in five seconds.'

Alan Birchenall adds, 'I liked the shoot-out because there was a bit of skill there. Do you take the keeper on or try to slide it past? The Americans were 25 years ahead with that rule.'

According to Smethurst, 'Sudden death destroyed the idea of being defensive. When you played for a draw it was for the opportunity to win the game. I don't remember missing too many in shoot-outs. You could hit them from ten yards or there were guys who would chip it, which keepers used to dread. I used to run left of the ball and stroke a bender two feet off the ground to the right and try to get the keeper caught on a forward step. It didn't have to be 60 miles an hour, guys like Jimmy Greaves knew that all their lives. A short, quick, forward release without back swing. Players like that, and chippers, didn't have too much bother. I have never met a player who likes penalties, but the shoot-out was different. There was not the same tension because you were released from that as you were running.'

Scotland international goalkeeper Bobby Clark played in the

NASL for San Antonio in the final season of traditional penalties and says, 'It was one of those things you lived with and it was exciting to do it. It was a chance to be a hero. I remember one game at Hartford and we had this enormous thunderstorm in overtime. They cancelled the game and we came out next morning for the penalty shoot-out. We won and then flew off somewhere else. I must have had an early night that night.'

Paul Hammond, who played in the 35-yard shoot-out era, says, 'I didn't like it but I agreed with it being introduced. Some guys would just blast it. I would try to stay on my line as long as possible and come out in the last few seconds and block them.'

The American sporting obsession with statistics also found its way into the NASL, with everything from assists to goalkeepers' goals-conceded-per-game averages being logged. Noel Cantwell felt it could be counter-productive for the players, especially the Americans. 'People there were very interested in stats and thought they had played well if they had an assist. But coaches knew who had helped to make a goal or who had been to blame.'

The weather during American summers presented another big difference for players who learned their trade in the hard school of bitter English nights in mid-winter. Former Crystal Palace defender Stewart Jump, who had to adapt to the heat of Tampa, says, 'We would play at home in 94 degrees and 80 per cent humidity, and I remember one game in Washington when it was 107 degrees on the field. The players had heatstroke at the end. Astroturf held the heat and you could feel it through your shoes.'

Ex-Everton forward David Irving's abiding memory of a short spell in Tulsa is the heat. 'It was 100 degrees at night and the heat on the Astoturf was 130 degrees. On TV they were actually frying an egg on the pitch before the game to demonstrate how hot it was.'

Alan Birchenall remembers playing a game for San Jose at Hawaii, where 'at one end all you could see was the crossbar shimmering in the heat'. But he also remembers one of the advantages of football in warm weather. 'Every weekend there would be four or five pool parties going on. And you had to train in the evenings so you would finish training at nine o'clock and then go out with the lads. It was tremendous.'

For Scotland striker John O'Hare, training sessions during his two hot summers at the Dallas Tornado proved tougher than he had been accustomed to under Brian Clough at Derby and Nottingham Forest. 'Cloughie didn't work his players hard,' he recalls. 'We worked hard in pre-season, but once the season started we didn't have too many hard slogs. But our coach in Dallas, Al

Miller, was really disciplined and the heat made it difficult.'

With the huge distances between teams, training sessions had to be scheduled around the demands of travel, one of the less attractive aspects of the NASL for the visiting player. Charlie Cooke says, 'I loved playing in America, but the travelling took some of the fun out of it at times. You were playing twice a week and playing all over the country. It was not like a bus trip from Milwall to Chelsea. It is not just the time on the plane. There is getting to the airport, checking in, waiting for luggage. When you are three-quarters of the way through a season you are getting a little tired of it.'

To relieve that boredom, the British players created a school-trip atmosphere. Public relations director Vince Casey highlighted Chris Turner as the practical joker of the New England Tea Men in media releases and the former Peterborough defender rarely failed to live up to his billing. Casey recalls, 'We had a guy on our staff called Arthur Smith. He was a balding guy who smoked and he could put on an austere British-type manner. On one trip we had to walk out to the tarmac to get on the plane and Chris had put Arthur in a wheelchair. He was flopping over to one side with a cigarette hanging out of his mouth. Chris told the guy taking the tickets, "This is my father, he has been very ill. Can we get him on the plane early?" They got a big runway for the wheelchair and after getting everything ready the airline guy opens the door and Chris and Dennis Viollet just let go of Arthur and he goes shooting down and crashes onto the tarmac. I thought the attendant was going to die and he thought he was going to lose his job. Arthur lies there for 30 seconds and then gets up and marches up the stairs into the plane.

'Turner was also master of the 50-cent trick. As somebody was rushing through the airport for their plane Chris would flip the coin so that it would ping off the ground. Ninety per cent of the time the guy rushing to get the plane would stop, thinking the money had fallen out of his pocket. They would insist it was their half dollar and sometimes Chris would argue and sometimes let them have it.'

Turner was the victim on one occasion, however, as Casey recalls. 'In Anaheim, we used to take vans or buses to practice and once in a while a limo would come. I was in front of the hotel and a limo pulls up for a wedding. Turner comes down after a nap and all he had on was very short shorts. He sees me and asks if this is the transportation and I say, "Yes." Chris piles in and sits in the back, thinking, "How great is this? Going to practice in a limo." It was dark in there and you couldn't see his blue shorts, so he looked naked. So the limo driver comes out and sees what he thinks is a naked tall guy sitting in the back of the limo. He went crazy and was going to call the police!'

The light-hearted atmosphere around the Tea Men was typical of the mood among the British players in the NASL. For the most part well-paid and well-treated, to be an NASL player in the mid- to late-'70s was not a bad way to be earning a living. But it was not all parties and practical jokes. The players discovered that when they decided it was time to organise a union.

17. ☆ Strikers United

For the first few weeks of the 1979 NASL season, the term 'striker' took on a whole new meaning. Maybe it was a sign of having arrived in the higher echelon of American sport, but soccer found itself embroiled in the kind of labour dispute that was becoming common in the major US leagues. Ironically, the seeds for a withdrawal of labour that put NASL players, albeit briefly, on picket lines instead of forward lines were sown by Ed Garvey, head of the National Football League Players Association (NFLPA). In 1977, Garvey, a labour lawyer, approached Washington Diplomats player John Kerr and suggested that the country's soccer players should form a union along the lines of the one put together to represent the NFL workforce.

Added to the payroll of the NFLPA, Kerr met with representatives of every team in Washington DC and the North American Soccer League Players Association (NASLPA) was formed. With Garvey and Kerr as its directors, the union was denied recognition by the team owners, who objected to a union for their sport being run by the NFL. Having been denied official recognition for the better part of two years, the NASLPA asked its members to vote for strike action at the beginning of the 1979 season. The strike was a brief one, lasting only five days, and affected only one set of games – those scheduled for 14 April – but it catapulted the union into the media.

'It was a frustrating time because we were aware that some clubs were getting edgy,' says Phil Woosnam, the NASL commissioner. 'The players' union pushed some people over the top. Owners worried that it would get too expensive and that there would be constant demands from the union. It came at the wrong time.'

While the league and the owners considered the long-term

implications, the initial problem for the clubs was how to play the games without a full complement of players. In Fort Lauderdale, due to face the Washington Diplomats, George Best and newly signed Peruvian World Cup star Teofilio Cubillas crossed the picket line to play in the Strikers' 4–0 defeat. But coach Ron Newman was forced out of retirement at the age of 43 to play for a team that included his son, Guy, assistant coach David Chadwick and a handful of other players making their only appearance of the season. 'The players had promised us they would play but said they had been threatened that they would lose their visas and be sent back to Europe if they didn't go on strike,' says Newman. 'Phil Woosnam said that we must field a team, so we got local kids, including a goalkeeper who had hardly played. What pissed me off was that at the end of season we lost our division by nine points. We could have got those points in that game. Nobody ever said thanks or gave me the game back.'

The response to the strike call among the players was mixed. The English-dominated Tulsa Roughnecks and Vancouver Whitecaps were largely unaffected, while Rodney Marsh was one of the few players to withdraw his labour at the Tampa Bay Rowdies. The Seattle Sounders faced an almost total walk-out, forcing another coach, Jimmy Gabriel, back on to the field, while the players that Don Megson fielded in the Portland Timbers' 2–0 loss to a makeshift Minnesota Kicks were, without exception, playing in their only game of the season.

The New England Tea Men's British contingent was split, with Peter Simpson, Keith Weller, Brian Alderson and Roger Gibbins providing a foundation of first-choice players. But new recruits were needed as well and public relations director Vince Casey remembers accompanying coaches Noel Cantwell and Dennis Viollet on an emergency scouting mission to the area's Portuguese soccer communities. 'We were friends with the Portuguese writers covering the local league and we went down to a restaurant to meet these guys who were going to play with us in Philadelphia a couple of days later. To be polite, Dennis asked if they would like something to drink, thinking they would order ginger ale or Coca-Cola. They answered, "Scotch and soda, Budweiser and a gin and tonic." This in front of the coach they were going to play for two nights later. I still have a great team picture of us in Philadelphia and there is one guy in it with a huge pot belly. I think he was the guy who ordered Scotch and soda. He only lasted the first half.'

Public reaction to the players' strike was predictably negative. Marsh recalls, 'It turned the fans off because soccer wasn't ingrained in them. They thought, "Who are these bunch of guys who've come over and gone on strike? Who do they think they are?" That was a problem. I was asked what my opinion was and I said, "I'll just do whatever the majority of the players at this club want to do because we have to be unified."'

The strike ended with still no sign of official recognition for the union, leading the NASLPA to file a grievance with the National Labor Relations Board. Finally, on 1 September, that body would officially recognise the NASLPA as the union of the league's playing force. The NASL, though, still refused to deal with Garvey, viewing him as a front for the NFL. The league was ordered to begin negotiating a deal with the players' union that would set the standard for salaries and playing conditions around the league and, despite an unsuccessful venture into the US Court of Appeals, the owners were forced to comply. It would take until early 1981, following several other legal battles, for the agreement to be concluded.

While the legal battles were kicking off and the Vancouver Whitecaps were preparing their run to their first NASL championship, the league had been celebrating a two-year deal with ABC, a marked increase on the exposure provided by the previous TVS package. ABC would air nine broadcasts, including the Soccer Bowl.

Viewers of NASL action, in the stands and on television, found themselves watching more of the world's biggest stars in 1979. As well as Johan Cruyff's decision to play in Los Angeles, West German legend Gerd Müller, top scorer in the 1970 World Cup finals and scorer of the winner in his country's 1974 final victory against the Netherlands, was joining Best and Cubillas in a star-studded Fort Lauderdale forward line. By the end of the season Müller had scored 19 goals, while Cubillas had found the net 16 times and added 18 assists. Coach Chadwick recalls, 'I had never seen double touch play like Cubillas. He would open his foot looking like he was going to pass and then he would turn it and flick it inside you. When Ron Newman signed Müller and Cubillas I don't think he ever thought they could be so deadly. They couldn't talk to each other in the locker room, but they could work together so well they didn't need to communicate.'

Keith Weller, who teamed up with Müller the following season after leaving New England, adds, 'Gerd was a funny character. Most of the guys from non-English speaking countries picked up English quickly, but he either couldn't or didn't want to speak English. He would go off at you in German.'

In Washington, Gordon Bradley was beginning his second season in charge of the Diplomats after ending his seven-season connection with the New York Cosmos. In 1978, his additions to the squad had included ex-Newcastle man Paul Cannell, who finished as the club's top scorer with 14 goals, and former Villa winger Ray Graydon, whose goal against Norwich had won the 1975 League Cup final. But he discovered that trying to sign a world figure of the Beckenbauer or Cruyff stature was a perilous pastime.

He recalls, 'Cesar Menotti, the Argentina manager, said to me at one time, "If you feel like coming down to Buenos Aires and talking to Diego Maradona, it might be the right time to move." That was when he was 21. I spent quite a lot of time with him but it didn't pan out as we had hoped for. Menotti's office was telling us it was a good time to get him out, but he wanted to spend a couple more years in Argentina and eventually went to Napoli. Menotti was a father figure to him and was all for trying to persuade him to come to the US.'

The bid to sign Maradona ended only in disappointment. But when, a few months later, Bradley went south again to attempt to sign Daniel Passarella, who had lifted the World Cup for Argentina in 1978, it almost ended in disaster. 'I went to their equivalent of the FA Cup final, which was played home and away. River Plate won the first game 4–1 and were going to Rosario Central in an almost meaningless game. I went to the game with an Argentinian friend called Victor and I went wearing red and white, a red collar and a white shirt – I didn't realise they were the colours of the River Plate shirt.

'River Plate won 3–1 and after the game a person knocked me on the shoulder from behind. When I turned, he smacked me right in the face. My friend looked back and I pointed at someone. Victor went after the guy and caught him, an 18-year-old kid. Police cars came and guns were firing and the whole thing was going upside down. We were thrown into a police car and driven up a one-way street the wrong way. They were firing guns into the air and putting guns to our heads. They drove us into the countryside and were threatening to kill Victor. He said to them, "Do you know who this guy is?" They took us to a jail three hours outside Buenos Aires. It had a clay floor and bars and we were put in different cells. I was thinking that nobody in the world knew where I was. We were frightened, to say the least. Victor said to the lieutenant at the jail, "You are going to be in so much trouble if you don't listen to me." The lieutenant had some knowledge about what was going on and let Victor make a call to his uncle and he called a lieutenant in another part of Argentina. The other lieutenant was told by Victor's uncle, "You had better let them go."

'Sure enough, calls were made and we were let out. Victor said everything was OK, except for the guy who had been pointing the gun at us. "I want him to apologise," Victor said. I replied, "Victor, shut your mouth and let's get out of here." But the guy was made to apologise in Spanish to me and now he had to take us back. Victor said, "If that guy is going to take us back, we have got to head straight back to Buenos Aires instead of the ground."'

Bradley survived to hold meetings with Passarella and River Plate officials at the Sheraton Hotel in Buenos Aires. 'We were offering $1.5 million and I was on the phone almost every minute with Madison Square Garden, who owned the Washington team. River Plate said he was worth more, so we offered $1.7 million. Their attorney said, "Do you want to go to $2 million?" Passarella said, "Coach, get me out of this country." I told him I couldn't help him, that the club wanted $2 million and we had offered $1.7 million. He cried on my shoulder. The hotel was filled with press and they found out I was negotiating. There was a headline in a paper, "British bandito trying to steal our captain."'

The most significant arrival in the American capital for the 1979 season was English attacker Alan Green, returning to Washington for the first time in two years after a permanent transfer from Coventry. Backed up by Cannell's 10 goals, Green's haul of 16 helped the Diplomats into the play-offs, where their hopes were immediately ended by Los Angeles.

Another effective NASL scorer was Jeff Bourne, who tallied 18 goals and 15 assists for an Atlanta Chiefs side that had moved home from Colorado but was never in the play-off hunt. Bourne's tally took his record to 54 goals in three NASL seasons, compared to 14 goals in 86 League games at Derby and Crystal Palace.

Bourne, who joined Derby from Burton Albion, admits, 'I was just a local lad in Derby and I think I was a bit in awe of everyone when I was there. We had 14 internationals in the squad. I think playing in America, away from the spotlight, being a bigger fish in a smaller pond, brought out the best in me.'

Having celebrated his 30th birthday during the 1978 season, Bourne, then a Dallas player, was asked to guest for the New York Cosmos on a European tour. 'I'd heard that their coach, Eddie Firmani, fancied me as a player and asked Dallas if they would allow me to go with them. During the tour, the coach, Al Miller, called and said, "I have sold you to Chicago." We had an argument and I said, "I am not going anywhere." I think the club were in difficulties and realised I was one of their assets. In the end I went to Atlanta, where Ted Turner was the new owner.'

Bourne had played for an American coach at Dallas, but found

Atlanta's Dan Wood difficult to get on with. 'He was just a college coach and didn't have much idea about the professional game. When we went on a road trip, he said to me, "It's your turn to get the bags from the baggage claim." I said, "Fuck off. I will get my own, but not the American kids'." Later in the season, he asked everyone what they thought was going wrong. The Americans said, "We don't like the way Jeff Bourne takes the mickey out of us in training." I used to nutmeg them because if they had their legs open it was the natural thing to do. They had to learn to deal with things like that.'

It was halfway through the season before the Detroit Express were able to welcome back Trevor Francis, fresh from his European Cup heroics, but he proved well worth waiting for as he scored 14 goals in 14 games. Another cup-winning goalscorer landed in Detroit in the shape of Roger Osborne, Ipswich's match-winner in their FA Cup triumph a year earlier. Keith Furphy top-scored with fourteen goals, while former Scotland striker Ted MacDougall added nine after his late arrival to partner Francis. Now 32, MacDougall had hit the headlines with Bournemouth in 1971 when he scored a record nine goals in an FA Cup tie against Margate. His high-profile move to Manchester United had not worked out, leading to a transfer to West Ham after six months and only five goals. A nine-month residence at Upton Park proved no more successful but MacDougall's touch returned at Norwich and Southampton, where his combined total of League goals was a more than respectable 93 in 198 games. Veteran full-backs Mick Coop, the ex-Coventry man, and Tony Dunne, a European Cup-winner with Manchester United 11 years before the success of Francis and Forest, featured in the back four, but Detroit once again got no further than the first round of the play-offs.

At the Houston Hurricane, Finnish coach Timo Liekoski brought about a revival and his team posted 22 wins, the most of any team in the American Conference. Defender Stewart Jump, in his second year with a team short on star names, says, 'Timo bought in some good players. We were able to run and work hard. When you are playing with people with a good attitude, it goes an awful long way.'

Houston, though, were to suffer their first home loss of the season to Philadelphia in the play-offs and suffered an early exit as Scottish striker Davie Robb found the net in each game after finishing the season as the Fury's top scorer with 16 goals. Lining up alongside Robb was Frank Worthington, another of those crowd-pleasers whose ability and personality made them an ideal fit for the NASL. Beginning his career at Huddersfield and being denied a move to Liverpool when he failed the Anfield medical, Worthington had earned eight England caps during five years at Leicester, where the mere numbers of his Filbert Street career – 72 goals in just over 200 games – could not begin to do justice to the balance, skill and arrogance of one of the First Division's great showmen.

Worthington, who had spent two seasons at Bolton by the time he arrived in Philadelphia, succeeded where Peter Osgood had failed a year earlier, notching ten goals and seven assists during the regular season and scoring one more in the play-offs before the Fury's title hopes were ended by the Rowdies. 'We had a bad side,' he recalls. 'Our coach was Yugoslav and didn't speak English and it all went wrong. There was a big controversy after the game in Toronto. They needed nine points to reach the play-offs and we wanted three. They won 4–3, but under the American points system we both got our quota. At the end, both teams celebrated and then came suggestions that the match was rigged, which it wasn't.'

Alan Hudson was another of that group of '70s stars whose glittering skills stood out in a decade that featured its fair share of dull, dour and downright ugly football. It seems inevitable that such a wayward talent would follow Marsh and Best to the NASL, although it took until 1979, after a falling-out with Arsenal, before it happened.

A teenage sensation with Chelsea, Hudson missed out on the 1970 FA Cup final, and a possible World Cup place, because of an ankle injury. He re-established himself as the midfield genius of one of the game's most exciting teams, helping Chelsea to win the 1971 European Cup-Winners' cup and qualify again for Wembley, where they lost in the 1972 League Cup final to Stoke. It was to Stoke that Hudson was transferred for £240,000 early in 1974, two months before Peter Osgood also left Stamford Bridge for Southampton. A member of Don Revie's England team that beat world champions West Germany 2–0 at Wembley in 1975, Hudson played only once more for his country and was sold to Arsenal late in 1976 for £200,000. He was in danger of becoming a forgotten man before forcing his way back into the Arsenal team for the 1977–78 season and inspiring the Gunners to the FA Cup final with several months of sublime play, earning a brief recall to the England party. But after clashing with Gunners manager Terry Neill in the aftermath of the Londoners' surprise Wembley defeat, Hudson's Highbury days were numbered and a £100,000 transfer to Seattle was arranged. His career in top-class English football was effectively over at the age of 27, although he would return eventually to play a few more games for Stoke.

Hudson's new contract doubled his Highbury pay packet and took him to a land where he 'settled in as if I was born to be there'. In his book, *The Working Man's Ballet*, Hudson writes, 'This really was the best experience of my life so far, with the opportunity to play week in, week out, against the best players in the world.'

Hudson's return from his first NASL season was 11 assists, many of them setting up ex-Chelsea teammate Derek Smethurst, who led the side with 13 goals after escaping his purgatory at San Diego. Former long-serving Luton man John Ryan contributed 12 goals from right-back, while Ron Davies marked the final year of his NASL career by scoring only 1 goal in 22 games. At the end of a disappointing season for the club, the Sounders' owners suggested to coach Jimmy Gabriel that it was time to move on.

There were several other coaching changes afoot in the NASL, including the end of John Sewell's five-year reign at the California Surf. Former Palace teammate, Peter Wall, was asked to take over. 'We did OK in '78, but the crowds were not what the club expected,' Wall recalls. 'At the end of the year they decided the team was not attractive enough nor had enough entertaining players. There was a large German population in Anaheim and the management thought John was resistant about getting German players.

'We started slowly in 1979 and the general manager called me in and said he didn't like the way we were playing. They were going to fire John and offer me the job, but I said I couldn't take it because John had brought me here. But they got me together with one of the main owners and, after a long meeting, I said, "OK, I will do it, but I am not going to sign a new contract. Just pay me so many dollars each time we win." We lost six of the first seven games! I did change our style of play and had more attacking players, instead of being a more English-type defensive team who would win 1–0. I thought it was better to lose 4–3 and get the odd win.'

Laurie Abrahams arrived from Tulsa, to whom he had been traded from New England in the off-season, scoring eight goals in ten games for the Surf. He recalls, 'My first game at Memphis, we were two goals down in no time but won 3–2. I scored a goal and then they took me off, but it was a mistake – they were trying to take off someone with a similar number. Tampa and Fort Lauderdale battered us for six goals each but it didn't wear the team down at all. If we had been beaten like that in Tulsa heads would have gone down, but Peter did a good job in that respect. The Surf was a young team, the guys lived there for good and the majority seemed to get on.'

Gerry Ingram scored ten goals after a trade from Chicago and, with six wins in the last seven games, the Surf made it to the play-offs, where they were beaten in two games by San Diego.

Another coaching change occurred in Memphis, where Eddie McCreadie handed the baton to his former Chelsea teammate Charlie Cooke, although not by choice. McCreadie, capped 23 times by Scotland, was a popular figure with the Rogues' public, but lost the support of team owner Harry Mangurian as a result of the players' strike. McCreadie had been left with only one regular player for the April 14 game at Detroit and his decision to put on a uniform himself for a game that the Rogues lost 6–0 was interpreted as his way of sending a statement to the stay-at-home players. Mangurian was reportedly unhappy with the way things had transpired around the strike and fired McCreadie a month later.

Cooke says, 'I don't know what happened but suddenly Eddie wasn't manager any more. By that time I had got used to the way the clubs acted. They seemed to act on a whim, whatever took the owner's fancy. It wasn't like in Britain where you had a contract and they stuck to it. I didn't really know why I had been traded from Los Angeles because I thought I had been doing OK. That was one of the weaknesses of the league, that you never really knew what went on.' The Rogues would finish with the worst record in the league, only six wins in thirty games.

Meanwhile, a change in the regime at Minnesota did nothing to knock the Kicks off their course to a division title. Freddie Goodwin had moved into the role of general manager, with Roy McCrohan, a Norwich City stalwart during the '50s, taking the position of head coach. The usual haul of goals from Alan Willey and Ron Futcher, 21 and 14 respectively, saw the Kicks cruise to the play-offs, where they under-achieved again, beaten twice by Tulsa.

In his first season in charge of the Roughnecks, former Derby winger and Vancouver assistant coach Alan Hinton built a team that, despite more defeats than victories, made it to the play-off quarter-finals. Hinton had added to the British players he inherited by signing former England left-back and Baseball Ground teammate David Nish, whose £225,000 transfer from Leicester in July 1972 had made him Britain's most expensive player. Defenders Terry Darracott and Bob 'Sammy' Chapman were less heralded First Division defenders at Everton and Nottingham Forest respectively, while winger Alan Woodward's powerful shooting had earned him 158 League goals for Sheffield United.

Midfielder Steve Powell and centre-forward Roger Davies had played alongside Hinton at Derby.

Davies, a tall, gangly striker who had never quite managed to dislodge John O'Hare from the Derby number nine jersey, had been relieved to escape from Leicester, the club that had brought him back to England after a move to Belgium's FC Bruges. Plagued by a back injury, Davies had managed only half a dozen goals in 26 games for Leicester, but he beat that total by two in fewer games in his first NASL season. Wayne Hughes, a young midfielder from West Brom, scored 12 goals, while Abrahams struck 10 times before his departure.

Hinton, however, was not to get the chance to build on his first season, despite the efforts of his loyal players. 'It was a strange year,' says Davies. 'They had promised people they would do this and that, but things wouldn't happen. Then Alan got the sack. They said it was down to poor results and I don't know whether that was true or not. The players heard what was coming and we rang up radio stations and spoke up for Alan and tried to pre-empt it.'

Abrahams, however, argues that the atmosphere in Tulsa had been far from conducive to winning. 'There was a lot of finger pointing and I am not saying I wasn't part of it,' he admits. 'The players were only there on loan and were thinking about going home.'

The Portland Timbers' 1979 campaign was to be their last under Don Megson, who recalls an unhappy year. 'I went over there with a lad called Keith Williams, who was a pioneer. But the money situation was becoming too much for him and he was not a multi-millionaire, so he sold out.

'The new people were not really on the ball. Gates were not going up, money was not increasing for better players and I couldn't do the things I wanted. They made me go out and look for a world star because everyone else had one. I looked at Holland's Robbie Rensenbrink but I found out he'd just had a cartilage operation and was not ready. I said, "He is not right for us." The next day we are sat in the general manager's office and he says he has signed him. As a manager from an English background, that was not the way I was used to working. Besides, the Portland crowds liked players like Peter Withe because they liked to see someone jumping and challenging and heading the ball. I said, "Most people don't know who Rensenbrink is and they don't know the difference between him and someone who will fight all day for them." As the 1980 season was starting, my wife's mother died and I decided to go back home.'

Megson may not have seen the new season in Portland, but

Rensenbrink, the Dutch World Cup forward, was in place to attempt to brighten up an attack that had been led by Clyde Best's eight goals in 1979.

In Toronto, where a change of ownership had seen the controversial Metros-Croatia name replaced by the more acceptable 'Blizzard' before the 1979 season, Keith Eddy had been installed as coach, taking his team to the play-offs, where they fell in the first round to his former New York Cosmos team. The biggest name in the line-up was Peter Lorimer, whose fierce shot every schoolboy in every playground in England tried to copy in the late '60s and early '70s. He had scored more than 150 League goals in a 16-year Leeds career, winning 21 Scotland caps and countless medals as a part of Don Revie's great, but unloved, team. The other British players in the team included Jim Bone, the former Partick Thistle and Norwich forward, who had earned a couple of Scotland caps, and the veteran NASL defender Charlie Mitchell.

Eddy recalls, 'When I took the job five weeks before the season they had two players and I got rid of them. It was fun for about a year and a half. I was all over the world looking for players on a shoestring. We went to play the Cosmos and I looked at my team, and my star midfielder was from Bath. Lorimer was the only real player I had. My biggest coup was going and getting him. He and Jimmy Adamson, who was manager at Leeds, hated each other and I got him for nothing. Jimmy was glad to get him out of his hair.

'We started with a won–lost record of 1–7 and all of a sudden we turned it around and won seven games. It was the same goddamn team. In the end the highs were too high for me and the lows too low. It came to a head a couple of years later when my daughter came to me and said her mum had told her not to bother me if we lost. I went down to the club the next day and quit.'

The 1978 MVP, Tea Men striker Mike Flanagan, remained in England in 1979, where he finished the summer by signing for Crystal Palace for £722,000, thus setting up his partnership with Clive Allen – a dream for all those headline writers old enough to remember the days of the music hall. Without their leading striker, the Tea Men failed to score as they lost their first five games. They missed out on the play-offs, Keith Weller finishing as top scorer with nine goals.

By the time Weller arrived in Fort Lauderdale during the 1980 season, the Strikers had parted company with Ron Newman. After three seasons in which the Strikers qualified for the play-offs every year, Newman was removed from his position at the completion of the 1979 campaign following a clash with owner Joe Robbie. 'The press were saying we should have won the championship with players like Best, Müller and Cubillas,' says Newman. 'Those players would give the fans something to watch and could add something to the team, but they would not help you win a championship.

'I was asked to go to a meeting with the owner. There were other things I was upset about and needed straightening out. The meeting became a focal point in the media and everything the press said in my favour, Joe thought I was saying. He hated me more and more but he didn't want to fire me because he would have to pay me. They wanted me to accept the position of director of player personnel to get me out of my coaching contract and they called a press conference about it. I told the press, "It's an important position so I guess it must have an attractive contract and I am looking forward to seeing it. But I can't do that until the old one has been satisfied." They had no intention of offering me a better contract. They would have let me hold the new position for a month and decided it was not working out and got rid of me.

'Eventually it came down to our attorneys to sort it out, but it was like sharks versus minnows. My attorney told me that my contract was watertight but said that Robbie was so wealthy he would just keep it in the courts rather than pay me. Which was exactly what he did. It seems that Robbie would only be liable for my contract between jobs and, as I couldn't afford to be out of work for long, his plan worked and by the time I paid attorney fees I only got a few dollars. An interesting side story was that while the court case was going on, the radio announced one morning that a top attorney of Robbie's had been stabbed seven times by a house guest. I remember jokingly warning people not to mess with me! The attorney survived.'

The Strikers' British players mourned Newman's departure. 'There was no reason for Ron to go; it was a bad decision,' recalls David Irving. 'We lost a lot when Ron left. He was a big part of the Strikers and, even if not in a coaching capacity, he could still have been there. He put his heart and soul into the club and it was a sad day for the Strikers when he went, and poor business.'

Overall, the NASL's 1979 season was one of ups and downs. Many feared the early-season strike would have a lasting effect on the public's support for the league, although attendance showed only a slight dip and the season reached an exciting conclusion with the Vancouver Whitecaps ending the New York Cosmos' two-year dominance.

But there were obvious problems developing at some franchises. The large turnover of coaches demonstrated that – as do Steve Earle's memories of the Tulsa Roughnecks' winter trip to Europe, which ended up as chaotic as a Sunday League team's end-of-season jaunt to Majorca. 'By the time we got to Holland they were selling off the players. We started the tour with 18 and only had 12 when we got to England. People were interested in young Wayne Hughes and the club needed the money, so we kept giving him the ball to make him look good. He had a nightmare. He went from a £100,000 player to £60,000 in one game. We were due to play on a Tuesday, Wednesday and Thursday at Leicester, Derby and Lincoln. We got Jon Sammels, Keith Weller and Kevin Hector to play and drew with Derby and Leicester. They'd had enough and didn't go to Lincoln. We were left with a bunch of Americans and old farts like me and we got beat 9–2.'

Despite such problems, the NASL would open its 1980 campaign with an unchanged line-up, maintaining a 24-team format for a third, and final, year. But the bubble was about to burst.

18. ☆ We Can Be Heroes

The list of the highest individual scorers in North American League history includes four British players. But there is no place for Best or Marsh, Tueart or Francis, or any of the other household names from the Football League. Instead, the quartet of Brits enshrined among the NASL's most prolific players comprises Alan Willey, Ron Futcher, Paul Child and Laurie Abrahams. All were either toiling in the lower divisions or fighting for first-team football when they crossed the Atlantic to find goals, celebrity and longevity. The fact that their feats remain largely overlooked when fans back home remember the star-studded NASL is something they have learned to accept.

'Could I have been the same in England? I don't know,' says Willey. 'But I do know I would not change a thing. I am proud of what I achieved. The guys that people recognise when you talk about the NASL had already made their names and came over at the tail end of their careers. We were trying to prove ourselves. Those star players didn't have to push as hard.'

Elected in 2003 to American Soccer's Hall of Fame, Willey, in third spot, is the highest-placed of the British players in this top-ten scoring list (goals are worth two points and assists worth one point):

Player	Seasons	Games	Goals	Assists	Points
1. Giorgio Chinaglia	8	213	193	81	478
2. Karl-Heinz Granitza	7	199	128	101	357
3. Alan Willey	9	238	129	48	306
4. Ron Futcher	9	201	119	58	296
5. Ace Ntsoelengoe	11	244	87	82	256
6. Paul Child	10	241	102	47	251

7. Ilija Mitic	9	166	101	37	239
8. Steve David	8	175	100	28	228
9. Laurie Abrahams	7	162	76	64	216
10. Mirko Stojanovic	7	179	83	45	211

If timing is one of the strengths of a striker, then Willey proved he had it in abundance when Minnesota Kicks coach Freddie Goodwin made a trip to Middlesbrough during the 1975–76 season. 'He went to see Frank Spraggon in a reserve game, but I scored a couple of goals and he said he was interested in me as well. I was only 19 and Middlesbrough was the furthest I had ever been from Sunderland, where I was from. I had not long made my debut for Middlesbrough and I was coming on as sub for ten minutes at a time, so Jack Charlton, the manager, thought it would be good for me to get some playing time in America.'

Despite his immediate success in the NASL, scoring 16 goals in his rookie season, Willey was not expecting to return. 'I was back in Middlesbrough and I was leading scorer after five or six games with five goals. We went to Liverpool and Jack left me out because he wanted to play defensively for a point. We got a 0–0 draw and from then on I was in and out and back to where I was a year before.'

Willey was unable to win a regular place in a forward line of David Mills, Alan Foggon and John Hickton, so when Goodwin called again he decided to return to Minnesota. The goals flowed once more, 14 in 20 games. 'I think I was successful because I was getting a chance to play more,' he explains. 'It was hard coming on as substitute and getting into the rhythm of the game. The pace was not as fast as in England and there was not as much pressure in America. The fans didn't know much about the game and would always cheer you. If you have a bad game in England, the crowd is on your back. And at that time I was about 165 or 170 pounds and the fields in England were like quagmires, which made it hard for a smaller player like me.'

Returning to England, Willey realised his days at Ayresome Park were numbered under new manager John Neal. 'I went back after the '77 season with Stan Cummins, who played for the Kicks that year, and we got back on a Saturday. Middlesbrough were at home and Neal asked who we were. He said, "Why don't you come in and let's see how fit you are." We had just walked off the plane after a full season and now we had to do 12-minute runs. I got into the first team a couple of times and scored five goals against Rotherham, but I was not on the team sheet the following Saturday.'

Willey moved back to Minnesota on a permanent basis, scoring 21 goals in the regular season of 1978 and adding another seven play-off goals, including his incredible five-goal performance against the Cosmos. In 1979, he matched his total of the previous year.

Kicks teammate Alan Merrick describes Willey as 'one of the most underrated players ever to come out of England'. He claims, 'He was everything Michael Owen is. A great striker of the ball, great attitude and work rate. A quality player that nobody in the world knows about. He was head and shoulders above any of the other young English players over here.'

Ankle injuries slowed Willey's production to seven goals per year in 1980 and 1981, when he was sold to the Montreal Manic after only six games. 'The team had been sold and Freddie Goodwin was on his way out,' Willey explains. 'One of the last things he did was to trade me. We were at practice and Freddie came over and said, "Can I have a word?" I knew what was coming and he said they had traded me.'

Willey produced returns of 15, 13 and 15 goals in his final three NASL seasons, the last of which was back in Minnesota for the relocated Strikers. Having settled in the state as a computer systems engineer, he admits that one team in England would have had him boarding a plane to England without a moment's pause during his successful NASL career. 'I would have gone back to Sunderland in a heartbeat. That was my team. If I was not in the Middlesbrough team on a Saturday I would go to Roker Park. There was talk of it at one time but then they had a change of manager.'

Willey's long-time partner, Ron Futcher, had not even been among Goodwin's first choices when the Kicks coach approached Luton manager Harry Haslam about borrowing some players. 'He wanted guys like Jimmy Husband and John Aston, but they didn't want to go at that time,' Futcher recalls. 'I was just 19 and had not played much that year, so Harry asked if I wanted to go and get some experience. I watched a promotional film and said I would go. Right away I thought it was fantastic.'

A return of 14 goals in the Kicks' first season proved that Futcher was anything but second best and he became an instant crowd favourite with his no-nonsense style of play. 'And in those days I had long blond hair so I stood out. If you mix it, get involved with opponents and don't back down to anybody, the crowds love it.'

Futcher's approach dovetailed perfectly with Willey's eye for goal, as Luton and Kicks colleague Alan West explains: 'Alan was very sharp and Ron was the old-style centre-forward, very strong. They were a good combination and both were brave and prepared to get in the box when it mattered.'

Kicks goalkeeper Geoff Barnett adds, 'Ronnie was a battler and Alan was a better finisher. You don't see combinations like that much anymore, with players making runs for each other to create space.'

Futcher continues, 'Alan and I became close friends and I really enjoyed our partnership. Alan was quicker than me and I was the one who worked on the flick-offs. We were young and nerveless and were just out there enjoying it. I was getting $300 a week, treble what I was getting back home, and wasn't worried too much about results.'

Futcher shrugged off defeat in the 1976 Soccer Bowl – 'we were pleased just to get there and I got a lovely ring for it' – and continued to rattle in the goals for a Kicks team that 'could beat anyone in the regular season but always under-achieved in the play-offs'. After the 1979 season, by which time he had scored 46 NASL goals and had seen his English career progress to Manchester City, he accepted the Kicks' offer of a three-year contract to become a full-time American-based player. The demise of the Kicks brought that contract to a premature end and saw him heading for Portland, where he scored 13 goals for the Timbers in their final season. 'After Portland folded I didn't get picked up so I called Harry Haslam to see if he could put my name about. Lawrie McMenemy offered me a 12-month contract but then Terry Hennessey, who had become coach at Tulsa, called and offered me an 18-month deal. I wanted to get back to America so I took it.'

At the Roughnecks, where Futcher scored 33 goals in two seasons, Laurie Abrahams became the latest goalscorer to benefit from his teammate's imposing presence. 'It was great playing with Futch because he would kick you as soon as look at you,' Abrahams remembers. 'He could get wound up sometimes, but he was a diamond off the field.'

Once the NASL folded following his second year in Tulsa, Futcher returned to play out his career in England with six different teams in eight years. Not many fans at places like Bradford and Burnley realised they were watching a man whose 119 NASL goals had placed him ahead of some of the world's biggest names in the league's record books. 'People thought the NASL was just the Cosmos and Earthquakes and Rowdies,' he says. 'I was in Minneapolis, a Midwest town that never got much attention. But if the league hadn't folded I would have stayed in

America. I went to Pittsburgh for a trial for the indoor league but I was still only 28 and had been tapped up by clubs in Europe so I came back.'

☆

Among those who never returned to England was Paul Child, whose journey to America began when, as a 13-year-old Birmingham City fanatic, he signed for his favourite team's biggest rival. 'The club I was playing for as an amateur became something of a farm team for Aston Villa,' he explains, although he delayed signing as a professional until he had completed a diploma in carpentry. 'I was a regular in the reserves and when I was 19 the opportunity came to play at the Atlanta Chiefs through Vic Crowe.'

After two seasons playing for the former Villa player and coach in Atlanta, scoring eight goals in each, Child was offered the chance to return to America full-time. 'At Villa I was playing with guys like Brian Little and John Gidman, who went on to make it. The club felt I was getting too old and let me go, with the option that if I came back they would get first rights on me.'

It was the new San Jose Earthquakes who acquired Child's services and were rewarded with 15 goals. 'In my first year there I was lucky to be one of the top scorers and they promoted me that way. They took me to every function, promotion and press conference to show me off. I played in golf tournaments in San Francisco. They put me in situations where at first I was very nervous – on television or speaking in front of large crowds. It taught me a lot about selling the game. I must have sounded strange with my Birmingham accent and not the greatest education, but I caught a lot of people's attention because I was scoring goals and we were selling out stadiums.

'I wanted to show that Villa had made a mistake in getting rid of me. When I had the chance to play against the best players in the world it pushed me to the next level, to be as good as I could be.'

The 1975 season, when he scored only four goals and lost his place in the team, showed Child that success could not be taken for granted. 'They had built me up and I put so much pressure on myself. I was expecting to score two goals a game. When the season started I had a couple of bad misses. Even the Michael Owens of the world go through a roller-coaster sometimes. I remember being three yards away against Dallas, having plenty of time, and I drilled it against the bar. Then they started pulling me out of games and that screwed my confidence. But the biggest thing as a pro is learning your strengths and weaknesses. I was not going to dribble around three players; my job was getting on the end of crosses and putting my head in when I knew I was going to get kicked.'

That approach paid off to the tune of forty-two goals over the next four seasons and Earthquakes colleague Laurie Calloway says, 'Paul would kick his grandmother if he had to. He was very intense and aggressive and left messages with goalkeepers. He did not have a lot of finesse and he was not one to get the ball down and create something out of nothing, but he was not frightened to stick his head in among the feet. If you had to list Paul's number one ingredient, it would be heart.'

Former Villa youth-team colleague Mick Hoban, who had teamed up with Child at Atlanta, adds, 'Paul was a very physical player, very athletic. He had fantastic upper-body strength. People like Souness, Beardsley and Talbot came to America and were able to go back with a reputation. Paul was in the same ilk, but he loved it here. He was a John Wayne type, knocking people over and picking them up. The Americans could not necessarily see the more subtle things, but Paul would knock down three players in the box and the crowd would love him. In his own community he was a local hero. He was an affable chap, worked hard and did well financially. I think he felt that after making a name for himself in America, he didn't want to go over to England and start again.'

As the Earthquakes looked to improve precarious finances, Child, their most valuable asset, was sold to Memphis for the 1980 season, scoring 12 goals for his new team. 'I was one of those stupid players who was loyal,' he says. 'I would have been in San Jose to the end if they had not sold me. In Memphis, I had a chance to sign a three-year guaranteed contract for more than $100,000 a year. I had never known that kind of money. In my first year in San Jose I was on $800 a month. I thought everything was great in Memphis. Charlie Cooke was coach, there were a lot of English players and we had a pretty good team. I was ready to buy a house and the owner decided he was folding the team. I was out on my ear.'

Child played one more season in the NASL, returning to Atlanta to score 13 goals for the Chiefs. He reflects, 'I realised I was maybe not going to make it in England so I made sure I became Americanised quickly. It is a shame that a lot of people never realised what I achieved in the NASL and maybe I could have gone back and played regularly in England. But one of the great things for me was when I went back to San Jose recently I met Landon Donovan and Brandi Chastain from the US men's and women's teams and they told me they used to watch me. When you are remembered in the places where you played, you feel it was all worthwhile.'

☆

Child, Willey and Futcher were already established NASL stars when a young Charlton Athletic forward called Laurie Abrahams was signed by former Coventry manager Noel Cantwell for the New England Tea Men's first season in 1978. The product of a tough upbringing in London, Abrahams admits, 'I hadn't looked at football as a career. I had no desire to play professionally at 17 or 18. I liked to play but didn't think I would like the business.'

Abrahams's talent could not be ignored, however, and he progressed from playing for the Ship and Anchor pub in Dagenham, via non-League football, to the books of Charlton Athletic. He recalls: 'Charlton had a training ground owned by Unilever and one of their companies was Lipton Tea, who had just bought the New England franchise. Noel was there putting the team together and I knew Mike Flanagan and Colin Powell from Charlton, so it was a no-brainer to go when I was asked.'

After seven goals and ten assists in his rookie season, Abrahams moved to the Tulsa Roughnecks. 'The Tea Men had a deal that said if I stayed with them they would have to pay an extra amount to Charlton. I had a call asking if I wanted to play in a friendly for Tulsa on tour at Portsmouth. I went down there and met Alan Hinton and Terry Hennessey, their coaches. But it just didn't work out for me at Tulsa. Steve Earle and guys like that were good to play for. They were very helpful and would teach you things and I was scoring goals, but from a personality point of view I don't think Alan and I got on very well.'

Abrahams may not have been happy at Tulsa but he was effective, scoring 10 goals in 13 games before being traded to the California Surf, where he took his goals total for the season to 18. Asked about the secret of his success, Abrahams responds, 'I think it was any number of things and I am not smart enough to know what it was. One thing was the weather. I found it easier to play in San Diego in the summer than Hull in the winter.'

The 1980 season produced 17 goals, but after California coach Peter Wall's departure the following season, Abrahams's relationship with the club broke down. He finished with only five goals after sitting out most of the second half of the season. 'In the end they were trying to trade me,' he recalls. 'A couple of the management wanted me to play and a couple didn't. I didn't want to go and I had a no-trade clause. They started to mess around with me and, in some ways, when people do that I say, "Fuck you."

'It wasn't that I didn't want to play. After a game against Atlanta, there was a meeting at which it was decided that guys had to say whether they wanted to play or not. I wasn't there and when I turned up a couple of days later I was told I had to tell them if I wanted to play. I said, "I don't have to tell you that I want to play." So they said I was not going to play. Then, on a road trip, they said I was playing and I said, "No I am not. You said I wasn't going to play unless I told you I wanted to and I haven't."'

Abrahams is honest enough to admit, 'Even my best friends will tell you my attitude could have been better. I would not have stood for my attitude, but then I would not have played the games people tried to play. I have lived with my decisions and suffered from some of them.'

Wall adds, 'Laurie was a weird guy with a strange personality and was hard to deal with, but he was as quick as lightning and as good a finisher as I had ever seen. Most people would hate his attitude. He didn't like to train too hard, but when it came to the big day he would produce. But after a short period of time he would rub you up the wrong way. I spoke to Noel Cantwell and he said he couldn't put up with him after one season.'

Cantwell explains, 'Laurie was a bit of a Jack the lad. He would play well for a week or two and then disappear, then come out with something exceptional. He knew the game, but I don't think he took the football seriously.'

California teammate Mark Lindsay recalls, 'Laurie had been a tailor and he made me laugh one day by saying, "I am going in there to negotiate a new contract. If they don't agree I will go back to making trousers." I said, "You are going to leave California to go back to that? Bollocks you are." In his own way, he was very competitive. He always said what he thought and sometimes that led him into trouble.'

A second spell with Tulsa under coach Terry Hennessey proved more successful than his first residence at the club, with Abrahams having 28 goals and an NASL championship to show for it. 'Terry knew what I was like and he didn't like the way I trained,' he says. 'But there are some people you can play for and some you can't. When I went to Tulsa the first time, Terry called to wish me a good trip and I thought, "What a waste of time." I didn't realise it was just him being a nice guy and didn't understand what good manners were.'

Lindsay, who also played at Tulsa, remembers Hennessey being close to losing his patience with the eccentric Londoner. 'Terry said one day, "Laurie, you are the hardest player I have ever had to manage. The minute you stop scoring you will be gone." Laurie's answer was, "All you have to do is get those clowns to get the ball to me."

'Laurie would analyse games so that when reporters spoke to him he could say, "I got two balls in the first half and four in the second half and they were crap. I need better service." A lot of people take Laurie the wrong way. The first impression is that he is a very harsh guy. He is very blunt, very dry humoured, and a lot of people don't get past the first five minutes with him, but he is a very nice man.'

After the Roughnecks ran into money trouble and Hennessey left the club, Abrahams spent the NASL's final season at the San Diego Sockers, scoring only one goal in nineteen games. 'A couple of the players there got US citizenship in the off-season and I had to sit on the bench. San Diego was a strange team with lots of factions.'

It was an unfortunate way for Abrahams to end an NASL career that he looks back on with fondness. 'I never think about whether I could have been successful in England,' he says. 'I get people now who say, "Are you Laurie Abrahams?" and I say, "I used to be." I was just very lucky to find someone dumb enough to think I could do it for their team. Instead of being miserable about it, I just think about it as being a good time. How many people does that happen to?'

19. ☆ Who Shot the NASL?

On the second weekend of November 1980 there was only one question on the lips of most Americans: who shot J.R. Ewing? As a television audience of 83 million settled down to discover that sister-in-law Kristen was the guilty party, events no less dramatic were unfolding at the NASL's end-of-season meetings. But while television's favourite bad guy lived to continue womanising and waging war on the Barnes clan, the shots being administered to the NASL would ultimately prove to be fatal – even if it was to be a slow, lingering death.

The league's problems had been highlighted by the 1980 season, which saw the New York Cosmos win their third crown in four years. That just emphasised the hopelessness that some franchises felt at having to compete with the Warner-backed giants. As the season progressed it became clear that some of the clubs that had joined the league in 1978 were in dire straits. Meanwhile, ABC's television coverage failed to bring in the required audiences.

John Best, general manager of the Vancouver Whitecaps, says, 'The Cosmos were buying the best in the world and it was a problem to some of ownership. The Cosmos situation was not compatible with where the league was at that time. The basic fact was that franchises could not support their payrolls and that was really the demise of the league.'

Commissioner Phil Woosnam reveals that, for all their on-field success and financial backing, even the Cosmos were in the red. 'They were losing more than any other team because they were expanding so far ahead of other people,' he says. 'They created enormous things for us, but brought a lot of concerns, too. We couldn't stop them from trying to build overnight but the net effect was that costs and salaries were rising and there were disgruntled people everywhere. Since then there have been ideas like salary caps, but there was no legal way for us to do it then.'

With the backing of Madison Square Garden, the Washington Diplomats were one of the teams who had attempted to match New York in bringing the biggest names to the US, although their highest-profile signing for 1980, Johan Cruyff, had already spent one season with the Los Angeles Aztecs. His arrival in the Diplomats' dressing-room gave Gordon Bradley the distinction of being the only man in football to have coached Pelé, Beckenbauer and Cruyff at club level. 'My approach was that I respected those players and I wanted them to respect me,' says Bradley. 'I felt that if there were problems they would sit down and discuss them. They could knock at the door and I would see them there and then because I knew it must be serious. I never for one moment thought, "I am the coach of Pelé." I just wanted to see them be better than they were and give them every ounce of my knowledge. I was comfortable with it and I think they respected that.'

Even with ten goals and twenty assists, Cruyff was overshadowed at the Diplomats by the prolific scoring of Englishman Alan Green, whose 25 goals tied for third in the league. Matching that total was Roger Davies, who helped the Seattle Sounders win their division with a won–lost mark of 25–7, a league record that earned Alan Hinton the Coach of the Year award. Davies had followed his former Tulsa coach and Derby teammate to the Pacific north-west, along with full-back David Nish. The signing of Bruce Rioch, and Jeff Bourne's arrival for the final few weeks of the season, further strengthened the Baseball Ground connection.

Meanwhile, former Scotland winger Tommy Hutchison, his days at Coventry City nearing an end, was signed to take command of the left flank, providing 12 assists and earning a continuation of his First Division career at Manchester City. 'The spell in America was a great boost to me,' said Hutchison, snapped up by City when he lost his regular place at Highfield Road on his return from Seattle. 'Reputations that have taken years to build can vanish overnight if players fool around in the States. I had no intention of blowing my reputation with a few bad games, so I didn't regard my trip there as a holiday.'

League MVP Davies recalls that 'everything seemed to gel for us' and is full of praise for the contribution of former England midfielder Alan Hudson, who finished with 15 assists. 'I had seen him play before in the NASL. He could really play but he was trying to run the show, taking it deep from defenders. Now he had a back four of internationals behind him and could push on and do more damage further forward.' Bourne adds, 'Alan was one of the best midfield players I ever saw. He would look one way, but you knew he was going to knock it to you.'

Recalling his Sounders teammates in his autobiography, Hudson describes Rioch, an old First Division nemesis, as being as good as it was possible to find in his new position in the back four. But, off the field, he claims Rioch was trying to undermine Hinton's position as coach because of his own interest in the job. Rioch puts Hudson's comments down to a relationship that went sour at the end of their first season together. 'We got on very well in the first year but had a bit of a fallout in one of the play-off matches against Los Angeles. He took it personally and couldn't get it out of his system. It festered.'

Despite that situation, Rioch says, 'The reason we did so well was the phenomenal team spirit, as good as I have been involved in. We lunched together, barbecued together, swam together and lived in the same apartment complex. Tommy was outstanding for us, but Roger Davies was the hero. The Americans love the guys who get the touchdowns, make the baskets or score the goals. He was a lovely man as well, which helped. He was very popular with the Seattle public.'

Rioch's own form after moving into the back four earned him a place on the NASL all-star team. 'I had stood in at centre-half at Luton, Everton and Derby, so it wasn't new. I went to Seattle to play in the back four because they wanted an experienced player there. It helped playing alongside David Nish and Jimmy Ryan, who had been at Luton with me.'

Seattle's first play-off opponents were the Vancouver Whitecaps, who had scraped into the play-offs in third place in their division. Trevor Whymark had top scored with 15 goals, while Carl Valentine added 10. Kevin Hector had not returned until late in the season.

In goal for Vancouver was a 22-year-old Zimbabwean, Bruce Grobbelaar, who had played a couple of games in 1979 and won the position in the wake of Phil Parkes's departure. The joker's personality that would make him a folk hero at Liverpool was already in evidence. Coach Tony Waiters recalls, 'We worked him out at Derby's training ground because West Brom were releasing him. I asked Tommy Docherty if we could fire a few balls at him and it was obvious he had something special. The ability was there, but we hadn't tested his brains. Bruce didn't play much in 1979, but in one game he tried to show everything he knew. One shot was going outside the post and he dived and caught it, rolled over and it went under his body into the net. We loaned him to Crewe that winter and Liverpool got interested.

'He was very popular and a joker. When we were bringing him back from South Africa, I picked him up and told him how he had become this big mystery figure in our front office. He got this mask, the most horrible-looking thing, like someone 70 years of age. I took him to the front office and announced he had finally arrived and he walked in wearing the mask. People didn't know how to take it. He got me in 1980, after we had won at California to reach the play-offs. The players took the next day off and went to Disneyland. I had a call from the trainer saying Bruce had fallen off a ride and broken his arm. He even got a fake cast and had me going for three or four hours. He even did it for the media after I didn't play him in the last game of the season.'

Seattle had the last laugh on Grobbelaar, winning both games against Vancouver to set up a meeting with Los Angeles, play-off conquerors of Cruyff's Diplomats. The series featured two one-sided games, the Aztecs winning 3–0 at home and Seattle taking revenge with a 4–0 victory at the Kingdome, Steve Buttle, an ever-present midfielder, getting one of the goals. In the fourth of his six seasons in Seattle after failing a medical at Ipswich, the former Bournemouth midfielder could, according to Hudson, 'have been a real star had it not been for his wonky knee' and 'had a left foot that I can only imagine God gave him'.

The decisive mini-game saw Buttle and the Sounders go down in a shoot-out after drawing 1–1. 'They got lucky,' says Seattle goalscorer Davies. 'We hammered them, but it was just one of those games.' Rioch adds, 'We had done so well that year and thought we could go all the way. Suddenly it was over.'

Elsewhere, David Chadwick had taken the head coaching position in Atlanta, but the team's seven wins were the lowest in the league. In California, Laurie Abrahams's 17 goals and 15 assists helped fire the Surf to a play-off spot. Ex-Rowdies midfielder Mark Lindsay says of the Surf set-up, 'They were a club who took care of us and we didn't have to worry about people like Gordon Jago, who had their own agenda at Tampa.'

In Detroit, the links with Jimmy Hill and Coventry took young Sky Blues forwards Mark Hateley and Gary Bannister to the Pontiac Silverdome. Hateley, later to forge an England career, found his game ill-suited to Astroturf and scored only twice in 19 games, while Bannister enjoyed more success with 10 goals in 22 matches. It was not enough, though, to get Detroit beyond the regular season. Nor were the 12 goals from leading scorer Paul Child able to lift the Memphis Rogues out of the basement of their division.

The Minnesota Kicks had Freddie Goodwin back at the coaching helm, but they surrendered top place in the National Conference's Central Division to the Dallas Tornado and were then shut out by Tornado goalkeeper Alex Stepney in two play-off games.

In New England, the Tea Men's play-off push was spearheaded by 14 goals from Hartlepool striker Bob Newton. 'He was a big, strong centre-forward who was quicker than you would think,' recalls coach Noel Cantwell. 'He was one of those holiday players. Playing in Hartlepool and then coming to America, well, it was like Christmas every day to him. He was hard and tough and if there was a chance around goal he would take it.

'I remember playing Fort Lauderdale and they had a player who was a film star in South America and he was very good looking. He was an international player of top quality. Newton was a strong bastard who put himself about, a typical Third Division player. The ball was played into the box and Newton elbowed this guy and broke his jaw. There was a big shemozzle and in the papers in Boston it said Bob was going to be sued for $2 million. I told them, "I will tell you now, if he is sued for $2 he will not be able to pay it." The player didn't have an arse in his trousers.'

Newton was partnered up front by the former West Brom forward Tony 'Bomber' Brown. Approaching 35, Brown had scored 218 League goals in 16 seasons at The Hawthorns, including leading the First Division with 28 in 1970–71, when he won his only England cap. He was held to eight in the first of his two NASL seasons, but set up fourteen goals. The Tea Men, however, could not find the net in two play-off games against Tampa Bay.

In Portland, a familiar face returned to take charge of the team, but a late-season revival under Vic Crowe could not get the Timbers into the play-offs. Clyde Best scored 11 goals for a team that saw former Scotland and Manchester City left-back Willie Donachie beginning a three-year NASL stint. Meanwhile, Bill Foulkes took charge of his third NASL team, but could not guide the San Jose Earthquakes into the play-offs, even with George Best in the ranks.

The New York Cosmos, now without any British connections, duly won their division as Giorgio Chinaglia notched a goal for every one of his 32 appearances. Chinaglia also scored six goals in three games in the new mid-season Transatlantic Challenge Cup, a tournament in which the Cosmos won two games and drew one to finish ahead of Vancouver, Manchester City – who had Dennis Tueart back in their ranks – and Roma. Tueart scored in a 3–2 loss against his former team and City were then thrashed 5–0 by the Whitecaps, with Whymark scoring a hat-trick.

Chinaglia kicked off the play-offs with two goals in a 3–1 win at Tulsa. The Roughnecks, now coached by Charlie Mitchell, had sneaked into the post-season field by winning their last two games, a 2–0 win in the season finale against Vancouver having seen former Fulham centre-forward Viv Busby finally score his first NASL goal in 19 games. Busby and his teammates could only watch in awe as Chinaglia scored seven goals in New York's 8–1 victory at Giants Stadium and by the time Dallas and Los Angeles had been dispatched in later rounds, Chinaglia had scored an incredible sixteen goals in seven play-off games.

New York's opponents in Soccer Bowl were the Fort Lauderdale Strikers, whose success was the perfect answer to those who had criticised the dismissal of Ron Newman. Ironically, to reach the final, the Strikers had been forced to contest the American Conference championship with their former coach's new team, the San Diego Sockers. Newman saw his team lose the first game of the series in California before he made his return to Fort Lauderdale, where a sell-out crowd of more than 18,000 packed Lockhart Stadium.

Newman recalls, 'Soon after the start I was stood behind the players' bench when a policeman came up behind me and whispered to me to stand still as it was reported that there was someone in the crowd with a gun threatening to shoot me. My first reaction was to look round at this policeman, who was several inches smaller than me, and I am only 5 ft 8 in. I asked him if he was the biggest policeman they had. Realising I was stood behind the substitutes and that the gunman may not be a marksman, I suggested to the miniature policeman that we moved behind another bench a few yards away. So we shuffled along like Flanagan and Allen. It was later reported that the suspected assassin was thrown out of the stadium and the gun was a fake. Anyway, I needed a change of underwear at half-time.'

A hat-trick from Mexican striker Hugo Sanchez gave the Sockers a 4–2 victory, but the home team prevailed in the mini-game. Yet whoever won was only likely to provide fodder for the Cosmos, and so it proved as two more Chinaglia goals eased New York to a 3–0 victory and their third NASL title in four seasons. The Italian finished the season with a staggering total of 56 goals in 43 games.

Even though a respectable 51,000 fans had attended the final in Washington DC's Robert F. Kennedy Stadium, the league was concerned about the drop in New York's average attendance from 49,000 to 42,000. Meanwhile, Philadelphia and Atlanta had both averaged fewer than 5,000 per game. ABC had been unhappy with the low ratings for its broadcasts and decided it would show only the Soccer Bowl in 1981, an indication that there would be no more contract beyond that.

Derek Possee, the former Vancouver and Millwall forward, is among those who believe that the all-powerful NFL was exerting its influence over television networks like ABC. 'I am convinced there was a conspiracy with football, because the NFL was frightened to death that some of the soccer teams could get bigger crowds. Television had millions invested in the NFL and I think the league put pressure on them. I think it was a done deal that ABC would dump its soccer contract to keep the NFL happy.'

The NASL's problems made for an unpleasant atmosphere when the league met a couple of months after the Soccer Bowl. California Surf owner Bob Hermann, one of the old-school traditionalists, had already resigned as chairman of the board of NASL directors after being insulted in a meeting and Phil Woosnam says, 'Teams were caught up in thinking they could buy success. It was disappointing to think these intelligent businessmen couldn't all stick together with the same approach. We were trying to at least break even before we went off on ego trips.

'People like Lamar Hunt said that what was good for the league was good for the owners but there were a bunch of others who got in the wrong frame of mind. It was OK when only one was fighting that battle, but when half the room were taking that view we couldn't control it. People were getting concerned with the losses and the effect of the union and the tone within the room had changed. They had split into two. There were New York and others who didn't want controls and wanted to do whatever they wanted. The other faction was Lamar and Bob and the teams that were not financed as well, who felt the league was going to go downhill.'

While the poorer teams wanted to restrict the big boys' ability to spend money, the elite group, including Sonny Werblin, head of Madison Square Garden and owner of the Washington Diplomats, wanted to be rid of their poor relations. Gordon Jago, coach of the Tampa Bay Rowdies, remembers the meeting well. 'The strong boys said, "We are not going to stay in a league like this. Some teams are costing us money and there will be a domino effect." Washington wanted to reduce the teams, and Sonny Werblin was absolutely right. He said, "I have got Johan Cruyff and World Cup players and when we go to places like Atlanta we triple their gate. When they come to me, people in Washington won't go to see it. They are costing me money." He wanted the bigger teams to break away and have a four- or five-million budget. But the majority of people wanted to stick with the same teams.'

As Americans discussed the previous night's events on the Ewing ranch at South Fork, Werblin decided to saddle up and leave town, announcing that he was closing the Diplomats. 'It was tragic, but he was right,' says Jago. 'Even in Tampa, we could not compete with the big cities. The Cosmos had more internationals on their bench than we had in our team.'

The Houston Hurricane and Rochester Lancers followed suit, while the New England Tea Men announced a move to Jacksonville. The Memphis Rogues were to become the Calgary Boomers, while the Philadelphia Fury would also move north, to become the Montreal Manic. Woosnam's 24-team dream was in tatters and his former right-hand man, Clive Toye, was among those who had seen it coming.

'I'd been part of the league's long-range strategic committee,' Toye explains. 'We used to have a meeting once a month and we came out with this thick strategic plan. Phil was not on that committee, which was a mistake. Before 1978, we'd had six good clubs, six that were OK and six that were rubbish. We felt we needed to get rid of the last six, either by getting new ownership if the city was right or getting the team out of the city. Phil was going off on the parallel path of expansion. We presented our plan, which was contraction, and he presented his idea of expansion. With six new franchises playing $3 million, the idea of having $18 million to spread around had been too much for the owners. I still think it was a mistake. Instead of having two-thirds of our teams performing acceptably we now had 50 per cent that were not.'

Woosnam, however, remains angered by the criticism he has received for adding new teams. 'Not everybody believed in expansion, but I think there are ulterior motives in those who questioned it afterwards. Our intention was good and honourable and it was not like we did it round the corner. All the owners knew exactly what was going on. They had to approve everything we did. If people say now we shouldn't have gone to 24, well, so what? They voted for it.'

20. ☆ Beginning of the End

Ken Furphy, coach of the Detroit Express, was preparing his off-season calendar when he received a surprising phone call. 'It was Duncan Hill, Jimmy's son, who had taken over as general manager,' he recalls. 'He told me to leave Eddie Colquhoun in charge because I had to fly to Washington right away. They were discussing taking the team there. I couldn't believe it.'

Team owner Jimmy Hill reckoned his team had been losing $1 million a year in Detroit and blamed NASL commissioner Phil Woosnam and the directors of the NASL for the league's instability, claiming Woosnam was too busy finding new franchises to produce a comprehensive league strategy. The Coventry City chairman's final throw of his NASL dice was to accept offers to relocate to Washington to become the new Diplomats, the venture being partly funded by $500,000 from his Highfield Road club. Furphy continues, 'We had worked hard to build the club in Detroit, working with kids and creating a base of seven or eight thousand fans. The team in Washington had just folded and I thought, "How are we going to make money here when the last owners couldn't make it work?" The next thing I know, we are in Washington and it was a terrible move.'

The Diplomats started brightly in their new surroundings, winning eight of the first eleven games, but won only seven more in the remainder of the season and missed the play-offs. Southampton's Malcolm Waldron finished as top scorer with fifteen goals, while fellow Saint Trevor Hebbard added nine from midfield. Johan Cruyff played in only five games during the latter part of a season that Furphy recalls for its turmoil and uncertainty.

He says, 'Jimmy Hill came back on the scene and took over the team in the end. I remember a terrible game in about 100 degrees against Jacksonville. We lost in extra time and Jimmy came in and told everybody off and I had a bust-up with him upstairs. The outcome was that he took over selection. The players were calling the team the "Over-the-hill Gang".

'Later in the year we heard the club had declared bankruptcy. They owed about three or four hundred thousand dollars, but that was nothing over there. The players were in rented houses and it was a hell of a mess. I tried to sell a few players, acting on their behalf. I got £550 instead of two years' wages. I had to get out of my flat so I got a van and went down to Atlanta to live with my son. Within two weeks other teams started folding.'

Surprisingly, given their on-field consistency, the Minnesota Kicks were one of those teams, a year after being bought by a consortium headed by English businessman Ralph Sweet, formerly vice-chairman of Notts County. Geoff Barnett, the Kicks' former goalkeeper, had taken over from Freddie Goodwin as coach during the season. 'I had done fairly well as coach of the indoor team,' Barnett recalls, 'and one day the owner asked if I wanted to coach the outdoor team. I said I was not going to stab Freddie in the back, but obviously I had aspirations to coach outdoors. The next day he takes me into Freddie's office and tells him that he is giving me the job.'

The Kicks took second place behind the dominant Chicago Sting in the league's Central Division – the two-conference system having been scrapped. Ron Futcher scored 14 goals, supported by Don Masson, the ex-Queens Park Rangers and Scotland World Cup midfielder, and Steve Heighway, the leggy former Liverpool and Republic of Ireland winger. 'Heighway was unstoppable,' says Kicks defender Stewart Jump. 'Defenders had more space to cover over here and he could take them on and skin them. He was a good player at Liverpool and even better in America.'

But when a pair of 3–0 defeats against Fort Lauderdale ended their season at the quarter-final stage, the Kicks had played their final games. Municipal Stadium was scheduled to give way to a new indoor venue, the Metrodome, and the club was unable to negotiate a lease with the new facility. Sweet, who accused the NFL's Minnesota Vikings of squeezing the Kicks out of the Metrodome, claimed he had lost more than $1 million and the Kicks went into liquidation.

'I was in Europe scouting at the time,' says Barnett. 'I said to the owner, "What the hell am I doing here if you are folding the team?" It was a real tough time. Phil Woosnam was looking at prospective buyers and I was trying to keep the team together because if the players didn't get paid they would become free agents. We had about three champagne parties because we thought we had been saved. When we went it was the start of the demise of the league.'

Defender Alan Merrick, brought back to Minnesota by Barnett, says, 'We were still drawing crowds of 28,000. But the new ownership tied the club up in so much litigation.' A distraught Heighway, who had been building a house in the area, said, 'My world is falling upside down. I can't believe the Kicks would be allowed to just die.'

Futcher recalls, 'We knew something was going on about four or five weeks earlier. We had not been paid for about ten weeks and we thought the team might be sold. It was a terrible time. If you found another team they had to pick up your back-pay, but you lost all your money and went home if you did not find a new team. I remember Chico Hamilton ended up selling everything, including his car, in a garage sale.'

The Kicks' remaining assets were sold, including Futcher, who fetched $45,000 for the club's administrators when bought by Portland. Other sales ranged from the $58,000 received from Toronto for striker Ace Ntsoelengoe to $70-worth of megaphones.

Atlanta, California, Dallas, Los Angeles and Calgary were also playing their final seasons, the Chiefs winning the Southern Division on the back of 22 goals by former Manchester United striker and future United and Leeds coach Brian Kidd. The Chiefs could not survive the first round of the play-offs, however, beaten by the Jacksonville Tea Men, for whom Alan Green scored twice in each game. Green had enjoyed another productive season with 16 goals and coach Noel Cantwell says, 'I had him as a kid at Coventry. I liked to have pace up front, otherwise you had to be very organised. He gave us that pace.'

In California, the Surf went under after a season that had seen the departure of Peter Wall, the latest English coach angered by interference from on high. Wall explains, 'We had new ownership, the Segerstrom group, and after the first year they brought in a general manager who had been at a Six Flags amusement park and knew nothing about sport. He sold himself on telling the ownership we would get crowds of 20,000. He told me our team was not entertaining enough. It was a long and heated discussion. I said, "If you need a better team you have got to spend more money on players, but we won't get 20,000 even if we win Soccer Bowl."'

Wall's plea for the club to spend $180,000 for Tampa Bay's Jan Van der Veen fell on deaf ears. 'A week into the season I was told we needed entertaining players – Brazilians – and was told they were going to make a Swedish guy called Tom Lilledahl player-personnel director. I said, "As long as I am coach you are not." Seven games into the season they wanted to bring in Carlos Alberto. We didn't need him. He was a lovely man but he was coming to our club for the money. I stood my ground and said I didn't want Carlos or Paulo Caesar, who they also wanted. We came to a financial agreement and I walked out in May. Within a week they had signed Van der Veen along with Carlos and Paulo.'

Surf player Mark Lindsay remembers, 'They went out into the community and asked what brand of football people would rather watch. The South Americans and Mexicans said, "We don't like this English shit." Lilledahl introduced himself in a hotel room by saying we were not going to play an English style and that everyone was going to be traded. Peter was dumbfounded.'

Englishman Laurie Calloway, whom Wall had appointed as his number two, was next in line as head coach. 'I told Laurie to take the job if they offered it to him,' says Wall. 'But I warned him he wouldn't have any say and by September there might not be a club. It was a circus.'

Calloway recalls, 'We were basically a British and American team and had a good *esprit de corps*. They wanted to bring in all these foreigners. In the end we had an Egyptian putting his prayer mat down in the dressing-room praying to Allah and a Dutchman getting offended. Carlos and Paulo were unbelievable at times, but they thought they were playing with Brazilians. We had John Craven, who was as hard as nails and a brilliant defender, but couldn't trap a bag of cement. He didn't want to be playing short one-twos out of the box.' The Surf, who included Charlie Cooke on the wing, won only 11 out of 32 games, but the on-field problems came to an abrupt end with the closure of the team.

In Dallas, the Tornado won only five games under English coaches Mike Renshaw and Peter Short and, after 15 years in the league, owner Lamar Hunt decided he had seen enough. Meanwhile, qualification for the play-offs was not enough to save the Los Angeles Aztecs and Calgary Boomers from extinction.

The Montreal Manic were the surprise success of the season, drawing average attendances of more than 20,000. Eddie Firmani's team was spearheaded by Gordon Hill, who had been transferred from Manchester United to Derby for £250,000 and won six England caps since first playing in the NASL during his Millwall days in 1975. Hill registered 16 goals and 12 assists and former Manchester City man Tony Towers anchored the midfield with 9 assists. In the play-offs, Hill's four goals, including a 91st-minute penalty in the deciding game, helped win the best-of-three series against Los Angeles. But two more strikes from Hill and a couple of goals from Alan Willey could not stop a 2–1 series defeat against the Chicago Sting, who made it all the way to the Soccer Bowl, powered by the prolific goalscoring of German Karl-Heinz Granitza.

Chicago's first play-off victims were the Seattle Sounders, for whom former Norwich defender Kevin Bond, the penalty taker, was the leading scorer with 16 goals. Joining the familiar line-up of English faces in Seattle was midfielder Steve Daley, who had been Britain's most expensive footballer when he moved from Wolves to Manchester City for £1.5 million in September 1979 during a period of extravagant spending by Malcolm Allison. English goalkeeper Paul Hammond was a late-season addition.

Departing from Seattle during the season was Bruce Rioch, who recalls, 'During the winter I was corresponding with Roger Davies, who was playing in the indoor season. He said the atmosphere was not as good as it had been in my first year. He warned me to bear that in mind if I had thoughts about going back. I went out again but it wasn't as enjoyable, so when I was asked if I would like to go back to be player-coach at Torquay, I took the job.'

The Sounders achieved some success in an otherwise disappointing season by winning the transatlantic Challenge Cup after beating Southampton and Celtic in Seattle and drawing at the New York Cosmos.

In Vancouver, where former Leeds legend and ex-West Brom and Republic of Ireland manager Johnny Giles was in charge of the team, a won–lost record of 21–11 suggested that a second Whitecaps championship in three seasons might be possible. Giles had brought in several new, but familiar, faces, including two old Leeds teammates, Terry Yorath and Peter Lorimer, and ex-England and Queens Park Rangers winger Dave Thomas. Yorath became one of the few British players to maintain an international career from across the Atlantic when he jetted back to lead Wales against the USSR at Wrexham. 'As far as the pace of the game is concerned there is no problem,' he said. 'Where you must gear up is your level of concentration. When you return and face a side as good as the Russians you appreciate the gap.'

Ray Hankin scored 12 goals for the Whitecaps and Alan Taylor, the injury-prone striker who struck both of West Ham's goals in their 1975 FA Cup final victory, added 11. Only Peter Beardsley, a 20-year-old forward who scored 13 goals after being bought from Carlisle United, bettered those records. It was the first of Beardsley's three years in Canada, a residency that would be punctuated by a brief spell at Manchester United and would end with him finding a permanent home at Newcastle, from where he would launch his England career.

With a low centre of gravity, outstanding balance and ball control, Beardsley's potential was obvious to Hankin. 'Peter was a breath of fresh air,' he says. 'He had fantastic talent and made it so easy for me. He had quick feet and he could go past three or four defenders at a time.'

After the arguments and unrest of the previous season, Hankin also remembers the changed atmosphere at the club under Giles. 'Johnny changed the training format and how we played. His methods were very different to Tony Waiters', who had thrived on hard work. With Johnny we did a lot of ball work in training and he made it fun.'

But a single goal from Carl Valentine, the fourth Whitecaps player to have scored in double figures in the regular season, was all Vancouver had to cheer in two defeats against the Tampa Bay Rowdies in the first round of the play-offs. 'We had the quality in the team to go on and win,' says Hankin. 'We were the best team in the NASL but we blew it.'

While the Whitecaps had won their division, the Rowdies had only qualified for the play-offs thanks to a system that allowed a team finishing last in its division and losing more games than it won to enter the tournament field. The Rowdies had begun the season without former Luton midfielder Peter Anderson, who fired some parting shots at the club when returning to England to become player-manager at Millwall. 'My players at Millwall are treated better than those at Tampa,' he said. 'When we toured England last summer we had £2 a day spending money and had to do our own laundry.'

Kevin Keelan had arrived from New England to take over the goalkeeper's position, while former Tottenham full-back John Gorman would play well enough to be named in the league's all-star team for the third year running. The responsibility of providing the goals had fallen to former Swindon winger David Moss, on loan from Luton, and the 32-year-old Birmingham striker Frank Worthington.

While Moss scored nine goals and assisted on eleven, former England forward Worthington, whose previous NASL season had been in Philadelphia two years earlier, totalled 11 goals and 16 assists. Dubbed the 'Yorkshire Striker' by local media with a topical, if macabre, sense of humour, Worthington had arrived in Tampa talking about winning back his England place when he returned home. 'I feel I've done enough in the past to justify my claim,' he argued. But by the end of Tampa's inconsistent season, he was saying, 'The team has been unsettled and we've not put our game together. The service hasn't been as good as I'd like. I need the ball played to me and it hasn't been happening.'

The Tulsa Roughnecks, where former Wales midfielder Terry Hennessey took over from Charlie Mitchell as head coach, were helped to a play-off berth by 14 goals and 16 assists from the much-travelled and highly-skilled Duncan McKenzie, whose Football League career had just finished after stops at Nottingham Forest, Leeds, Everton, Chelsea and Blackburn. Less heralded was Dean Neal, a 20-year-old who scored 12 goals after signing from QPR.

Meanwhile, Ron Newman's San Diego Sockers and Vic Crowe's Portland Timbers had won through to a play-off meeting that was won by the Sockers. But San Diego missed out on a place in the Soccer Bowl when they came up against Chicago, despite winning the first game of the series through a pair of goals by former Polish World Cup captain and Manchester City midfielder Kazimierz Deyna. Predictably, the Sting's opponents in the final were the New York Cosmos, for whom Giorgio Chinaglia scored 29 regular season goals and 6 more in the play-offs.

New York's toughest opponents on the way to the final had been their old rivals from Tampa Bay. Few had expected the Rowdies to dispose of the Whitecaps, but Moss and Worthington contributed towards a 4–1 victory in the first game and a Moss free-kick and Keelan's safe hands secured a 1–0 victory in game two.

The first game of the quarter-final series was played in Tampa Stadium, where a burst of four goals midway through the game set up a 6–3 Cosmos victory. Having taken a two-goal lead in the second game in New York, the Rowdies were angered when Keelan was ruled to have allowed a shot to slip over the line to halve their lead. The keeper's heroics helped to keep the Cosmos in check for a further 40 minutes until New York broke through to equalise with five minutes remaining. The Rowdies edged the shoot-out and, with the mini-game system having been scrapped, the teams reassembled four days later in Giants Stadium, where the Rowdies' resistance was ended in a 2–0 home victory.

Five Chinaglia goals in two semi-final games saw the Cosmos overpower the Fort Lauderdale Strikers, for whom Ray Hudson, with 10 assists in the regular season, had once again played a key supporting role to more illustrious names like Teofilio Cubillas, scorer of 17 goals.

Soccer Bowl, played in front of 36,971 in Toronto, saw Chinaglia kept at bay, however, as the Sting finally overcame the defending champions in a shoot-out after 120 minutes of frustrating, scoreless action. ABC had not even aired the game live – showing it at lunchtime the following day – and it was no surprise when the company announced it was not renewing its contract for 1982.

The loss of its major television contract and the closure of several teams were not the only worries for the NASL. Although overall league attendance held steady at around 14,000, the Cosmos continued to decline, dropping to 36,000 per game, while Chicago had been one of the few teams able to capitalise on the summer's baseball strike to increase crowd figures.

Another ongoing threat to the NASL's stability was the emergence of the six-a-side version of the sport, played indoors on an enclosed field in an ice hockey-type environment. The Major Indoor Soccer League (MISL) had got that particular ball rolling in 1978–79 and had seen its most successful franchise, the Philadelphia Fever, average crowds of 8,500, more than some NASL teams could manage outdoors. As well as feeling obliged not to leave the field clear for a rival organisation, the NASL owners saw an opportunity to get their money's worth from players signed to 12-month contracts and a chance to keep the franchise in the public consciousness during the off-season.

The NASL's own indoor competition, therefore, had kicked off in 1980–81. But despite devoting resources and finances towards marketing their indoor teams, the NASL was being beaten at the gate by the MISL, which had also been quick to secure winter rights to NASL players not committed to year-round deals. Whitecaps general manager Tony Waiters argues, 'When indoor soccer raised its ugly head it was like mixing apples and oranges. The owners decided to take on the upstart MISL, so now teams were losing money in the winter as well as summer.'

By 1981, all but Philadelphia and New York of the NASL franchises had participated in the winter's 18-game schedule, but Woosnam admits, 'Indoor football split the ownership. Some thought it was the way to go, some didn't. The Cosmos didn't want to go into it and if you couldn't get the big guys it was a problem.'

Meanwhile, threatened with expulsion from FIFA, the NASL reluctantly bowed to pressure to drop the 35-yard offside experiment for the 1982 season and attempted to encourage the development of more home-grown players by increasing the number of Americans or Canadians fielded by each team to four. For years the rule had been three, but many teams had effectively reduced that number by fielding internationals who had qualified as American citizens, Giorgio Chinaglia in New York being an example. 'We need honest Americans in the league, not European thieves or phonies,' said US national team coach Walt Chyzowych.

With the NASL having dropped from 24 teams to 14 in 2 years, budgets being slashed around the league and reductions being imposed on imported players, the British professionals' great American adventure was drawing to a close.

21. ☆ All Over

On the NASL's diminishing number of playing fields, the league's final three seasons would feature yet another triumph for the New York Cosmos, a surprise success for the Tulsa Roughnecks and a second title for the Chicago Blitz. Away from the action, there was evidence of desperation as the NASL fought to halt its depressing march towards extinction.

Inevitably, the Cosmos remained the team to beat, their 1982 squad featuring the return of Steve Hunt for the first time since helping them win back-to-back titles in 1977 and 1978. His transfer to Coventry after the second of those victories had not produced the England recognition he had craved, and it would not be until he was back home again with West Brom that he would win his two international caps. 'I was told that a few experienced players would be added to the Coventry squad,' he said during another of the club's frequent relegation battles early in 1982. 'But that hasn't happened. It's difficult to make an impression with a side that's out of the spotlight. I miss playing in America. It is much more exciting and more geared to attacking play. I was an out-and-out winger there and I prefer that to the midfield role I've had to take on in England.'

Hunt's wishes were fulfilled when New York moved to get him back in Cosmos colours. This time he sported a neat, clean-shaven look instead of the long hair and moustachioed surfer style of years earlier. His impact, however, reminded everyone of his earlier spell at the club as he scored nine goals.

It was Hunt's goal that settled the decisive third game in the first round of the play-offs against Tulsa. In the semi-finals, the Cosmos came up against the San Diego Sockers, who were within one series of the Soccer Bowl for the third straight year. Ade Coker, the former

West Ham forward, had enjoyed a return to form with 13 goals for Ron Newman's men, but the team from California were again denied their day in the sun when the Cosmos beat them in two games.

The Seattle Sounders, champions of the Western Division, won through to contest the Soccer Bowl and earn a shot at revenge for New York's Pelé-inspired victory of five years earlier. Peter Ward was the spearhead of the Sounders attack, scoring 18 goals on his arrival from Nottingham Forest to win the league's MVP award. 'Defenders couldn't get anywhere near him,' says teammate Roger Davies. A prolific scorer at Brighton, where he bagged 79 League goals in 172 starts and earned an England cap as a substitute against Australia, Ward's transfer to the European champions in October of 1980 had brought limited success.

'Alan Hinton asked me to come over to America after he saw me score five against Manchester City in a reserve game,' says Ward. 'I didn't go over thinking I had anything to prove, I just fancied it and it was a decent amount of money. After a slow start, we played well. We didn't play any long ball stuff, we played a lot on the floor and that suited me.'

In Seattle's midfield, the former Wolves duo of Steve Daley and Kenny Hibbitt did their best to compensate for the long-term absence of Alan Hudson, Daley setting up 18 goals during the season and scoring twice in a decisive play-off win against the Toronto Blizzard.

Southern Division champions Fort Lauderdale Strikers, for whom Brian Kidd had scored 15 goals, were Seattle's opponents in a keenly contested semi-final series. Beaten 2–0 at home, Kidd having scored one of the goals, the Sounders kept their championship hopes alive with a 4–3 extra-time win in Florida, where Ward equalised with 43 seconds left in the 90 minutes and Davies doubled his season's total of goals by finding the net twice. Overtime was needed again in the decider in the Kingdome before Hibbitt scored the game's only goal.

The final in San Diego, watched by fewer than 23,000 fans, was settled when Giorgio Chinaglia, scorer of 20 regular season goals, found the net to give New York a 1–0 victory and their fourth title in six seasons. 'They were more experienced at the top level and they were the better team,' says Seattle goalkeeper Paul Hammond. 'Their goal might have been my fault because I charged out and I was a bit slow in going down.'

Ward argues, 'I thought we outplayed them, but just couldn't score. I remember going up to Carlos Alberto, who was magnificent, and asking for his shirt. He said, "Only if you give me yours." I thought he was kidding but he came into the locker room after the game and swapped shirts.'

Soccer Bowl '82 was to be the last title shot for both teams. The Cosmos, who saw Hunt return to England but welcomed back Franz Beckenbauer at the age of 37, suffered a surprise defeat to Montreal to end their 1983 campaign. Their final season, with Eddie Firmani returning to coach the team and Giorgio Chinaglia departing, saw them fail to qualify for the play-offs for the first time since 1975. With crowds down below 13,000 per game, the Cosmos had even tried unsuccessfully to lure Pelé out of retirement.

For Seattle, it was an even sorrier tale, their appearance in the 1982 final marking the beginning of the end for one of the NASL's most successful franchises. Coach Alan Hinton did not survive the winter of 1982–83 after the team's new owner, Bruce Anderson, decided to include more local players. His drive towards Americanisation even included banning the use of the English word 'pitch' to describe the field. Laurie Calloway, the former San Jose defender and California coach, took over the team. 'I had a reputation as being someone who thought we should bring in Americans quicker,' he explains. But Calloway's appointment was not welcomed by Hudson, who referred to 'two clowns' having taken over the organisation.

Calloway says, 'Alan Hudson resented me and wouldn't do what I asked him to do. I didn't agree with the philosophy of the league, which had been favouring the Brits coming over towards the end of their careers and, in some cases, stealing money. Some didn't perform. I told Alan I wanted him to be the main man, but we didn't see eye to eye. He slagged me off but I won't get into it with him because I have too much respect for him. He was a great player.'

Hudson was gone after one game of the 1983 season, while Davies was traded to Fort Lauderdale before the new season kicked off. Davies recalls, 'After I won the MVP award I tried to get a no-cut, no-trade contract, but the general manager, Jack Daley, had said, "You won't need that as long as I am here." But then he got sacked. They got rid of me and Alan because we were the highest-earning players.'

As the 1983 season progressed, it was clear that the Sounders, with their attendance down by several thousand on previous years, would struggle to make the play-offs, despite thirteen goals from Ward, nine by well-travelled English forward David Kemp and the signing of former Manchester City and England goalkeeper Joe Corrigan. And there were concerns off the field. 'The owner wanted to save money but probably should have done it more slowly,' says Calloway. 'The team had financial problems and there were doubts about the guy's ability to keep the team going. In the end people were not being paid. I had to be a counsellor to wives asking me when their money was coming. We were playing to get into the play-offs in the last two games and the wives went in for their money and there was none. Joe Corrigan said, "You don't expect us to play with no wages." We got them to play but their hearts weren't in it and we lost two games we could have won. If you don't get paid, some players are just going to say, "This is bollocks." A couple of weeks later the team folded.'

Peter Ward recalls, 'We'd had an inkling, but none of us had been around that kind of situation and atmosphere, so we didn't really believe it. We'd seen players in England wondering if they were going to get a new contract, but not this. It was a shock because we'd still done OK with the crowds.'

At least the Sounders had made it into the 1983 season, which is more than could be said of the Edmonton Drillers, Jacksonville Tea Men and Portland Timbers, who all played their final seasons in 1982. In Portland, crowds hovered around 7,000 in what had once been 'Soccer City, USA'.

The signing of Scottish World Cup star Archie Gemmill, a League Championship winner at Derby and Nottingham Forest and holder of 43 international caps, had been unable to drag Noel Cantwell's Tea Men from the foot of their division and dissuade them from dropping down to the American Soccer League. Mark Lindsay, signed from San Jose, recalls, 'It was the most volatile team I played for. We had Argentinian players and Archie made a couple of comments they didn't like. There were more fights there than at any other period of my career.'

The Montreal Manics were another team who would not see the end of the NASL era. After making the play-offs in 1982, they were there again the following year. Top scorer Alan Willey and Tony Towers each scored in a 4–2 win against the Cosmos and more than 20,000 in the Olympic Stadium saw a shoot-out victory complete a surprise series win. But defeat against Tulsa in the semi-final series was the club's last action.

The Roughnecks, tucked away from the spotlight in the media outback of Oklahoma, had long been many people's tip to go to the wall. Instead they were on their way to their finest hour. In 1982, Terry Hennessey's players had forced their way into the play-off field on the back of 17 goals by Laurie Abrahams and a team-high 11 assists by David Bradford. A year later, they rose to the top of the Southern Division after Ron Futcher arrived to partner

Abrahams. The ex-Luton man scored 15 times in the regular season and his double in the second game of the first round series was enough to kill off Fort Lauderdale, where David Chadwick had returned as head coach and Kidd had once again been the star performer with 18 goals. Abrahams recalls, 'Ron was lucky to be on the field for the second game because he had chased after someone earlier on.'

In the first game against Montreal, the Roughnecks prevailed in a shoot-out after Futcher scored their only goal in a 1–1 draw and former Luton midfielder Lil Fuccillo had been sent off. 'He had been booked for a nothing foul and then got another card,' says Abrahams. 'We lucked out with a draw.' A defeat at Montreal set up a deciding game back at Tulsa's Skelly Stadium, where Futcher struck twice in a 3–0 win to put the Roughnecks through to Soccer Bowl, to be played in Vancouver.

It was a remarkable achievement by Hennessey's team, who had the lowest payroll in the league. Says Futcher, 'Our team spirit was fantastic, even though we didn't have the best players technically. Everyone played at the top of their game and teams could not deal with the humidity in Oklahoma. We were winning games in the last 20 minutes because they were knackered.'

Even more amazing than the Roughnecks' success was the league's decision to allow Futcher to play in the final. 'I was booked in the semi-final, which took me to the number of yellow cards you needed to be banned,' he explains. 'But our owner complained that it would devalue the final if the better players did not play.'

Citing the 'best interests of the game', the NASL rule-makers allowed Futcher to take the field in front of a crowd of 60,051. The striker continued his scoring spree with the second goal in a 2–0 win against Toronto as the Roughnecks were crowned as one of the NASL's more unlikely champions. Abrahams concludes, 'Overall, we were very, very fortunate to win it. Montreal had done us a favour by beating the Cosmos, who we couldn't beat. They were our bogey team.'

Toronto, champions in 1976 but rarely in the hunt since then, had begun their own resurgence with the appointment of Bob Houghton as head coach in 1982. Houghton, a former Fulham junior who decided early in his career to turn to coaching, had come to prominence in his native England when, still only 30, he led Swedish side Malmö to a 1979 European Cup final place against Nottingham Forest. He returned home for an unsuccessful spell as manager of Bristol City that lasted less than two seasons. His Toronto team, which included former Manchester United and

Northern Ireland full-back Jimmy Nicholl and ex-Liverpool 'Super Sub' David Fairclough, advanced to the play-offs in his first season. The feat was repeated a year later when David Byrne, son of former England and West Ham forward John 'Budgie' Byrne, led the individual points list with 13 goals and 18 assists.

The signing of Nicholl, born in Hamilton, Ontario, before his family moved to Belfast, had been significant for the Blizzard in light of the regulations introduced by the NASL before the 1982 season. Players like Nicholl, who had Canadian citizenship, enabled teams to meet their quota of home-based players without loss of quality, but did nothing to hasten the development of the US and Canadian national teams.

With that in mind, and in a development that smacked as much of desperation as innovation, 1983 saw the introduction of Team America to the NASL. Based in Washington DC, the club was intended to give the US national side the experience, training and cohesion that would help them on the international stage – as well being a patriotic marketing ploy. Defender Alan Merrick, who had been in the US long enough to acquire American citizenship, jumped at the chance to represent his adopted country. 'I knew I wasn't going back to England and I felt like an American,' he says. 'It was a novel opportunity.'

But many of the better American players, like New York Cosmos midfielder Ricky Davis, chose not to leave successful teams for an experimental one. 'I thought he had let us down,' says Merrick. 'The concept was good and it needed guys like Ricky to help the United States Soccer Federation's marketing, to give it a focal point.'

Other newly qualified Americans were striker Alan Green and goalkeeper Paul Hammond, who recalls, 'One of the highlights was meeting Ronald Reagan in the Oval Office. I sent the pictures back to my mum in Nottingham. But everyone wanted to beat us and there was a bit of animosity because we were not really the US team.'

Former NASL commissioner Phil Woosnam adds, 'About six teams would not release their players. They couldn't visualise that if the national team does well, then suddenly the sport is important for the media and the kids.'

Lack of quality players, a won–lost record of 10–20 and average crowds of 11,000 ensured that the new team was a one-year experiment only. Bizarrely, the Montreal Manic management liked what they saw enough to announce that they would act as Team Canada in 1984. It was a suicidal move in the pro-French city of Montreal at a time of great activity among Quebec separatist movements. As the crowds drifted away, the club's fate was sealed and the new team would never see the light of day.

If Team America's failure was a disappointment, it was nothing compared with the blow suffered by Woosnam, the NASL and the cause of American soccer during the winter of 1982–83. In his role as vice-president of the USSF, Woosnam had been the driving force behind the American bid to stage the 1986 World Cup finals after Colombia decided it could not fulfil its commitment to host the event. 'We had been inviting big names to present the trophy at Soccer Bowls, like Sir Stanley Rous and Sepp Blatter from FIFA and Henry Kissinger. We staged the world all-star game after the 1982 finals. All of it was done with the thought that one day we would be ready to hold the World Cup.

'After Colombia threw it back in December '82, I knew we were ready because if you put on a competition like that in this country it is successful. The person at FIFA we dealt with more than anyone else said, "If you put the best presentation together you will get it." I spent all my time on the presentation. I got another guy out of the league office and we ran all over the country getting stadiums, mayors, everything. Our presentation consisted of two thick flip-books, with photographs, statistics and God knows what. But the nine-page, hand-written presentation from Mexico won the day. You would never have believed it. Getting the World Cup would have counter-influenced the negative things that were going on. From then on I knew it was going to be tough.'

He was not wrong. By the time the 1984 season rolled around, the NASL, which had gone from 14 teams in 1982 to 12 a year later, was down to 9 clubs. And Woosnam himself had departed.

The man whose energy helped to keep the NASL in business in the late '60s and had, wisely or otherwise, driven it towards expansion throughout the '70s, cleared out his office after the 1983 season and said farewell to the organisation that had been his life for a decade and a half. For the previous year, Woosnam had been kept around the league's New York headquarters mainly to help his replacement find his feet after the NASL owners decided that a new face was required to front their business. While Woosnam was working on the American World Cup bid, Howard Samuels had been installed as the league's new commissioner.

'You have to accept it. It happens in all walks of life,' reflects the Welshman, his baritone voice still resonating more of the valleys than the Atlanta suburbs where he makes his home. 'I stayed on to help the new guy and then I tried to look onwards and went and did the marketing for the USSF.'

Samuels came from a military background, which apparently made him ideal for the trench warfare that NASL survival had become by the time he was installed as league president and chief executive officer in June 1982. Later that year, the NASL owners had decided to save on Woosnam's salary by adding commissioner to the role of a man who had been an aide to three US Presidents.

As the 1984 season approached, Samuels was bent on introducing a salary cap and raising the number of North American players required on the field to five. He and the team owners went as far as warning the players' union that the league would fold unless they accepted a reduction in squad size from 24 to 19, a 15 per cent pay cut for any player earning more than $40,000 and an overall team salary budget of $600,000 – although there was scope to have one star player's salary fall outside of that figure. The players initially rejected the offer before finally, less than three weeks before the season kicked off, agreeing to everything but the individual salary reduction.

Along with wages, the season was also shrinking, from 30 to 24 games, to allow for a longer indoor season. That change of emphasis saw the Fort Lauderdale Strikers head north to Minnesota, where a better indoor venue was available. The Strikers took Alan Willey back to the city where he had been such a force for the Kicks and his 15 goals, plus 8 by Brian Kidd, helped them win 14 of their 24 games, although that was not enough to make the 4-team play-off field. The support for the team was disappointing compared to the 20,000-plus who had consistently turned out to support the Kicks. There was one huge crowd, a 52,621 turn-out for the game against the Tampa Bay Rowdies, but that was a somewhat false figure.

Coach Dave Chadwick recalls, 'The Beach Boys were in concert right after the game. We won it with a Brian Kidd goal and we had won four of our first five games. We were on a great run. But next game we had only 6,000. Where the hell had everyone gone? You could see the players as they came of out of the tunnel. It was horrific. They were all fired up to play and it was like a needle in a balloon.'

Occupying the top two places in the Western Division above the Strikers were the San Diego Sockers and Vancouver Whitecaps. San Diego's division title meant a fourth semi-final place in five years and owed much to Ade Coker's 16 goals.

The Whitecaps had endured a frustrating three seasons. In 1982, they had won more games than anyone in their division but finished only third because of their failure to pick up as many bonus points for goals as their rivals. What goals they did score had been spread around between Ray Hankin, with 11, and Peter Lorimer and Carl Valentine, who scored 10 apiece. Former West Brom skipper John Wile was the linchpin of the defence.

In 1983, the Whitecaps had returned to the top of their division with 24 wins, the most in the league, only to lose to Toronto in the first round of the play-offs. David Cross, the bearded former Norwich, Coventry, West Brom and West Ham centre-forward, led the attack with 19 goals, while Peter Beardsley's 8 took his tally to 28 in his 3-year stay in Canada. Other players added by coach Johnny Giles included ex-Sunderland, Manchester City and England stopper Dave Watson and Dutch midfielder Frans Thijssen, who had helped Ipswich lift the UEFA Cup in 1981 and been named England's Footballer of the Year.

Vancouver began the 1984 season with Giles, who had returned for a second stint as West Brom manager, being replaced by former Seattle coach Alan Hinton. Peter Ward made the same short journey from the defunct Sounders to register 16 goals and 10 assists. The Whitecaps won fewer games than Minnesota, but edged ahead because of scoring more goals, ten of them provided by Cross.

The defending champions, Tulsa Roughnecks, never threatened to repeat their feat of a year earlier after very nearly failing to start the new season. The team's owners, figuring they had lost $8 million on their venture, decided to fold the franchise without even paying the players their Soccer Bowl bonuses. Samuels, however, had other ideas, claiming it would be 'a kick in the teeth' if the league began the 1984 season without its champions. Although Samuels' own efforts at raising the capital to save the team appeared doomed, a local disc jockey galvanised his listeners into raising $65,000 – just enough to keep the team in business.

Dutch World Cup player Wim Suurbier replaced Terry Hennessey as head coach and, for the second time in his NASL career, striker Laurie Abrahams was pleased to get away from Tulsa. 'The club was having a ruck again. Terry left and the management was arguing about money,' he says. Strike partner Ron Futcher signed off his NASL career with a flourish of 18 goals, but 10 defeats in their first 13 games doomed the Roughnecks to a lowly finish.

Bringing up the rear in the Western Division were the Golden Bay Earthquakes, who had made the play-offs a year earlier after changing their name from San Jose in an attempt to appeal to a wider fan base. Former Luton striker Godfrey Ingram's 16 goals had been one of the main reasons for their success in 1983, but he began the following season with Minnesota. After scoring only twice in 12 games for the Strikers, he returned for the last eight games of the Earthquakes' undistinguished season.

In the Eastern Division, the Chicago Sting took the honours ahead of Toronto, even though they scored only one more goal than they conceded. The Sting had been unable to maintain their championship-winning form after their 1981 triumph, finishing last in their division in 1982 – despite Gordon Hill's nine goals after a trade from Montreal – and making an early play-off exit a year later. Toronto's second place finish owed much to David Byrne, who scored 12 goals and made 13 more.

Occupying last place in the division were the Tampa Bay Rowdies, which was hardly the result Rodney Marsh had expected when he accepted the offer to coach his former team. Marsh's return had fulfilled the promise he made to Tampa reporters when he warned them after his farewell testimonial game in 1979, 'I'll be back.'

While Marsh had been enjoying success as coach and chief executive of the semi-professional Carolina Lightnin', the Rowdies had been a pale imitation of the team he graced in the NASL's boom years. In 1983, no team had achieved fewer than the Rowdies' seven victories under American coach Al Miller, who had succeeded Gordon Jago after his 1982 team had won only 12 games. Jago's final match had been an embarrassing 9–2 defeat at Toronto.

The Rowdies' owners, Cornelia and Dick Corbett, felt that a dose of the Marsh personality was the tonic required to revive their ailing team. His English contingent included former Manchester City teammate Tony Towers and ex-Bolton forward Stuart Lee, while Mark Lindsay returned to Tampa Bay to play seven games after taking the job of player-coach. Lindsay admits that his move was inspired by the inevitability of the NASL's closure. 'I could have stayed in San Jose, but I was more cynical as my career went on. Everyone knew the league was winding down and my idea was to get back to Tampa, play out my career and settle down in my house.'

Even Marsh, their talisman, could not revive the Rowdies' fortunes and their only high spot was when South African-born teenager Roy Wegerle, a future US international, was named Rookie of the Year after totalling nine goals and seven assists. Marsh got straight on the phone to England and helped Wegerle launch his Football League career with a move to Chelsea.

The final NASL play-offs saw Toronto dispose of San Diego in two games, while Chicago and Vancouver played out a much more exciting series. After former Wolves goalkeeper Paul Bradshaw kept a clean sheet and Carl Valentine earned a single-goal Whitecaps victory in the opening game in Chicago, the Sting hit back by winning 3–1 in Vancouver and taking the decider 4–3 in the Windy City.

Soccer Bowl had gone the way of so many features of the NASL's previous, more successful, era, replaced by a best-of-three series that at least ensured home team participation. The Sting became the NASL's last-ever champions – and the only team apart from the Cosmos to win the title more than once – with a pair of close-fought victories, 2–1 and 3–2 over Bob Houghton's Blizzard team. Toronto keeper Paul Hammond recalls, 'Many people didn't like Bob because they thought he was too defensive. We lost both games and it was disappointing because I thought we were the better team.'

It was obvious, however, that the real battle was taking place away from the field. The league was fighting for its life. While the 1984 Olympic soccer tournament was attracting crowds of 100,000 to games at the Pasadena Rose Bowl in California, attendance had continued to slump in the NASL. Hammond remembers, 'There were rumours rumbling all around during that year. I was lucky that the teams I was with were financially sound, but we heard stories about players not getting paid or being two weeks behind and it was unnerving.'

San Diego, Minnesota and Chicago announced plans to move to the MISL. The Whitecaps said they could not continue, selling off everything apart from their Soccer Bowl trophy. And, in March 1985, the previously unthinkable happened when the Cosmos, sold by Warner Communications to none other than Giorgio Chinaglia, joined the defections to the MISL. 'That was the end,' says Alan Hinton. 'When the Cosmos pulled out, the league was finished.'

The possibility of a new franchise in Seattle would still have left the league with only five teams. The death of Howard Samuels early in 1985 from a heart attack also meant that the NASL was without a figurehead to attempt to keep the league in business.

In the final week of March, the inevitable announcement was made: the NASL was ceasing operations. The news was greeted by most American sports fans like the passing of a fragile, elderly aunt. Even to those who cared, it was hardly a shock. As for the rest, well, it came as a surprise to learn that the ailing old girl had still been alive at all. After close to 4,000 games, and almost 18 years after Geoff Hurst's hat-trick showed America the potential of the world game, it really was all over.

☆

Almost two decades on from the NASL's final curtain, opinions remain divided about the cause of the league's downfall. Rapid expansion, apathy of the television networks, inept local management, the dominance of the Cosmos, failure to develop North American players, ill-advised attempts to push through home-grown players too quickly, the strike of 1979, the failed American World Cup bid – all played a part at certain times and all feature when those involved in the NASL look back at the league's demise.

Former Vancouver Whitecaps coach Tony Waiters argues, 'I thought it was crazy to expand in 1978. In 1977 it looked as though the league had a real chance of succeeding. It became unbalanced, with more teams struggling than succeeding. Phil Woosnam always said it was not his decision but he must have been able to influence the owners into standing put if he'd wanted to.'

Clive Toye, the former sportswriter who signed Pelé for the New York Cosmos, remains convinced of the folly of expansion. 'Those new teams were Johnny-come-lately carpetbaggers who had no idea of how we had got to where we were. They thought you could sign big players and people would come. Bullshit. We built a constituency in New York before we signed Pelé. Some of the good guys in the league sold up because it was not the league they wanted to be in. It was the one thing Phil and I clashed over in our philosophies. We parted ways and haven't spoken much since.'

Jimmy Gabriel, who coached the Seattle Sounders and San Jose Earthquakes, blames the industrial action of 1979. 'When the union man came in and said they had to get the players organised, the wonderful feeling between fans and players was lost and the game never recovered. The players just wanted a union and the owners didn't want them to have one. It was stalemate and in the end it ruined the league.'

Alan Ball, who helped the Whitecaps win Soccer Bowl with a mostly British team, says, 'I thought the Americans started to take the game back for themselves. It went from two American players to three and then to five, but they were moving too fast. People wanted to see big stars.'

Former Tea Men coach Noel Cantwell disagrees, saying, 'One of the things that could have been done differently was having more young American players in the team. With only one or two, the game was not going to make progress as quickly as they wanted. Maybe four Americans in the team earlier on would have improved the standard and encouraged more people to come.'

Peter McParland, one of the overseas stars of the NASL's early years, says, 'I think they made a mistake by going into the big time too quickly. They paid big bucks and I don't think that was wise. Slow and steady progress would have been better. They should have aimed for a mix of players to build it up and not gone after the big stars. The odd one was fair enough, but they brought in a lot of fellows who were just out to get a few bob.'

Former Vancouver coach and San Antonio player Bob McNab says, 'Owners of all the other sports clubs here in America will accept vast losses, but only if the value of their franchise increases. The value of the NASL franchises never increased because the league never got a major long-term TV contract.'

Geoff Barnett was coach at the Minnesota Kicks, one of the league's best-attended franchises, when that team folded. 'Our problem was that we had a very low average ticket price,' he says. 'It was about four dollars per ticket so for thirty bucks you could take the whole family for a day out. The club was scared to increase the prices in case people stopped coming so we always had low revenue.'

Peter Wall, who played for and coached the California Surf franchise, says, 'People had to recognise that the Cosmos had Warner Brothers behind them so money was no object. They could buy who they wanted, but then other people thought they could do that too. They paid out money to compete and at the end of the day owners looked at the balance sheet and saw how much they had lost. It became a crumbling tower.'

So the NASL failed to last the distance. But a league that captured the public's imagination, changed the landscape of American team sport and became a focus for the soccer world, if only for a few years, can hardly be written off as a failure. Certainly none of the vast British contingent in what amounted to a world all-star league would ever call it that.

Phil Woosnam turned down a transfer to Chelsea to accept what turned out to be an opportunity to run the NASL for almost 15 years, prompting the comment that 'his greatest asset and his greatest defect was a vision that outreached the league's tenuous grasp'. It seems appropriate, therefore, to give him the final word.

'The NASL established a foundation for the sport that they will never take away,' he concludes. 'Certainly many of the American players today are here as a result of the NASL. Brandi Chastain fell in love with the sport because she fell in love with Giorgio Chinaglia. The fact that Major League Soccer is here now is a consequence of what went on in the NASL, with Pelé and

Beckenbauer, British guys like Best and Marsh, and, equally, those like Ron Newman, who went around saying, "Let's get something organised."

'A lot of people gave their lives to it. It was a great challenge, some great people were involved, we accomplished a lot and we had some great years. We didn't get past the finish line, but we came pretty close.'

Postscript

It may have come too late for Phil Woosnam and the North American Soccer League, but the World Cup finally arrived in the United States in the summer of 1994. At last, so the theory went, the nation would catch the football fever that had been afflicting the rest of the world for more than a century.

As it happened, few Americans paid much attention to the opening match between Germany and Bolivia. Instead, tens of millions were glued to the televised police pursuit of a white Ford Bronco belonging to murder suspect and former American football hero O.J. Simpson. But a tournament that began and ended with a missed penalty kick – Diana Ross's embarrassing effort in the opening ceremony and Roberto Baggio's failure in Italy's shoot-out against Brazil – had more than its share of memorable moments. It was, as Woosnam had always predicted, magnificently organised, played in wonderful arenas in front of huge and enthusiastic crowds. The football, until the goalless final at least, was of vintage quality and there was even the opportunity for patriotic flag-waving when the United States upset Colombia, one of the pre-tournament favourites, before running Brazil close in the knock-out stage. As an introduction to soccer for the non-believers, there was not much that could have been bettered. Now it was time for the pay-off.

The award of the World Cup to the United States, ahead of Brazil and Colombia, had been made by FIFA on the understanding that it would be accompanied by the establishment of the country's first professional league since the NASL played its final game in 1984. But with the sport's governing body, and American soccer fans, becoming increasingly impatient for the deal to be fulfilled, it was the spring of 1996 before Major League Soccer finally took to the field.

The years since professional soccer had been played outdoors in the United States had been frustrating for the remaining fans of the sport. At one point, only the Western Soccer League, with its four teams, was playing a decent standard of the game outside of the nation's colleges. At grass-roots level, the number of players had never been so high, yet soccer was seen as a cheap and safe participation sport for youngsters of any sex, size or shape, while the 'real' athletes moved on to the world of gridiron or baseball.

Professionally, all that remained was the indoor game. The Major Indoor Soccer League, until its closure in 1992, continued to feature many British players who had decided that their futures lay in America. But while players like Alan Willey, Paul Child and Peter Ward put a roof over their heads by playing with a roof over their heads, the revival of the outdoor game was being planned – in the shape of America's bid to host the 1994 World Cup. The success, albeit brief, of the NASL and the huge crowds for the 1984 Olympic soccer tournament in Los Angeles helped the United States Soccer Federation convince FIFA of the viability of their scheme. And on the playing side, America's hosting of the event was conveniently validated by the national team's qualification for the 1990 finals in Italy. It was a feat achieved mostly with players from college soccer and from the semi-professional American Soccer League, which had re-formed in 1988. Among its founders was the former British sportswriter and New York Cosmos general manager Clive Toye.

To prepare its players for the 1994 finals without the benefit of a top-level domestic league, the USSF signed many of the country's best players to central contracts and embarked on a programme of year-round warm-up games aimed at providing continuity and competition. It was only ever intended to be a short-term solution, however, and once the World Cup had been and gone the urgency to launch the new league intensified.

Major League Soccer had earned FIFA approval as the country's top-level professional competition and set about demonstrating that it had learned some valuable lessons from the NASL's demise. Limitations on overseas players to five per team, a centrally controlled system for signing players, and salary limits of $1.25 million per team and $175,000 per player were all part of the structure when ten teams took the field for the inaugural MLS season.

By the time the league was entering its eighth season in 2003, very little had changed since that first year. Average attendance was holding steady at around 15,000 per game, while television coverage was being offered on cable sports station ESPN 2, with the

MLS Cup final – the modern version of the Soccer Bowl – broadcast on the ABC network.

Unlike the NASL, there has been no rush to expand. Numbers did rise to 12 for a couple of seasons, only for the teams in Miami and Tampa Bay to be closed down. Following the same thinking employed by the NASL on many occasions, the Miami Fusion had been located in the belief that the large Hispanic population in southern Florida would turn out to cheer their local team. But although it proved to be a misplaced assumption in the case of Miami, the Los Angeles Galaxy have enjoyed considerable support from the Mexican section of that city's population. The Galaxy, MLS champions in 2002, were even considered worthy of inclusion in the English magazine *Four Four Two*'s 'World Premiership' in the spring of 2003. The product on the field remains predominantly home-grown. Very few established world stars have been seen in the league, the most notable being German World Cup captain Lothar Matthäus, wild-haired Colombian striker Carlos Valderrama and Bulgarian World Cup forward Hristo Stoitchkov. The limits on overseas signings and the improved lot of the professional player in England and Scotland have combined to keep the British presence to a minimum. Whereas the average First Division player in the '70s dreamed of having his mortgage paid off by the time he retired, the modern Premiership squad member could pay cash for a new house every year. There is no longer a desire to seek out a summer 'earner' and, with its salary cap, American professional soccer is hardly the place to get rich quick.

Former Celtic, Rangers and Scotland striker Mo Johnston did spend six seasons at the Kansas City Wizards, where ex-Rangers, Tottenham and Scotland defender Richard Gough was a teammate. Manchester City and West Ham midfielder Ian Bishop and former Arsenal League Cup hero Steve Morrow have been among other British imports, while John Spencer, the former Chelsea, Queens Park Rangers, Everton and Scotland striker, was in his third season of leading the Colorado Rapids attack in 2003.

For a while it appeared as though the MLS might take a step down a path trodden by the NASL when Paul Gascoigne was given a week's trial by Washington DC United following the 2002 season, but the decision was made not to sign a player who would undoubtedly have raised the league's profile.

Had Gascoigne played for Washington, his coach would have been fellow Geordie Ray Hudson, the ex-Newcastle midfielder. Hudson was in his second season at United in 2003, having previously coached the Miami Fusion, and is one of a small group who span the NASL and MLS eras. Another is Hudson's former coach at the Fort Lauderdale Strikers, Ron Newman – winner of more games than any other coach in NASL history – who led the Kansas City Wizards through the first couple of MLS seasons. Meanwhile, Roy Wegerle, the South African-born forward who was the NASL's final Rookie of the Year and spent most of his career in England, was one of the US internationals who returned from foreign fields when the MLS kicked off.

A notable British name in the MLS during 2003 was that of former Liverpool and Scotland defender Steve Nicol, who took over as head coach of an ailing New England Revolution team the previous year and led them to the MLS Cup final. Nicol has seen enough in two years in America to believe that the MLS is rapidly closing the gap on the rest of the world. 'I think we and the other MLS teams could hold our own in Division One of the Nationwide League,' he says. 'There may be too much depth in the Premiership for us to compete with the big teams, but maybe we could give the lower teams a run for their money. There's certainly a possibility that in ten years' time there could be a whole wealth of talent. The young guys coming through now are a real step up from what they had ten years ago. If they continue at that rate they'll have a great national team and a strong league.'

Nicol warns that 'if they think for one minute that soccer's made it here, then it will just go down the pan' and endorses the league's continuing policy of shying away from NASL-style importing of ageing superstars. 'It doesn't look good for the league if they bring in retired guys, although people like that can pass on something to this country. There's a fine dividing line between someone who's coming here for a rest and someone who is going to work hard and do their stuff.'

While the MLS continues to combat that issue, and other problems faced by the NASL, some of its predecessor's obstacles remain. Most significant is the simple fact that the overwhelming majority of Americans remain uninterested in watching professional soccer on a regular basis. The MLS's determination to develop American players has undoubtedly raised the standard of the national team, but the fact that the USA is now good enough to reach the quarter-finals of the World Cup remains of only passing interest. To a sporting public used to seeing its nation triumph on the world stage, nothing less than winning the World Cup seems likely to achieve the surge of interest that Phil Woosnam always argued would result from national team success. In fact, the 1999 World Cup victory of the US women's team, in front of 90,000 fans in Los Angeles, captured the imagination to a far greater extent than the men's achievement in the Far East three years later.

Postscript

For now, however, professional soccer is at least re-established in the United States and, thanks to a sensible, safety-first business plan, appears to have a decent chance of achieving longevity. But the edge, excitement and anti-establishment feel of the NASL is still missed by many. The conservative MLS even allows games to end in a draw!

The North American Soccer League dared to be big; it screamed to be heard in the brash and boisterous world of American sport. Perhaps the kind of caution and common sense exhibited by Major League Soccer would have kept it in business for longer. But, as any of the NASL's British contingent will tell you, it wouldn't have been half as much fun.

Appendix

NASL Championship Games, 1967–84

1967 (NATIONAL PROFESSIONAL SOCCER LEAGUE)
Baltimore Bays 1 (Viollet), Oakland Clippers 0. Attendance: 16,329
Oakland Clippers 4 (Djukic 3, Marin), Baltimore Bays 1 (St Vil).
   Attendance: 9,037
(*Oakland won 4–2 on aggregate*)

1967 (UNITED SOCCER ASSOCIATION), LOS ANGELES
   COLISEUM
Los Angeles Wolves 6 (Knowles, Burnside 3, Dougan, Shewan o.g.),
   Washington Whips 5 (Smith, Munro 3, Storrie). Attendance:
   17,824

1968
San Diego Toros 0, Atlanta Chiefs 0. Attendance: 9,360
Atlanta Chiefs 3 (McParland, Scott, Motaung), San Diego Toros 0.
   Attendance: 14,994
(*Atlanta won 3–0 on aggregate*)

1969
No championship game. Championship won by Kansas City Spurs

1970
Rochester Lancers 3 (Costa 2, Marotti), Washington Darts 0.
   Attendance: 9,321
Washington Darts 3 (DeLeon, Nana, Browne), Rochester Lancers 1
   (Costa). Attendance: 5,543
(*Rochester won 4–3 on aggregate*)

1971

Atlanta Chiefs 2 (Uriel, Motaung), Dallas Tornado 1 (Molnar).

Dallas Tornado 4 (Tinney, Juracy 2, McLoughlin), Atlanta Chiefs 1 (Largie).

Atlanta Chiefs 0, Dallas Tornado 2 (Renshaw, Moffat). Attendance: 4,687

(*Dallas won series 2–1*)

1972

New York 2 (Horton, Jelinek), St Louis Stars 1 (Frankiewicz). Hofstra Stadium, New York. Attendance: 6,102

1973

Dallas Tornado 0, Philadelphia Atoms 2 (Best o.g., Straub). Irving Stadium, Texas. Attendance: 18,824

1974

Los Angeles Aztecs 3 (De Rienzo, Banhoffer, McMillan), Miami Toros 3 (Wright, o.g., Aranguiz). Orange Bowl, Miami. Attendance: 15,507

(*After extra time. Los Angeles won on penalties*)

1975

Tampa Bay Rowdies 2 (Auguste, Best), Portland Timbers 0. Spartan Stadium, San Jose. Attendance: 17,009

1976

Toronto Metros-Croatia 3 (Eusebio, Lukacevic, Ferreira), Minnesota Kicks 0. Kingdome, Seattle. Attendance: 25,765

1977

New York Cosmos 2 (Hunt, Chinaglia), Seattle Sounders 1 (Ord). Civic Stadium, Portland. Attendance: 35,548

1978

New York Cosmos 3 (Tueart 2, Chinaglia), Tampa Bay Rowdies 1 (Mirandinha). Giants Stadium, New Jersey. Attendance: 74,901

1979

Vancouver Whitecaps 2 (Whymark 2), Tampa Bay Rowdies 1 (Van der Veen). Giants Stadium, New Jersey. Attendance: 50,699

1980

New York Cosmos 3 (Romero, Chinaglia 2), Fort Lauderdale

Strikers 0. RFK Stadium, Washington DC. Attendance: 50,768
1981
Chicago Sting 0, New York Cosmos 0. Exhibition Stadium, Toronto. Attendance: 36,971
(*After extra time. Chicago won in a shoot-out*)

1982
New York Cosmos 1 (Chinaglia), Seattle Sounders 0. Jack Murphy Stadium, San Diego. Attendance: 22,634

1983
Tulsa Roughnecks 2 (Pesa, Futcher), Toronto Blizzard 0. Empire Stadium, Vancouver. Attendance: 60,051

1984
Chicago Sting 2 (Margetic, Rojas), Toronto Blizzard 1 (Wilson). Attendance: 8,352
Toronto Blizzard 2 (Paskin, Bettega), Chicago Sting 3 (Simanton, Margetic 2). Attendance: 16,821
(*Chicago won series 2–0*)

Sources

Interviews

Laurie Abrahams, Ken Adam, Alan Ball, Geoff Barnett, John Best, Alan Birchenall, Jeff Bourne, Gordon Bradley, Laurie Calloway, Noel Cantwell, Vince Casey, David Chadwick, Paul Child, Bobby Clark, Charlie Cooke, Chris Dangerfield, Roger Davies, Peter Dinsdale, Steve Earle, Keith Eddy, Roy Evans, Ken Furphy, Ron Futcher, Terry Garbett, Gordon Jago, Stewart Jump, Paul Hammond, Ray Hankin, Mick Hoban, David Irving, Graham Leggat, Mark Lindsay, Bobby McAlinden, Bob McNab, Peter McParland, Don Megson, Alan Merrick, Ron Newman, John O'Hare, Derek Possee, Bruce Rioch, Neil Rioch, Jon Sammels, Peter Simpson, Derek Smethurst, Brian Tinnion, Clive Toye, Tony Waiters, Peter Wall, Colin Waldron, Peter Ward, Keith Weller, Alan West, Trevor Whymark, Alan Willey, Peter Withe, Phil Woosnam

Books

Arriverderci Swansea: The Giorgio Chinaglia Story, Mario Risoli (Mainstream, 2000)

Banks of England, Gordon Banks (Arthur Baker, 1980)

Blessed, George Best (Ebury Press, 2001)

Bring Back The Birch, Alan Birchenall with Paul Mace (Polar, 2000)

Children of the Revolution, Richard Whitehead (Sports Projects, 2001)

Chronicle of America (Longman Chronicle, 1989)

Deadly, Doug Ellis (Sports Projects, 1998)

Doog, Derek Dougan (All Seasons, 1980)

Football League Players' Records, 1946–92, Barry J. Hugman (Tony Williams Publishing, 1992)

Football's Strangest Matches, Andrew Ward (Past Times, 1999)

I Did It the Hard Way, Tommy Smith (Arthur Baker, 1980)

The Jimmy Hill Story, Jimmy Hill (Hodder & Stoughton, 1999)

NASL: A Complete Record of the North American Soccer League, Colin Jose (Breedon Books, 1989)

Priceless, Rodney Marsh (Headline, 2001)

Rothman's Football Yearbook (Queen Anne Press, various)

The Seventies Revisited, Kevin Keegan (Leeward Queen Anne Press, 1994)

Sporting News Chronicle of 20th Century Sport, Ron Smith (Hamlyn, 1997)

Working Man's Ballet, Alan Hudson (Robson Books, 1997)

Other Publications

Charles Buchan's Football Monthly, Daily Mail, Daily Mirror, Goal, Kick: The Official Magazine of the North American Soccer League, Shoot, The Sun, The Times, World Soccer

Internet Sites

American Soccer History Archives (www.sover.net/~spectrum)

Soccer Base (www.soccerbase.com)